WHEN THE SHOE FITS

ABOUT THE AUTHOR

Osho's teachings defy categorization, covering everything from the individual quest for meaning to the most urgent social and political issues facing society today. His books are not written but are transcribed from audio and video recordings of extemporaneous talks given to international audiences over a period of 35 years. Osho has been described by *The Sunday Times* in London as one of the '1000 makers of the 20th century' and by American author Tom Robbins as 'the most dangerous man since Jesus Christ'.

About his own work, Osho has said that he is helping to create the conditions for the birth of a new kind of human being. He has often characterized this new human being as 'Zorba the Buddha' – capable of enjoying both the earthy pleasures of a Zorba the Greek and the silent serenity of a Gautam Buddha. Running like a thread through all aspects of Osho's work is a vision that encompasses both the timeless wisdom of the East and the highest potential of Western science and technology.

Osho is also known for his revolutionary contribution to the science of inner transformation, with an approach to meditation that acknowledges the accelerated pace of contemporary life. His unique 'Active Meditations' are designed to first release the accumulated stresses of body and mind, so that it is easier to experience the thought-free and relaxed state of meditation.

WHEN THE
SHOE FITS

COMMENTARIES ON THE STORIES
OF THE TAOIST MYSTIC CHUANG TZU

OSHO

WATKINS PUBLISHING
LONDON

First published in the UK in 2004
Reprinted 2006

Watkins Publishing, Sixth Floor, Castle House,
75–76 Wells Street, London W1T 3QH

Distributed in the USA and Canada by Sterling Publishing Co., Inc.
387 Park Avenue South, New York, NY 10016

Text Copyright © The Osho Foundation 1974
www.osho.com
Osho is a registered trademark of Osho International Foundation

Throughout this book Osho comments on original
Tao sutras from the following source:
The Way of Chuang Tzu by Thomas Merton
New Directions books published for James Laughlin
by New Directions Publishing Corporation
333 Sixth Avenue, New York 10014
Simultaneously in Canada by the Abbey of Gethsemani
First published as a ND Paperback 276 in 1969
5th printing
Also London Unwin Books:
George Allen & Unwin Ltd., Ruskin House
Museum Street, London W1
Published 1970 © under Berne Convention
© 1965 the Abbey of Gethsemani

3 5 7 9 10 8 6 4 2

Designed and typeset by Jerry Goldie
Printed and bound in Great Britain

British Library Cataloguing-in-Publication Data Available

Library of Congress Cataloging-in-Publication Data Available

ISBN 13: 978-1-84293-085-4
ISBN 10: 1-84293-085-0

www.watkinspublishing.com

CONTENTS

CHAPTER 1

WHEN THE SHOE FITS

Chu'i the draftsman could draw more perfect circles freehand than with a compass.

His fingers brought forth spontaneous forms from nowhere. His mind was meanwhile free and without concern with what he was doing.

No application was needed, his mind was perfectly simple and knew no obstacle.

So, when the shoe fits, the foot is forgotten; when the belt fits, the belly is forgotten; and when the heart is right, 'for' and 'against' are forgotten.

No drives, no compulsions, no needs, no attractions: then your affairs are under control.

You are a free man.

Easy is right.

Begin right and you are easy.

Continue easy and you are right.

The right way to go easy is to forget the right way and forget that the going is easy.

Chuang Tzu is one of the rarest of flowerings, rarer even than a Buddha or a Jesus. Because Buddha and Jesus emphasize effort and Chuang Tzu emphasizes effortlessness. Much can be done through effort but more can be done through effortlessness. Much can be achieved through will but much more can be achieved through will-lessness.

And whatsoever you achieve through will, will always remain a burden to you; it will always be a conflict, an inner tension, and you can lose it at any moment. It has to be maintained continuously – and maintaining it takes energy, maintaining it finally dissipates you.

Only that which is attained through effortlessness will never be a burden to you, and only that which is not a burden can be eternal. Only that which is not in any way unnatural can remain with you forever and forever.

Chuang Tzu says that the real, the divine, the existential, is to be attained by losing yourself completely in it. Even the effort to attain it becomes a barrier – then you cannot lose yourself. Even the effort to lose yourself becomes a barrier.

How can you make any effort to lose yourself? All effort is born out of the ego, and through effort ego is strengthened. Ego is the disease. So all effort has to be left completely, nothing is to be done; one has to lose oneself completely in the existential. One has to become again like a small child, just born, not knowing what is right, not knowing what is wrong, not knowing any distinctions. Once distinctions enter, once you know this is right and that is wrong, you are already ill, and you are far away from reality.

A child lives naturally – he is total. He does not make any effort, because making an effort means you are fighting with yourself. A part of you is for and a part of you is against – hence the effort.

You can achieve much, remember. In this world, particularly, you can achieve much through effort because effort is aggression, effort is violence, effort is competition. But in the other world nothing can be achieved through effort, and those who start with effort finally also have to drop it.

Buddha worked for six years, continuously meditating, concentrating – he became an ascetic. He did all that can be done by a human being, not a single stone was left unturned – he staked his whole being. But it was an effort, the ego was there; he failed.

Nothing fails like the ego in the ultimate; nothing succeeds like the ego in this world. In the world of matter nothing succeeds like the ego; in the world of consciousness nothing fails like the ego. The case is just the opposite – and it has to be so because the dimension is just the opposite.

Buddha failed absolutely. After six years he was completely frustrated, and when I say completely, then I mean completely. Not even a single fragment of hope remained; he became absolutely hopeless. In that hopelessness he dropped all effort. He had already dropped the world, he had already left his kingdom; all that belongs to this visible world he had left, renounced.

Now after six years of strenuous effort he also left all that belongs to the other world. He was in a complete vacuum – empty. That night his sleep was of a different quality because there was no ego; a different quality of silence arose because there was no effort; a different quality of being happened to him that night because there was no dreaming.

If there is no effort, nothing is incomplete – then there is no need to dream. A dream is always to complete something: something which has remained incomplete in the day will be completed in a dream because mind has a tendency to complete everything. If it is not complete then the mind will always be uneasy. Effort is put into many things and if they remain incomplete, a dream is needed. When there is desire, there is bound to be dreaming, because desiring is dreaming – dreaming is just a shadow of desiring.

That night, when there was nothing to be done – this world was already useless, now the other world was also useless – all motivation to move ceased. There was nowhere to go, and there was no one to go anywhere. That night sleep became *samadhi,* it became *satori;* it became the ultimate thing that can happen to a man. Buddha flowered that night and in the morning he was enlightened. He opened his eyes, looked at the last star disappearing in the sky, and everything was there. It had always been there, but he had wanted it so much that he couldn't see it. It had always been there, but he had been moving so much in the future with desire that he could not look at the here and now.

That night there was no desire, no goal, nowhere to go, and no one to go anywhere – all effort ceased. Suddenly he became aware of himself, suddenly he became aware of reality as it is.

Chuang Tzu says from the very beginning: Don't make any effort. And he is right, because you will never make such a total effort as Buddha. You will never be so frustrated that the effort drops by itself; it will always be incomplete. And your mind will always go on saying, 'A little more and something will happen, just a little more … The goal is near, why are you getting dejected? Just a little more effort is needed, because the goal is coming nearer every day.'

Because you will never make so absolute an effort, you will never be completely hopeless. And you can continue this half-hearted effort for many lives – that is what you have been doing in the past. You are not here for the first time before me. You are not here for the first time making some effort to realize the true, the real. You have done it many, many times, a million times in the past – but you are still hopeful.

Chuang Tzu says: It is better to drop effort in the beginning. It has to be dropped: either you drop it in the beginning or you will have to drop it at the end. But the end may not come soon! So there are two ways: either make a total effort, so total that all hope is shattered and you come to realize that nothing can be achieved through effort – there is not even a single small fragment still lingering somewhere in the unconscious, saying, 'Do a little more and this will be achieved.' Either make a total effort then it drops by itself, or don't make any effort at all. Just understand the whole thing. Don't move into it at all.

Remember one thing: you cannot come out of it if it is incomplete; once entered, it has to be completed. Because the mind has a tendency to complete everything – not only the human mind, even the animal mind. If you draw a half circle, incomplete, and a gorilla comes and sees it and some chalk is there, he will immediately complete it.

Your mind as such has a tendency to complete – anything incomplete gives you tension. If you wanted to laugh and you could not, there will be tension. If you wanted to cry and could not, there will be tension. If you wanted to be angry and could not, there will be tension. That's why you have become one long illness; everything has been left incomplete! You have never laughed totally, you have never cried totally, you have never been angry totally, you have never hated totally, you have never loved totally. Nothing has been done totally – everything is incomplete. Nothing is total. It lingers on, and then there are always many things on your mind. That is why you are so ill at ease; you can never feel at home.

Chuang Tzu says: It is better not to start because once you start it has to be completed. Understand, and don't move in a vicious circle. That is why I say that Chuang Tzu is a rare flowering, rarer than a Buddha or a Jesus, because he achieved simply by understanding.

There is no method, no meditation for Chuang Tzu. He says: Simply understand the 'facticity' of it. You are born. What effort have you made to be born? You grow. What effort have you made to grow? You breathe. What effort have you made to breathe? Everything moves on its own, so why bother? Let life flow on its own; then you will be in a let-go. Don't struggle and don't try to move upstream, don't even try to swim; just float with the current and let the current lead you wherever it leads. Be a white cloud moving in the sky – no goal, going nowhere, just floating. That floating is the ultimate flowering.

So the first thing to understand about Chuang Tzu before we enter his sutras is: Be natural. Everything unnatural has to be avoided. Don't do anything that is unnatural. Nature is enough, you cannot improve upon it, but the ego says, no, you can improve upon nature; that is how all culture exists. Any effort to improve upon nature is culture, and all culture is like a disease – the more a man is cultured the more dangerous he is.

I have heard that a hunter, a European hunter, was lost in a forest in Africa. Suddenly he came upon a few huts. He had never heard that a village existed in that thick forest; it was not on any map. So he approached the chief of the village, and said, 'It is a pity that you are lost to civilization.'

The chief said, 'No, it is not a pity. We are always afraid of being discovered – once civilization comes in we are lost.'

Nature is lost once you make an effort to improve upon it – that means you are trying to improve upon God. All religions are trying to do that – to improve upon God. Chuang Tzu is not in favor of that. He says nature is ultimate, and that ultimate nature he calls Tao. Tao means that nature is ultimate and cannot be improved upon. If you try to improve upon it you will cripple it – that is how we cripple every child.

Every child is born in Tao, then we cripple him with society, civilization, culture, morality, religion … We cripple him from every side. Then he lives, but he is not alive.

I have heard that a small girl was going to a party, a friend's birthday party. She was very small, just four years old. She asked her mother, 'Were there such parties and dances when you were alive?'

The more cultured and civilized, the more dead. If you want to see perfectly dead men and yet still alive go to the monks in the monasteries, go to the priests in the churches, go to the Pope in the Vatican. They are not alive: they are so afraid of life, so afraid of nature, that they have suppressed it everywhere. They are already in their graves. You can paint the grave, you can even make a marble grave, very valuable – but the man inside is dead.

A drunkard was passing through a graveyard and he saw a beautiful grave made of pure white marble. He looked at the grave, looked at the name on it. The grave was that of the famous Rothschild. He laughed and said, 'These Rothschilds, they know how to live!'

Culture kills you, culture is a murderer, culture is a slow poison – it is a suicide. Chuang Tzu and his old master, Lao Tzu, are against culture. They are for nature, pure nature. Trees are in a better position than you … even birds, fishes in the river, are in a better position because they are more alive, they dance more to the rhythm of nature. You have completely forgotten what nature is. You have condemned it to the very root.

And if you want to condemn nature you have to start by condemning sex, because the whole of nature arises out of it. The whole of nature is an overflowing of sex energy, of love. The birds sing, the trees flower – this is all sexual energy exploding. Flowers are sex symbols, the singing of the birds is sexual, the whole of Tao is nothing but sex energy – the whole of nature propagates itself, loves itself, moves into deeper ecstasies of love and existence.

If you want to destroy nature, condemn sex, condemn love, create moral concepts around life. Those moral concepts, howsoever beautiful they look, will be like marble graves, and you will be there inside them. Some drunkard may think that you know what life is, that you know how to live, but anyone who is in his state of awareness cannot even call you alive. Your morality is a sort of death; before death kills you, the society kills you.

That is why Chuang Tzu's message is one of the most dangerous, the most revolutionary, the most rebellious – because he says: Allow nature! And don't give any goal to nature. Who are you to create goals and purposes? You are just a tiny part, an atomic cell. Who are you to force the whole to move according to you? This is most dangerous for people who are religious; for people who are moralistic puritans, this is a most dangerous message. This means: break all the barriers, allow nature to erupt. It is dangerous.

I have heard that a head nurse was introducing a new nurse, who had just come from college, to the hospital. She was taking her around the hospital to show it to her. She introduced the various wards: a cancer ward, a tuberculosis ward, and so on. Then she came to a big hall, and she said, 'Look, and remember well, this is the most dangerous ward of all … this is the dangerous ward.'

The new nurse looked, but she couldn't see what the danger was. So she asked, 'What is the matter? Why is this the most dangerous ward? Even in the cancer ward you didn't say that it was dangerous.'

The head nurse laughed and said, 'These people are almost healthy. That's why this is the most dangerous ward. So be alert – health is always dangerous.'

Priests are afraid of health because health is immoral in their eyes. You may or may not have heard of one of the thinkers of this century, a German thinker, very famous in his day – Count Keyserling. He was thought to be a religious philosopher and he wrote in his diary, 'Health is the most immoral thing' – because health is energy, and energy is delight, energy is enjoyment, energy is love, energy is sex, energy is everything that is natural. Destroy the energy, make it feeble and dim. Hence so many fasts – just to destroy the energy, just to prevent so much energy from arising that it starts overflowing.

Religious people have always thought that health is dangerous. Then to be unhealthy becomes a spiritual goal.

I repeat again, Chuang Tzu is very rebellious. He says: Nature, energy, the ecstasy that comes from overflowing, and the balance that happens spontaneously, is enough. There is no need for effort. So much beauty happens all around in nature without any effort: a rose can be so beautiful without any effort, a cuckoo can go on singing without any effort. Look at a deer, alive, full of energy, fast. Look at a hare, so alert, so aware, that even a Buddha may become jealous.

Look at nature: everything is so perfect. Can you improve upon a rose? Can you improve upon nature in any way? Only man has gone wrong somewhere. If the rose is beautiful without any effort on its part, why not man? What is wrong with man? If stars remain beautiful without any effort, without any of Patanjali's yoga sutras, why not man? Man is part of nature, just as stars are.

So Chuang Tzu says: Be natural, and you will flower. If this understanding enters you, deeper and deeper and deeper, then all effort becomes meaningless. Then you are not constantly making arrangements for the future, then you live here and now ... then this moment is all, then this moment is eternity. And buddhahood is already the case, you are already a buddha. The only thing that is missing is that you have not given it any chance to flower because you are so engaged in your own projects. A flower flowers without any effort because the energy is not dissipated in any projects; the flower is not planning for the future, the flower is here and now. Be like a flower, be like a bird, be like a tree, a river, or the ocean – but don't be like a man. Because man has gone wrong somewhere. Nature, and to be natural – effortlessly natural, spontaneously natural – that is the essence of all the teaching that Chuang Tzu is going to give to you.

Now we will enter his sutra. Listen to every word as deeply as possible, because your mind will create barriers, your mind will not allow you to listen. The mind is society within you. Society is very cunning: it is not only outside you, it has penetrated within you. That is what your mind is, and that is why all those who know are against the mind and for nature – because mind is an artificial thing, implanted in you by the society.

So when you listen to Chuang Tzu your mind will create barriers. Your mind will not like to listen because what he says is so against the mind. If you allow it, if you put aside your mind and allow it to penetrate you, the very listening will become meditation, the very listening will transform you. There is no other thing to be done, just listening.

Chuang Tzu believes in understanding, not in meditation. And if I say you have to meditate, it is only because I feel that understanding is so difficult for you. Meditation will not lead you to the goal – no method can lead you to the goal. There exists no method, no technique. Meditation will only help you to understand. It will not lead you to the truth; it will only destroy the mind, so that whenever there is truth you can see it.

Chu'i, the draftsman, could draw more perfect circles freehand than with a compass.

Chuang Tzu talks about a draftsman of the name Chu'i, who could draw more perfect circles freehand than with a compass. Really, the compass is needed because you are afraid. If you are not afraid, you yourself can draw a perfect circle without any help.

In nature, circles exist everywhere – everything moves on a circular path. The circle is the easiest phenomenon in nature – and no compass is used. The stars don't consult a map; they don't carry a compass and yet they go on moving in a circle. If you give them compasses and maps I am certain they will be lost – they will not know where to go and what to do.

You must have heard the story of the centipede?

A centipede walks with a hundred legs. A frog, who was a philosopher, saw the centipede; he looked at and watched him and became very troubled. It is so difficult to walk even with four legs, but this centipede was walking with one hundred legs – this was a miracle! How did the centipede decide which leg to move first, and then which one next and then which one after that? And one hundred legs! So the frog stopped the centipede and asked him a question: 'I am a philosopher and I am puzzled by you. A problem has arisen which I cannot solve. How do you walk? How do you manage it at all? It seems impossible!'

The centipede said, 'I have been walking all my life, but I have not thought about it. Now that you ask, I will think about it and then I will tell you.'

For the first time thought entered the centipede's consciousness. Really, the frog was right – which leg should be moved first? The centipede stood there for a few minutes, couldn't move, wobbled, and fell down. And he said to the frog, 'Please don't ask another centipede this question. I have been walking my whole life and it was never a problem, and now you have killed me completely! I cannot move. And a hundred legs to move! How can I manage?'

Life moves in a perfect circle … life moves perfectly, there is no problem. Chuang Tzu says of Chu'i that he could draw more perfect circles freehand than with a compass. You need a compass because you are not confident in life; you need moralities, precepts, principles, Bibles, Korans, Gitas to direct you because you are not confident of the inner force. That is your life. And these Bibles, Korans and Gitas have created the same situation for you that the frog created for the centipede.

So many precepts to be followed, so many principles to be

managed – so many moral concepts. You have so many things imposed on you that your inner life cannot be spontaneous. You go astray, not because of any evil force, but because of the do-gooders. It is not a Devil which is leading you towards wrong, it is your priests, your leaders, your so-called saints.

This is very difficult. It is easy to believe in a Devil, so you throw all the responsibility onto the Devil. There is no Devil, I tell you. And that is what Chuang Tzu is saying also.

Chuang Tzu says: There is no God, there is no Devil: only life exists. Priests create God and priests create the Devil because priests create the distinction between right and wrong. And once this distinction enters your mind you will never be right. Nature is right. Once the distinction enters your mind that this is wrong and that is right, you will never be right, you will never be at ease, you will never feel relaxed; you will always be tense. And whatsoever you do will be wrong because the distinction creates confusion. The whole of life is so silent and meditative, why is so much effort needed for you? It is because there is distinction.

Chu'i, the draftsman, could draw more perfect circles freehand than with a compass.

If you are not self-conscious your life moves automatically. That compass is self-consciousness: if you do anything self-consciously you will be in trouble. You talk, the whole day you go on chattering with friends and there is no problem. But if I ask you to come here and talk from this chair to the friends who have gathered here, you will be in the same position as the centipede. And yet you have been talking your whole life and there was never a problem.

Why does this problem come in? The problem comes in because now you are self-conscious. Now so many persons are looking at you, watching you, that now you cannot be at ease and spontaneous. Now you project, now you want to plan, now you want the people to like you. Whatsoever you say, you would like them to be impressed – now you are self-conscious.

Otherwise everybody is a talker, a born talker. People go on talking and there is never any problem. But once you put them in a pulpit and tell them to talk to an audience something goes wrong. What goes wrong? Nothing has changed but self-consciousness has entered, and self-consciousness is the problem.

> *His fingers brought forth spontaneous forms from nowhere. His mind was meanwhile free and without concern with what he was doing.*

> *No application was needed, his mind was perfectly simple and knew no obstacle.*

> *His fingers brought forth spontaneous forms from nowhere.*

Nowhere means everywhere, nowhere means the ultimate void; nowhere means the ultimate source, the very ground of life.

From where are you breathing so perfectly? Chuang Tzu says you are not breathing, rather, 'it' breathes you. *You* are not breathing, because what do you have to do with it? Nothing. 'I am breathing' is a false notion. It would be better to say, 'Nature, 'it', breathes me.' Then the whole gestalt changes. Then the whole emphasis is on nature, not on you, not on the ego, but on 'it', the vast, the infinite that surrounds you, the basis, the very basis – 'it' breathes you.

When you fall in love, is it really *you* who falls in love – or does 'it' fall in love through you? When you are angry, are *you* angry? Because when there is anger, you are not; when there is love, you are not. In anger, in love, in any passionate emotion, you are not. In anything alive, you disappear. Then 'it' exists – the Tao.

So a man of Tao is one who has come to understand that 'I' is the most useless thing. It only creates problems and nothing else – so he drops it. Really there is no need to drop it; once he understands, it drops – there is no 'I'. Then he lives, he eats, he loves, he sleeps, but there is no 'I'. 'It' lives through him. Then there is no burden and no tension and no anxiety; then he becomes a child; his mind is free, without concern. You cannot do anything without concern. Whatsoever you do the ego comes in, concern comes in, and then there is anxiety.

Look at this phenomenon: a surgeon operates, and he is a perfect surgeon. But if his wife is on the operating table he cannot operate; his hand trembles. At other times he works like a perfect mechanism, but when his wife is on the table he cannot operate – some other surgeon is needed.

What has happened? Concern has entered. With other patients there was no concern, he was detached. He was not concerned this way or that, he was simply a surgeon, a natural force working. The mind was not there; he was perfect. But now that his wife is there, concern has entered: Will the operation succeed or not? Will I be able to save my wife or not? Now these problems are there, his mind has a concern, now his hand trembles.

Your whole life is a trembling because you have been carrying so many concerns; and now you cannot draw a perfect circle. Whatsoever you write …

There is a science for reading your writing and, through it, your mind. There is a definite basis for it because when you write, your trembling enters it. And when you sign your name you are the most concerned. Then your trembling is there, and with a magnifying glass that trembling can be observed, can be detected. That trembling can show much about you because whatsoever you are doing, you are doing it. It will carry *you*, it will carry indications about *you*. Just by seeing your handwriting much can be known about your personality.

If a buddha signs his name it is going to be absolutely different. There will be no trembling because there is no concern. And even through the signature it can be said whether it belongs to a buddha or not. Whatsoever you do, your trembling follows you like a shadow. Who is creating this trembling?

You come to me and you say, 'I am not at peace; my mind is not silent.' How can it be unless you drop your concern? You want your mind to be stilled, you want your mind to be made silent, clear, transparent. Without dropping the concern it is impossible because there will still be a trembling.

The only thing that can be done without changing your concern is to suppress all the trembling inside. So if you watch you will feel that on the surface everything is placid, calm, but deep down you are trembling, continuously trembling. Deep down fear and trembling continue. They are born out of concern.

And what is the concern? It is about how others are impressed by you. But why are you so worried about others, so worried that you cannot live at all? Everybody is wondering what others are thinking about them, and the same is the case with the others. They are worried about you, and you are worried about them.

Once it happened that Mulla Nasruddin was walking on a path. It was a lonely path, the sun had set, and darkness was descending. Suddenly he felt afraid because a few people were coming in a band, and he thought, 'These must be robbers … and there is nobody else here but myself.' So he jumped over a wall that was just nearby and found himself in a graveyard. A newly dug grave was there so he climbed into it, somehow calmed himself, closed his eyes, and waited for the people to pass so he could go home. But the people had also seen that somebody was there. Mulla had jumped suddenly, so they also became afraid: What was the matter? Was somebody hiding there, or doing something mischievous? So they all jumped over the wall.

Now Mulla was certain: 'I was right, I judged rightly, they are dangerous people. Now nothing more can be done; I must pretend that I am dead.' So he pretended. He stopped his breathing because you cannot rob or kill a dead man.

But the people had seen him jump so they became very worried. What was he doing? They gathered around, looked in the grave, and asked, 'What is the idea? What are you doing? Why are you here?'

Mulla opened his eyes, looked at them; then he felt certain that there was no danger. He laughed, and said, 'Now, here is a problem, a very philosophical problem. You ask me why I am here, and I would like to ask why you are here. I am here because of you, and you are here because of me!'

It is a vicious circle: you are afraid of others, others are afraid of you, and your whole life becomes a mess. Drop out of this nonsense, drop out of this vicious circle; don't be concerned with others. Your life is enough, don't be concerned with others. And I tell you that if you can live unconcerned your life will flower, and then others can share in it. You would like to share, and you can give much to others, but first you must stop thinking about others and what they are thinking about you.

This 'about' is very dangerous. Nobody is at ease, nobody is at home. Because of others, everybody is chasing everybody else – and life has become a hell.

His fingers brought forth spontaneous forms from nowhere. His mind was meanwhile free and without concern with what he was doing.

Do! Don't be concerned about what you are doing. Do it so whole-heartedly that the very doing becomes a bliss. And don't think of great things; there is no such thing as great or small. Don't think that you are to do great things, play great music, paint great paintings, that you are to become a Picasso or a Van Gogh, or something else – a great writer, a Shakespeare or a Milton. There is nothing – no great things, no small things. There are great men and small men but things are not great and small.

16

And a great man is one who brings his greatness to every small thing that he is doing: he eats in a great way, he walks in a great way, he sleeps in a great way. He brings the quality of greatness to everything. And what is greatness? Nature! Nothing is greater than nature. Eat like an emperor. That does not depend on the quality of the food, it depends on the eater, the way he celebrates it. Even with just bread, butter and salt you can be an emperor.

It happened that Epicurus had a garden just near Athens. He was also one of the rarest of men, just like Chuang Tzu. He didn't believe in God, he didn't believe in anything, because belief is nonsense. Only foolish people believe. A man of understanding has faith, not belief. Faith is different. Faith means trusting life, trusting it so absolutely that one is ready to go with it, anywhere.

He had a small garden, and he lived there with his disciples. People thought that he was an atheist, immoral. He did not believe in God, he did not believe in the scriptures, he did not believe in any temple; he was an atheist. But he lived in such a great way. His life was superb, magnificent, even though he had nothing, even though they were very poor. The king heard about them and wanted to see how they lived, and how they could be happy without belief. If you cannot be happy even with a belief in God, how could these people be happy without God?

So he came one evening to visit Epicurus' garden. He was really surprised, amazed – it was a miracle. They had nothing, almost nothing, but they lived like emperors. Like gods they lived. Their whole life was a celebration.

When they went to the stream to take their bath, it was not simply a bath; it was a dance with the river, it was getting in tune with the river. They sang and they danced and they swam and they jumped and they dived. Their eating was a celebration, a feast, and they had nothing, just bread and salt, not even butter. But they were so thankful that just to *be* was enough; nothing more was needed.

The emperor was very much impressed, and he asked Epicurus:
'Next time I come, I would like to bring some gifts for you. What would you like?'

Epicurus said, 'Give us time to think. We never thought that anybody would give us gifts, and we have so many gifts from nature. But if you insist, then bring a little butter, nothing else. Just that will do.'

Life can become a celebration if you know how to live without concern. Otherwise life becomes a long prolonged disease, an illness which culminates only in death.

His mind was meanwhile free and without concern with what he was doing.

No application was needed, his mind was perfectly simple and knew no obstacle.

You need to learn everything because you have forgotten your nature completely. Now psychologists are proposing that there must be training for love, because people are by and by forgetting how to love. Much literature has come into existence: 'The Art of Love', 'How to Love'. People have even completely forgotten sexual orgasm, sexual ecstasy. No animal needs any training! Even trees seem to be more intelligent than you.

Everything has to be taught, even the very basics of life have to be taught. That means that somehow we are uprooted. We have lost contact with nature; a gap exists.

And if you are taught how to love, your love is going to be false. Real love should be spontaneous. How can you be taught to love? If you are taught, then you will act according to the rules and the natural flow will not be there.

Nature does not flow according to your rules; it has its own rules. You have simply to be with it and it starts functioning. The day is not very far away when we will have to teach people how to breathe. Right now you laugh about it, but if you went back and asked Epicurus, 'Will there be a time when people will have to be taught how to achieve orgasm?' he would have laughed. Because animals achieve it without any teaching; no Masters and Johnsons are needed, no Kinsey Report is needed. Animals simply love – love happens naturally.

Now there are clinics in the United States where they teach people how to achieve orgasm. And if through learning and training you achieve orgasm, remember well, it is not the real thing. Because then you are manipulating it, then you are controlling it, then somehow you are forcing it, and orgasm happens only in a let-go – and a let-go cannot be taught.

You cannot teach people how to go to sleep. If you try to teach them, then you will disturb their sleep because if they try anything, it will only be a disturbance. You simply go to sleep, you simply put your head on the pillow and go to sleep. If you do something, then that very doing will be the undoing. Life is just like sleep; life is just like breathing.

No application was needed, his mind was perfectly simple and knew no obstacle.

When your mind is clear it has a clarity, you need not follow any rules. You need not carry any scriptures in the head – you simply look. Everything is transparent, because you are clear.

So, when the shoe fits, the foot is forgotten; when the belt fits, the belly is forgotten; and when the heart is right, 'for' and 'against' are forgotten.

Remember, this is one of the greatest mantras: 'When the shoe fits, the foot is forgotten.'

Whenever you are healthy you don't know anything about your body – the body is forgotten. When there is some illness, only then can you not forget the body. Do you know if there is any head without a headache? When there is a headache you cannot forget the head. When the shoe is pinching, then it doesn't fit. When you don't have any headache, where is the head? You completely forget about it. Whatsoever is healthy is forgotten but whatsoever is ill is remembered – it becomes a continuous note in the mind, a continuous tension in the mind.

A perfect man of Tao does not know himself; *you* know, because you are ill. Ego is illness, a substantial illness, because you continuously have to remember that you are somebody. This shows that you are in a deep 'dis-ease'. Dis-ease creates the ego; a perfectly healthy natural being forgets completely. He is like a cloud, like a breeze, like a rock, like a tree, like a bird – but never like a man. He is not, because only illness, like a wound, has to be remembered.

Remembering is a mechanism for safety and security: if there is a thorn in your foot, you have to remember. The mind will go continuously again and again to the spot because the thorn has to be thrown out. If you forget it, the thorn will remain there and it will become dangerous; it may poison the whole body. When there is a headache the body tells you to remember it, something has to be done. If you forget it, the headache may become dangerous.

The body shows you whenever there is some illness, something wrong – it attracts your attention. But when the body is healthy you forget it; you become 'bodyless' when the body is healthy. And this is the only definition of health: health is when there is no consciousness of the body. If there is any sort of consciousness of the body, then that part is not healthy.

The same applies to the mind. When your consciousness is healthy, there is no ego – you don't know anything about yourself. You don't go on reminding yourself that 'I am something,' you simply relax. You are, but there is no 'I'. It is a simple 'am-ness', an 'is-ness', but there is no 'I', no crystallized ego. The self is not there. So:

... when the shoe fits, the foot is forgotten; when the belt fits, the belly is forgotten; and when the heart is right, 'for' and 'against' are forgotten.

This is one of the deepest things to be understood: 'When the heart is right, "for" and "against" are forgotten.'

When the heart is wrong, ill, then you go on continuously being burdened, worried: this is right and that is wrong – and the right should be followed, the wrong should be avoided. The whole of life becomes a struggle how to avoid the wrong and how to achieve the right. And this is not the way to achieve the right! This is the way to miss it forever.

Look ... You have anger, sex, greed. If you say anger is wrong, then your whole life will be passed in an angry state. Sometimes you will be angry, and sometimes you will be angry because of your anger – that will be the only difference. Sometimes you will be angry, and when the anger is gone you will be angry because of the anger; you call this repentance. And then you will decide never to be angry again, but you will be angry again, because both states are anger. Sometimes you are angry against someone else, sometimes you are angry against yourself because you were angry.

If you are against sex and you say that it is wrong, as the whole world has said, then you will be sexual, and after your sexuality has passed you will feel guilty. In that guilt you will ponder and think about sex again and again; it will become cerebral. So sometimes you will be physically sexual, and sometimes cerebrally sexual – sometimes sexual in the body, sometimes sexual in the mind.

Once you make a distinction, once you make a conflict, you will be divided.

Once I was staying with Mulla Nasruddin. A very beautiful widow came to see him to ask for his advice. She said, 'I am in trouble and you have to help me. I am in love with a very handsome man, younger than me, but he is poor. And an old man who is very, very rich and ugly is in love with me. So what should I do? Which one should I marry?'

Mulla Nasruddin closed his eyes, pondered, and said, 'Marry the rich man, and be good to the poor.'

This is how all conflict arises, this is how you choose both the alternatives. Then you become divided. Whenever you say that this is right and that is wrong you are already divided, and your whole life will be a conflict – from this polarity to the other you will move like a pendulum.

Don't be against anything. Why? Because whenever you are against anything it means that deep down you are for it, otherwise why be against it?

A man who is not angry deep down will not be against anger. Why should he be? A man who is not greedy deep down will not be against greed. Why should he be against it? There is no problem for him, it is not a choice, he has not made any distinction. Remember, it is always greedy persons who are against greed, sexual persons who are against sex, angry persons who are against anger, violent persons who are against violence. Then what do they do? They create an opposite goal.

If you are violent, nonviolence will become the goal. And how can a violent man become nonviolent? What will he do? There is only one possibility: he will be violent against himself, that's all. What else can he do? A violent man … how can he be nonviolent? An angry person … how can he be without anger? And if an angry person cultivates non-anger, in his non-anger there will also be anger, because you cannot cultivate anything without *you* entering it. The anger will enter the non-anger; the violence will enter the non-violence.

If you look around, if you watch rightly, you cannot find more violent people than those who have nonviolence as their goal. And you cannot find more sexual, pervertedly sexual people than those who have *brahmacharya*, celibacy, as their goal.

Chuang Tzu says: Don't make distinctions, otherwise you will be divided. Once divided, you are two, split.

A person who is split cannot be natural. Nature exists in unity, it is a deep harmony, there is no conflict at all. Nature accepts everything – there is no choice, it is a choiceless let-go. Don't choose.

And this is the miracle: if you don't choose to be against anger, then when anger comes you are simply angry. Don't choose against anger. When anger comes simply be angry, and when anger goes, let it go. Don't repent, don't let it continue inside the mind, don't make it a continuity, don't be against it. When anger comes, it comes! What can you do? When it doesn't come, it doesn't come! You have no choice.

Then a miracle happens. Without choice you become so alert that your energies are undivided. And when energies are undivided they are so powerful, so tremendous that anger becomes impossible – because anger is part of weakness. Remember this: the weaker you are, the more angry; the stronger you are, the less angry. If you are absolutely strong, there will be no anger. Remember this: the weaker you are, the more greedy – really, the weak has to be greedy to protect himself – and the stronger you are, the less greedy.

When the energy is total in you, not divided, not split, you are a unity. Greed disappears, because greed belongs to a weak mind, a split mind. And when you are split, there will be anger and you will fight against it, and a bigger split will be created and more energy will be dissipated. And you will become full of inner turmoil, anarchy – not one harmonious note anywhere. Everything will be out of tune.

And the more you make an effort to bring it to a tuning, the more trouble there will be – because you have missed the first step, and you will go on missing it to the very last. The first step is that…

when the heart is right, 'for' and 'against' are forgotten. So what to do? Forget 'for' and 'against' and let the heart settle. One thing is certain, you have been fighting against anger for so long but still you are angry – so try Chuang Tzu's way. You are not going to lose anything.

You have tried to be nonsexual and you remain sexual; on the contrary, you have become more perverted. Sex has become more poisoned – so try Chuang Tzu, you are not going to lose anything. Be sexual when sex comes. Just as when hunger comes you eat food, so when sex comes be sexual. Don't make any choice, don't say this is wrong. It is good. Accept it – it is part of nature. And suddenly the moment will come when you will be a unity and sex will be transformed automatically into love. Because a man who is in unity…

Try to understand what this unity means. Every man and every woman is bisexual: every man is both man and woman inside, and every woman is both man and woman inside. No one is simply man or woman; they cannot be, because one parent was a man and the other parent was a woman, and you carry both within you – half and half. Half your mother and half your father is carried within you, so you are both male and female – half and half. This is the deep split. And if you create more of a split, this split will widen more and more. Drop all splits, don't create any fight – don't choose. Be angry and accept it, be sexual and accept it, be greedy and accept it. What else can you do? Nature has given these things to you so accept them, and their consequences of course.

If you are angry, then someone else will be angry – accept the anger and the consequences. Then your split drops, and by and by your inner bisexuality becomes a harmony; a circle is created, an inner orgasm happens – your female and your male meet inside. And when they meet inside you have become one; now a new being is born. This oneness has love as its shadow. You cannot love; your love is a facade, a deception. Your love is just a trick, your love is just to attain sex. That's why when you attain sex, love disappears.

Once you have had sexual intercourse with a woman or a man, love disappears. Again after twenty-four hours energy will come; you will accumulate energy, and there will be sex again – you will become loving again. So love is just a means to have sex; that's why you cannot love your own wife or husband – very difficult. How can you love? The need has disappeared. Love is just a courting, just a foreplay to persuade the other person to have sex. For a wife or a husband no persuasion is needed, they are taken for granted. A husband can demand, a wife can demand, there is no need to persuade. So love disappears. There is no need to court. It is almost impossible to see how a wife can love the husband, how a husband can love the wife. They can only pretend. And that pretending becomes a heavy, heavy thing on everybody. Pretending love! Then your life feels meaningless.

That's why people get into extramarital relationships: it gives you a little energy again, a little feeling of love, because with the new person you have to court again. You cannot take the other for granted, you have to persuade. Before you seduce, persuasion will be needed. Your love is just a persuasion. It cannot be otherwise, because love happens only when you have become a unity – not before. The word 'sex' is very beautiful. The original root of the word 'sex' means division – sex means division.

If you are divided inside, then sex will be there. When you hanker after a woman or a man, what is happening? Your one part is hankering to meet the other part but you are trying to meet the other outside. You can meet for a single moment, but again you will be alone, because outside there can be no eternal meeting. Sex is bound to be just momentary because the other is the other.

If you meet your inner woman or man inside then the meeting can be eternal. And when all divisions are lost this meeting happens. This is an alchemical transformation: your woman and man meet inside and you become one. And when you are one, you will have love. Love is a quality of a Buddha or a Christ or a Chuang

Tzu. You are just playing with false coins, you cannot love. And the more you understand it, the better it is, because then you will not be fooled and you will not be fooling others. Once you are a unity, Chuang Tzu has happened to you also, and:

> *... when the heart is right,*
> *'for' and 'against' are forgotten.*
>
> *No drives, no compulsions, no needs,*
> *no attractions: then your affairs are under control.*
> *You are a free man.*

Right now you have obsessions, compulsions, you have to do certain things. Continuously the body forces you, the mind forces you to do them. If you don't do them then you feel uneasy; if you do do them, you feel guilty – there seems to be no way out. If you move into sex you feel guilty, you have done something wrong; if you don't move into sex you feel uneasy because energy gathers and where can you release that energy? Then the energy moves inside and forces you, compels you. Your life is one of compulsions and obsessions. And whatsoever you do you will be in trouble, because if you move into sex you will feel frustrated; all dreams will be shattered, nothing will be achieved. You have been imagining so much, you were projecting so much, but the real thing is never in any way equal to that which you were dreaming of.

The more you dream, the more the actual will be frustrating, and then you feel: Why waste energy? Why get into relationships and unnecessary complexities? Because when the other is allowed in, he will bring his own problems. So every relationship becomes a burden, it is not freedom – because every relationship arises from compulsions.

Only a man whose heart is at ease, one who has become a unity, is a free man. That doesn't mean that he will go to the Himalayas, or escape to Tibet. No! He will be here, but he will be here with a different quality. He will love, he will have compassion, there will be relationships, but he will remain free. No relationship comes out of obsession, it is just his sharing; he shares his being. He has too much so he gives it. And if you accept his gift he feels deeply grateful to you. Look … your love is just a technique to obtain sex, his love is not to achieve anything. His love is not to get anything from you, his love is just a sharing. He has it, he has so much that he gives some to you. And the more he gives, the more it grows. His being moves in a different dimension.

Just look … go into the garden and see. If flowers are left on the plants, then more flowers will not come. I have been observing it. I have never allowed anybody to pluck flowers, but if on a rosebush five flowers have grown and you don't pluck them, no more will come, and those five will soon die. If you pluck five, ten will come; if you pluck ten, twenty will come. The more you pluck, the more flowers the tree will give you.

The same is the case when you are a unity: you have become a flowering tree. The more you give, the more you find will come; the more you share, the more you grow in it. Bliss grows higher and higher, ecstasy goes deeper and deeper – share it, because unshared, everything dies.

But the basic thing is, don't be 'for' and 'against'; then you will be a free man.

Easy is right.

For you the case is just the opposite. You always choose the difficult because the difficult gives you a challenge and challenge gives you the ego. Difficult is right for you; easy is never right. Because with the easy there is no conquering, the ego cannot feel fulfilled. The more difficult a task, the more the ego feels exhilarated, ecstatic. It has to be done – Everest has to be conquered, the moon has to be conquered.

Somebody asked Edmund Hillary, who was the first to reach

the top of Everest, 'Why? Why so much effort? For a hundred years man has been trying and trying and many have died! They never came back. Why this desire to climb Everest? And what is there?' There is nothing!

For a hundred years many people simply died, lost their lives, never came back, but again, every year, a group would go and try. And this is beautiful: no Indian has ever bothered, and Everest is in India! No Tibetan has ever bothered, and Everest is on the boundary of Tibet! Why? Groups come from the West every year. When Edmund Hillary climbed it and came back, he was asked why. He said, 'Because Everest was there, and unless it is conquered, I cannot feel easy. It remains there, unconquered, a challenge to the ego. Just because it is there, it has to be conquered.'

The difficult attracts. The more difficult it is, the more it attracts you. It becomes more valuable because through it, if you conquer it, you will achieve a greater ego. Even if you fail you will achieve a greater ego because you at least tried, while others have not tried at all.

If you achieve with the easy, nothing is achieved, because the ego cannot feel greater. And if you fail much is lost, because everybody will say, 'Such an easy thing, and you couldn't achieve it?' Ego is always attracted magnetically to the difficult, but easy is right. So ego is never attracted towards the right, it is always attracted towards the wrong.

A person becomes a criminal because crime is difficult, a person becomes a politician because politics is difficult, a person becomes mad about money because making money is difficult. People will go mad for anything that is difficult. Not that anything is achieved, but just because it is there like an Everest, a challenge; it has to be conquered.

Look at your successful people, those who have succeeded. Look at them! What have they attained? They may have reached Everest, okay, but there is nothing there. One has to come back.

Look at your presidents, prime ministers, Rockefellers: what have they achieved? Nothing! They know deep down that they have achieved nothing. But one thing they have done, the most difficult thing – history will remember them. History always remembers foolish people, because fools make history and fools write it! Chuang Tzu makes no history, because easy is right.

So how can you make history if you are easy? If you win a war and kill millions of people you make history. If you just brush your teeth in the morning how can you make history? And easy is right! You take a bath, and you sing a little song … how can you make history? You eat your food and you silently go to sleep without any dreams – how can you make history?

No! History takes no notice of persons who are easy and natural. History takes notice of people who are mad, obsessed with something, who create trouble in some way or other. And difficult is wrong, easy is right; be easy and don't try to be in history. Leave it for fools and mad people, you just stay out of it. Because you cannot have both. Either you can have life, or you can be remembered in history. If you have life, you will be just an easy and simple man doing simple and small things, and enjoying them. You will not create any trouble for anybody, nobody will take any notice of you. You will exist as if you never existed. That is what easy is – existing as if you are not existing, existing as if you are not, not in anyone's way. Nobody will know about you but there is no need. You will enjoy; you will attain to the highest peak of ecstasy. Easy is right...

Easy is right. Begin right, and you are easy.

And this is the criterion: Doing anything, if you feel easy doing it, it is right. If you feel uneasy doing it, something is wrong. If you are tense, it means you are living an uneasy life. If you cannot sleep, cannot relax, cannot let go, it shows you are living an uneasy life – you are after difficult things, impossible things.

Change your style of life, you are on the wrong path. Begin right and you are always easy, begin right and you are always at rest – that is the criterion. So always look at what happens when you do something: if you become peaceful, if you become restful, at home, relaxed, it is right. This is the criterion, nothing else is the criterion. What is right for you may not be right for somebody else, remember that too. Because what is easy for you may not be easy for somebody else, something else may be easy for him. So there can be no universal law about it. Every individual has to work it out for himself. What is easy for you? Don't listen to the world, because there are people who would like to impose their laws on you. These people are enemies, criminals.

Nobody who has understood life would like to impose anything on you. He will simply help you to be easy so that you can find what is right for you.

Continue easy and you are right.

And then live in such a way that you are always easy. Just like a small child, sleeping happily, eating happily, dancing happily, bubbling with energy – just easy. Remember, nobody will take any notice of you.

People may even think you are mad. Because if you are serious they think you are valuable; if you go on laughing and you make your life fun they think you are a fool. Let them think. You be a fool, but be easy. Don't be a wise man and uneasy, because no wisdom can flower in an uneasy life. That wisdom is false, it is borrowed. Be easy. And it is not difficult to be easy. Once you understand then you can find your path.

Continue easy and you are right.

Beautiful is Chuang Tzu, incomparable is Chuang Tzu, unique is Chuang Tzu! Because he says: Continue easy and you are right. He doesn't say: Be nonviolent, then you are right; be truthful, then you are right; don't be angry, otherwise you will be wrong; don't be sexual … He says: Be easy and continue easy, and you are right – and then you choose your own path. He gives you the essence, not particular directions, but just a universal truth.

The right way to go easy is to forget the right way …

Because if you are too concerned with the right way you will become uneasy. So even with Chuang Tzu be easy; otherwise you will become uneasy. And you are so efficient at becoming uneasy that you can even turn Chuang Tzu into a madness.

The right way to go easy is to forget the right way …

Just forget. Be easy, that is all.

And forget that the going is easy.

That too! Otherwise you will become too attached to easiness, and then easiness will also become a rock on your chest.

If you go to Chuang Tzu and say, 'Now I have become easy,' he will say, 'Go, throw this out! You are still carrying it.'

When you are easy, you are easy. No concept, no notion is made out of it. When you are easy, why say it, why even carry it? Because if you carry it, sooner or later it will become a wound. An easy man is simply easy, and forgetful. He does not know that he is easy, he does not know that he is right, he does not know that he is valuable in any way. He simply lives his easiness.

And whenever you come to a person who lives his easiness easily, simply, without being aware, you will be able to smell it. Tension has its own smell and easiness has its own smell; but you may not be impressed by it.

You are so tense, you are always impressed by tense people – people who act, people who are sitting on their thrones, like statues. Then you are impressed; the thing seems so difficult. Are you impressed by a child? Do you look at a child playing? Nobody is

WHEN THE SHOE FITS

impressed! Then you cannot be impressed by Chuang Tzu. Then you cannot be impressed by a really easy person because he may not make any impact on you.

But if you understand, you will smell a different vibration around a person who is easy. And how will you feel it? What will be the way? The way will be that near a person who is easy you will also feel yourself becoming easier, more relaxed.

A really relaxed man will make you relaxed, a tense man will make you tense. With a man who lives naturally you will feel that you are at home; he will not force you in any way, he will not try to change you in any way. He will accept you, he will be accepting. Through his acceptance you can learn acceptance, and if you can accept yourself, nature takes over. And once nature takes over, the ocean is not very far; the river is constantly flowing towards it.

CHAPTER 2

THE TOWER OF THE SPIRIT

The spirit has an impregnable tower which no danger can disturb as long as the tower is guarded by the invisible Protector who acts unconsciously, and whose actions go astray when they become deliberate, reflexive and intentional.

The unconsciousness and entire sincerity of Tao are disturbed by any effort at self-conscious demonstration. All such demonstrations are lies.

When one displays himself in this ambiguous way, the world storms in and imprisons him.

He is no longer protected by the sincerity of Tao. Each new act is a new failure. If his acts are done in public, in broad daylight, he will be punished by men. If they are done in private and in secret, he will be punished by spirits.

Let each one understand the meaning of sincerity and guard against display.

He will be at peace with men and spirits and will act rightly, unseen, in his own solitude, in the tower of his spirit.

O nly man is in suffering. Suffering exists nowhere else than in the heart of man. The whole of nature is joyous; the whole of nature is always celebrating without any fear, without any anxiety. Existence goes on existing, but man is a problem. Why is this so? And every man is a problem. If only a few were problems we could call them ill, abnormal, but just the contrary is the case – only a few are not problems. Rarely is there a man like Buddha, Jesus, or Chuang Tzu – one who is at home, whose life is an ecstasy and not a suffering and an anxiety. Otherwise everybody lives in suffering and in hell.

Somewhere man has gone wrong – not any particular man, but human society as such has gone wrong, and this has gone to the roots. Whenever a child is born the society immediately starts changing the child to the abnormal pattern – the unnatural pattern through which everybody else is suffering. Psychologists have been trying to probe deeply into the mystery of where a child goes wrong and they have stumbled upon the age of four. Somewhere near that age the child becomes part of society; somewhere around that age he is no longer natural. Before the age of four he is still part of the great world of trees, flowers, birds and animals; before the age of four he is still wild. Then he is domesticated; then the society takes over. Then he lives according to rules, morality, right and wrong; he is no longer total. Then everything is divided. Before he moves he has to decide deliberately how to move, what to do, and what not to do. The 'ought' has entered and that 'ought' is the disease. Discrimination has come in. Now the child is no longer part of the divine – he has fallen from that grace.

Try to understand: this is the meaning of the biblical story of Adam's fall. Before he ate from the tree of knowledge he was natural, he lived in the Garden of Eden. That Garden of Eden is here; these trees are still living in it; these animals are still part of it; the sun and moon and stars are still moving in it.

Here and now is the Garden of Eden – but you are out of it.

Why was Adam turned out? He ate the fruit of knowledge. And at the age of four every Adam and every Eve are turned out again.

It is not something that happened in the past; it happens every time a child is born – again the Adam comes into being, again the Eve comes into being. Up to the age of four there is no knowledge. By the age of four the child starts understanding what is what. Then he misses the path, then he is no longer natural, then the spontaneity is lost. Now he will live according to the rules.

Once you start living according to the rules you will suffer. You will suffer because you cannot love spontaneously, you cannot enjoy, you cannot dance, you cannot sing. Once you start living according to the rules you have to move in a fixed pattern – and life is never a fixed pattern. It is a fluidity, it is a liquid, flexible flow, and nobody knows where it is moving. Once you start living through rules then you know where you are moving. But deep down the movement has stopped. Now you are simply vegetating, now you are simply dying, because you are imprisoned. And the imprisonment is very subtle – unless you become absolutely alert you will not be able to see it. It is like an unseen armor around you.

One of the greatest revolutionary thinkers of this age, Wilhelm Reich, stumbled upon this armor. But he was proved by society to be mad and was thrown in jail. He died in jail in deep anguish. The anguish was this: whatsoever he said was true but nobody was ready to even listen to him. He came upon the same thing which Chuang Tzu talks about in this sutra – the imprisonment. Wilhelm Reich found that every mental disease has a bodily part to it, a parallel part in the body; in the body something has gone dead, solid. And unless that part of the body is relaxed, that block dispersed, and again your body energy becomes a flow, it is impossible to make your spirit free. The imprisonment must be broken; the armor must be thrown.

For example, look how the child is prohibited from the age of two. He is not allowed to play with his genital organs: 'Don't touch your penis, don't touch your vagina.' There seems to be a natural enjoyment in playing with one's own body. There seems to be an ecstasy, a natural ecstasy.

Look at a small child, boy or girl, enjoying his own body, sucking his own thumb, playing with his own body, and you will see what ecstasy is. Tremors of ecstasy move all over the body. You can even see the waves passing all over the body – the child is madly ecstatic. But this looks wild to us. Because we have forgotten how to be wild and natural, we will stop the child.

This stopping is for two reasons: one is that deep down we feel jealous. The second reason is that we were also stopped in our childhood, and man's mind is a repetitive mechanism. Whatsoever has been done to us by our parents we will do to our children. We feel guilt. Something is wrong. The child is happy and we feel something is wrong. Remember, whenever a child is happy don't make the association in his mind that something is wrong, otherwise deep down happiness will become something wrong.

That is what has happened. Whenever you feel happy you feel guilty, and whenever you feel sad you feel happy. What nonsense! Whenever you feel happy you feel something somewhere is wrong! 'I am doing something wrong.' Whenever you are sad everything is okay, it is as it should be. This is because whenever a child is happy, immediately, from somewhere, society enters and says no. The child has no conception of what is wrong and what is right; he has no morality. A child is amoral. He knows only happiness and unhappiness – he is wild. And when you say stop, what will the child do? Waves of happiness were moving all over the body from the head to the toe; from the first center of sex, to the seventh center of *sahasrar* – the kundalini was awake.

Every child comes into this world with his kundalini functioning. But you say stop, and what will the child do? He will hold his breath. Whenever something has to be stopped, breathing has to be stopped. He will not breathe, he will pull in his stomach because that is the only way to stop those waves. His diaphragm will become rock-like. Again and again he will pull in his stomach and not allow deep breathing. His diaphragm will become an armor. Now, beyond that block, breathing will never pass. If breathing goes deep it hits the sex center, and when it hits the sex center, naturally you feel happy all over the body; waves start moving, energy flows. That is why nobody breathes deeply.

When I tell people to breathe chaotically, they come to me and say that it is very dangerous. They feel afraid. What is the fear? The fear is that if you breathe chaotically, you will become wild again. The armor will be broken and the breath will hit the sex center again. This is how society suppresses you – it creates a gap between the sex center and the breathing. And if breathing does not reach the sex center, then all sources of happiness are blocked. Your stomach becomes rock-like. It does not allow anything to move down and your body is divided into two. You never identify yourself with the lower body. To you, lower is really something lower. Evaluation has entered. Upper means something higher, something good; lower means something bad. You never feel identified with your lower body, it is something bad – the Devil is there.

Adam was turned out, and every Adam and Eve are turned out of the garden. Why? Because they have eaten the fruit of knowledge, and the fruit of knowledge is the most poisonous. If you want to throw out discrimination – deliberate intentional division – you will have to throw out knowledge; you will have to become children again. Only then can the armor be broken. But there is going to be anguish if you want to try to break this armor, because this armor is your whole ego. You feel good because of it because you are moral; you feel that you have something superior to others because you are moral.

If you break this armor a chaos will follow. First you have to go mad and then fear comes, and if you are afraid you will again suppress, you will again put on the armor – you will even make it

37

stronger. Your imprisonment is very subtle, and now you have become afraid to come out of it. It protects you, it seems.

I have heard that in a primary school, the teacher was lecturing her pupils about the law of gravitation. She said in conclusion that because of the law of gravitation we are able to be on the earth. One small child was very puzzled. He stood up and said that he didn't understand – how did we manage to stick to the earth before the law was passed?

You think you are here because of the society; you think you are here because of morality, and all the nonsense that goes with it; you think you are here because of your Bible, Koran, Gita. No! Nature exists without any laws. It has its own intrinsic laws, but they are not laws passed by men. They don't need your sanction; they are there, and life goes on following them. If you don't interfere you will reach the goal immediately; if you interfere then you will be in trouble. So if you are in trouble, anguish and suffering, then know well that you have been interfering with nature. Nothing is possible unless you stop interfering.

This is the whole message of Chuang Tzu: Don't interfere with nature. Allow it, move with it, trust it. You come out of it; it is your mother, it is the source; and one day you will go back to it – it is the ultimate goal. And in the meantime, why create interference, why fight? This fighting is now almost ingrained.

You will have to go back to your childhood, you will have to regress. You will have to re-live those moments when society entered and forced you to interfere. So remember one basic thing: whenever something wrong happens on the path of life, you cannot just dissolve it by intellectual understanding – it is not so easy. It has become your life pattern. It is in your body and in your bones; you will have to go back. If you really want to become natural you will have to re-live the past – by and by move backwards.

All meditative methods help you to go back. Lie down in your bed at night and make it a one-hour effort every day. In the beginning it will be an effort, but soon effortlessness will happen and you will enjoy it. The more you go back, the more you will feel free and great.

Nature is vast, and all man-created laws are narrow. They are like tunnels: the more you move into them the narrower they become. And a moment comes of cul-de-sac – you cannot move anywhere, and the tunnel becomes your grave. That is how everyone is stuck.

If you really want to get unstuck, at night, before falling asleep, close your eyes and just go back and try to re-live the past. Move slowly, there is no hurry; you cannot do it in one day – it will take almost three months. Move slowly. Re-live – do not just remember. Remembering will not help because remembering is intellectual – you remain aloof, it doesn't touch you. Re-live.

What do I mean when I say re-live? Just go back as if it is happening again. In the beginning it will be 'as if', but soon it becomes real. Incomplete, your suppressed being is there, struggling to become free. Just go back, and soon, within three weeks, you will reach the point where you will know this barrier. Beyond this barrier you will know you were free, natural, and this barrier created the whole trouble. Since this you have never been natural. Somewhere you will find your mother, your father, standing at the barrier – that is why you have forgotten so completely.

If you remember, you will not be able to remember beyond the age of four because the barrier is so big. It has completely blocked things out. Otherwise, why can't you remember beyond the age of four? Why have you forgotten it so deeply? Your mind was there. You enjoyed, you suffered, you passed through many experiences – so why have you forgotten them all? You have not forgotten. Because of this barrier you have repressed everything deep down in the unconscious. That is why people go on saying that their childhood was very beautiful. You go on thinking that childhood was paradise. It was not – but it appears so to you because you can't remember. It is a blank.

Go slowly. By and by more things will come up. The whole dust of the past has to be stirred up. You will perspire, you will be scared; your whole mind will say, 'What are you doing? Come back, go to the future!' The mind always says go to the future, because then the past remains intact.

If you really want to become a meditator, first go to the past. If you have taken a wrong route somewhere at some crossroads, the only way is to go back to the crossroads and move again on the right path – there is no other way. Wherever you are now, from here you cannot suddenly take the right path. There is no right path – you have to go back.

And when I say re-live, I mean allow it to happen in the body. Remember the first day you touched your sex center and your father or mother told you to take away your hand. Remember their eyes, their face – everything that condemned you. Just see your father standing there again: the same face, the same eyes, the gesture, the condemnation – the whole thing. And not only this, but feel how you felt on that day – the shrinking, the narrowing of your consciousness, the wound they created, the condemnation.

A child is so helpless he has to follow your orders; whatever you say, he has to follow you. Even if it is against his nature he has to follow you. He is so helpless he cannot live without you; he depends on you.

See the whole helplessness. Feel it in your body. You may start crying, weeping. You may start kicking. Maybe you would like to hit your father – you didn't do it then and that is the incompleteness. You will not be able to forgive your father unless you hit him in this moment of re-living. That is why no child can forgive and forget his parents. They are always there because something wrong has happened with them. Go back, re-live those moments, and by and by you will be able to go deeper and deeper. Then suddenly the tunnel is no more – you have passed the barrier. You are under a wide infinite sky; you are a child again. Only then Chuang Tzu will be understood by you, not before. And Wilhelm Reich and his therapy can be helpful. You can use Wilhelm Reich beautifully on the path of Chuang Tzu.

Now the sutra: The Tower of The Spirit.

The spirit has an impregnable tower which no danger can disturb as long as the tower is guarded by the invisible Protector who acts unconsciously, and whose actions go astray when they become deliberate, reflexive and intentional.

Your spirit is protected by nature itself, you need not be afraid for it. You need not be afraid and insecure because your being is protected by the whole of existence; the whole cosmos helps you. But the help is unconscious, it is not deliberate. And you cannot manipulate it – you have to be in a let-go so that the cosmic force can work through you. If you become deliberate, you become tense. If you become tense, you become narrow. If you become narrow, the infinite cannot work through you. And whenever you become afraid, you shrink – physical shrinking happens.

Chuang Tzu says, inside you is the eternal, the immortal. No death can destroy it. There is no need to fear for it. You are afraid because you are not there in the tower – the invisible tower of the spirit. You have moved into the laws and regulations of the society and those laws and regulations cannot protect you, they only give you a feeling of protection. But nothing protects. The laws cannot make you secure, they only give you a feeling of security, which is false. Death ultimately comes and shatters all your securities. You will stay trembling, fear-filled, unless you come back to the source – the inner tower of the spirit. What is that tower? How does it function? It functions unconsciously.

A child is born. How does the child know that the nine months are over and he has to come out of the womb? How does the child know? He has no calendar, no watch, nothing of the sort. But when the nine months are over the child is ready to be born. He actually struggles to be born. That is why so much pain is felt by the mother. There is a real struggle. Conflict has started, and the mother shrinks – afraid of the pain that is going to happen to her body. So she also resists. That resistance, and the child trying to come out of the womb, creates the pain. If the mother allows, if she is not resistant, there will be no pain. In primitive societies there was never pain. The more civilized a woman, the more pain she feels. This is because she now lives according to laws and rules; now everything has become false and unnatural.

How does the child know when the time is ripe? How does a seed know when it is time to sprout? The seed may wait for the whole year until the right moment comes. The seed never goes to ask an astrologer or palmist; at the right moment the seed simply breaks down and loses itself in the earth. It just drops its protection and sprouts. How do the trees flower in the right season? How do the stars move? Look at this cosmos – so mysterious, so complicated, so complex, but moving so easily, so simply, so effortlessly. It is protected by Tao, by nature, by the spirit of nature itself. Man is foolish because he thinks himself very wise.

Then the child grows. And have you ever observed that every child is beautiful? It is very difficult to find an ugly child. Every child is beautiful. From where does the grace come? Later on it is difficult to find one beautiful person in one hundred. In the beginning all the hundred were beautiful – so what happened to the other ninety-nine? How did they become ugly? Why is every child beautiful? He is beautiful because of the movement; the flow is natural. Nature is beautiful. Artificial, unnatural, then you become ugly; deliberate, then ugliness enters.

A child lives unconsciously. When he feels hungry, he cries; when he feels sleepy, he sleeps. But we force rules and regulations on him.

I have heard:

One small child was crying, standing outside his house. An old lady passing asked him, 'What is the matter? Why are you crying? What has happened?'

The child said, 'My mother has lost the guidebook on how to raise a child, and now she is using her own mind.'

Now there are guidebooks on how to raise a child, how to be a mother, how to be a father. And every instruction is given. One wonders how children were born before there were these guidebooks. When these laws were not passed, how did we manage to get born at all?

The guidebooks give particular, specific rules. After every four hours milk is to be given to the child. The child is crying but the mother is to watch the clock, not the child, and the four hours have not passed. Now you are destroying the unconscious nature. Soon the child will follow your example – he will also look at the clock and when the four hours are up he will start crying whether he feels hungry or not! Early in the morning he has to go to the toilet. Toilet training is such a nuisance. How is the child supposed to have a bowel movement when he doesn't feel one? And his mother is standing there with a very condemnatory look on her face telling him to do it – on order! And the child is crying and weeping, and he doesn't know how to satisfy this mother – and she is simply mad! But sooner or later the child will force himself.

Psychologists have unearthed the fact that fifty percent of neurosis in humanity is because of toilet training. Fifty percent! The child starts forcing because he has to obey, and he feels guilty if he cannot do it right on time. And whenever he does it naturally, then too he feels guilty because guests were there – and he did it in the drawing room. And how is the child to know that the drawing room is not the right place? He lives unconsciously. He does not know which is the toilet and which is the drawing room. He does not know when guests are there and when they are not, and when he is allowed and when he is not. He does not live according to the rules, but he will obey because he has to follow. He is so helpless, and you are so strong; you will cripple him completely.

Look what happens when a child forces himself to go to the toilet: by and by the whole body becomes an artificial mechanism to be manipulated. Then nothing is natural. Then, somehow, he forces himself, just to satisfy his parents. When he is not feeling hungry he starts weeping and crying. You can see it happening.

Go to any house: small children are sitting at tables, tears pouring from their eyes, and eating. They don't feel the hunger right now – and they are right and the mother is wrong. This is how the child will move on a wrong path. Then, when it is the 'right' time, he will ask for food – and he is not hungry! When he is hungry he will control it because he is not allowed to ask. This is the way he will lose contact with nature, and to be out of contact with nature is to be neurotic.

A child is feeling alive, active; he wants to run and dance. The mother tries to force him to go to sleep. Have you ever thought that this is asking the impossible? Can you deliberately go to sleep – even you? Can the mother deliberately go to sleep? When there is no sleep, what will you do? The child will pretend, he will close his eyes and pretend, only to open them as soon as the mother has gone. This is training him for pretending and making him a hypocrite, all for absolutely useless things. Sleep cannot be forced – there is no way to do it. Otherwise why is there so much insomnia? Why are so many tranquilizers needed? Why do people spend the whole night tossing and turning in bed? And a child is expected to go to sleep by order, and get up by order, and in the *brahmamuhurt* – he should get up at five o'clock – all in order to be a good child, a goody-goody; otherwise he is a bad guy.

All those who are natural are bad guys, and all those who are artificial are goody-goody. Now the whole life of this being will suffer. He will go to this priest and that, this *swami* and that, from this master to that, and they will go on giving him things to do – this and that – but nothing will be of much help because his whole life-style is wrong, nothing can be added because the whole structure is wrong. The whole structure has to be dropped and a fresh start made.

But this seems too much. You have lived for forty, fifty years, and you have much invested in your life-style. And you come to me and I tell you to drop it completely. This is what I mean by *sannyas* – it is just a decision to drop the whole life-style; to change so completely that the past is dropped. And because you no longer identify with it, you drop all the investments you had there and all the profits that you were getting through them. There are profits, otherwise why should you carry such a burden? It pays. Society respects you – you are a respectable person. Society honors you when you follow society.

So when I say take a jump into *sannyas*, I mean change your whole life-style. Nothing less will do. I cannot change fragments because you are such a disease. Even if I try to change the fragment there is no point, because this fragment cannot change the whole – the disease is so big. It is more likely that the disease will change the fragment back again. Unless you are ready to drop totally, nothing can be done. You can meditate, you can do TM, you can close your eyes and do a mantra for ten minutes in the morning and ten minutes in the evening – you can go on befooling yourself in many ways, hoping that something will happen without spoiling your life-style.

That is how Mahesh Yogi is so influential in the West. He never touches your life-style. He never says change yourself. He says you are okay whatsoever you are. Just a little injection of TM and everything will be okay. It is just like taking a pill; your life-style is not touched, not at all. Whoever you are, wrong or right, just add this much mantra, to be done for ten minutes in the morning and evening – then everything is okay because the doors of paradise are open and just waiting for you. And man is so foolish that he goes on believing in such tricks. These are just tricks. They can help just like tranquilizers. They may help you to adjust to your wrong life-style – and that is the problem, they *may* help. They may give you an adjustment to your life-style, but your life-style is basically wrong. So it is better not to be adjusted to it than to be adjusted. They may give consolations but those consolations are poisonous, because then you will never change. You will be consoled in your life-style, and you will think that everything is okay because you are doing something – TM.

You will sleep a little better – I know a mantra can give you better sleep. You may become less prone to disease – that too is possible because you will be more adjusted to a wrong life-style. But this is not going to give you bliss. You may be less unhealthy, but this is not going to give you ecstasy. You may be able to prolong the suffering a little more. You will be less maladjusted, but you will never become an ecstatic being, a blissful being. You can become a blissful being only when you are ready to drop the whole life-style. Nothing less than *sannyas* can help.

> *The spirit has an impregnable tower which no danger*
> *can disturb as long as the tower is guarded by the*
> *invisible Protector who acts unconsciously, and whose*
> *actions go astray when they become deliberate,*
> *reflexive and intentional.*

Avoid deliberateness, avoid will, avoid intentions; move like a child, trusting nature. When you feel hungry, eat. When you don't feel hungry, don't eat. Nature guides you. When you feel sleepy, go to sleep. If you don't feel sleepy there is no need – just drop the idea. Move unintentionally and soon this neurotic style of life will be dropped and you will fall back to the source. That source is Tao.

The unconsciousness and entire sincerity of Tao are disturbed by any effort at self-conscious demonstration. All such demonstrations are lies.

Live, but don't make your life a demonstration. All such demonstrations are lies. Live, but don't become a showman. Don't allow
showmanship – there is no need. What others say is useless,
irrelevant; what you are is the only relevant thing. Live according
to your nature. Whatsoever others think about you is their problem,
you need not worry about it. Don't make your life a piece of showmanship. Once you start there is no end to it; then you will always
be making yourself false, and if people pay respect to a falsity, you
will become false. If they think that it is good and respectable you
will do a thing even when there is no natural reason.

If you want to become a painter and this is an unconscious
desire, become a painter and remain poor. Don't become a doctor
and become rich. You may become rich by being a doctor, but if you
didn't become a doctor because of an unconscious desire, if you
have only done it to satisfy your parents, society, friends, then
although you may become very, very rich, you will remain unfulfilled – and the ultimate thing is fulfillment.

I have heard about a doctor who became the greatest surgeon in his
country. He was made president of the National Society of
Surgeons. The day he was made president there was a great celebration in his honor. But he was sad.

A friend asked him, 'Why are you looking so sad? You should be
the happiest man in the world. You have become the greatest
surgeon and nobody can compete with you now. The greatest honor
that a surgeon can have is to become president of the National
Society. Why are you so sad?'

The surgeon replied, 'I never wanted to become a surgeon. I
have succeeded in something I never wanted, and now there is no
escape from it. If I had been a failure then there would have been
a chance, but now I am stuck.'

His friend said, 'You must be kidding. What are you saying?
Your family is happy, your wife is happy, your children are happy,

everybody is happy – and everybody has great respect for you.'

The surgeon said, 'But I cannot respect myself, and that is the basic thing. I wanted to become a dancer but my father and mother wouldn't allow it, and I had to obey them. I was a weakling. And I am not happy that I have become the greatest surgeon. I am unhappy because I am the lousiest dancer in the world. I cannot dance, and that is the trouble.'

Fulfillment comes through nature, not through society. You carry your destiny within yourself but it is an unconscious thing. Follow it. Nobody else will know that you have reached but you will be aware. You may not get a Nobel Prize because it has never been awarded to a fulfilled person. Nobody fulfilled has yet received a Nobel Prize – no Buddha, no Jesus – and it won't happen in the future either, because the Nobel Prize is given to somebody who has obeyed society very sincerely, and who has achieved society's aims, not his own. Look at the Nobel prizewinners and you will not find sadder men than those. Most of them commit suicide, and this is not accidental – it has deep meaning in it. Most of them feel unfulfilled. Prizes cannot fulfill you.

Allow the unconscious nature; don't force it consciously.

The unconsciousness and entire sincerity of Tao are disturbed by any effort at self-conscious demonstration. All such demonstrations are lies.

All your successful persons are lies. The so-called successful persons, look at them, and you will find nothing but lies.

Mulla Nasruddin was ill, so he went to the doctor. The doctor said to him, 'Nasruddin, do you drink alcoholic beverages?'

Nasruddin said, 'No' – and his hands were trembling. Even at that moment he was drunk – you could smell it on his breath.

So the doctor said, 'All right then. Do you chase after women?'

Nasruddin said, 'No' – and he had just come from a prostitute. You could see the lipstick on his face.

'Do you smoke, Nasruddin?' asked the doctor.

'No, never,' said Nasruddin – and you could see a packet of cigarettes in his pocket, and his fingers were brown.

'What do you do then?' said the doctor.

'I tell lies,' said Mulla Nasruddin.

And this is how all your successful men are: the greater liar you are, the greater will be your success. To succeed in this world you have to be a liar. But then you miss yourself. You succeed in this world but you become a failure in the other. And, finally, the other counts.

All such demonstrations are lies.

When one displays himself in this ambiguous way, the world outside storms in and imprisons him.

Once you show the inclination towards demonstration and show-manship, the world comes in and imprisons you immediately. You have become a victim.

He is no longer protected by the sincerity of Tao.
Each new act is a new failure.

Once you become interested in what others say about you, each new act of yours will be a failure. Here it may succeed, but this success is absolutely useless because you are never fulfilled by it, you never flower through it. You never come to the fulfillment of your destiny; your seed remains a seed. You may accumulate cuttings from newspapers about yourself, but those dead cuttings, certificates that you put on the wall of your sitting room, are not life. Faces that you carry with you when you go out, smiles that are false, are not life. And by and by, with every new act, you go deeper into lies. How do you think you can be blissful through these lies? You may attain much of the rubbish of this world but you will lose all of the real.

Says Chuang Tzu: Be in Tao, authentically in it, sincerely in it. There is only one sincerity needed of you, and that sincerity is towards Tao – your inner nature, your authentic being. No other sincerity is needed – let the whole world say you are insincere.

That is what Buddha's father said to him, because Buddha deserted his parents. That is what Buddha's wife said to him, because he deserted her. That is what his whole kingdom said to him, because he deserted the whole kingdom. But he was happy, and he remained sincere to his Tao, his nature. And he said: 'No other way is possible. If you suffer, you suffer because of your expectations – not because of me.'

You are here to fulfill yourself; others are here to fulfill themselves. If they expect something from you this is their problem; they will suffer, but you need not become false because of it.

Be sincere to your inner nature and help others to be sincere to their inner nature. This is what I call a religious man. A religious man is one who is sincere to his inner nature and helps others to be sincere to their inner nature. You are here to fulfill your destiny, and others are here to fulfill theirs. Don't expect anything from them; otherwise you will turn them into showmen, you will turn them into liars. Don't expect anything from anybody, and don't fulfill others' expectations of you.

This is arduous, but this is what *sannyas* is – this is what it is all about. Don't help anybody's expectation of you to grow. Don't even give them a hint that you will fulfill it. Whatsoever suffering you pass through, be ready to pass through it, but don't allow others to have expectations about you. Otherwise the world will close you in and there will be imprisonment.

Once you nod yes to doing something, then you are closed in. You are in the tunnel already, and now with every step, every new act, you will fall into a new misery, new unfulfillment, new lies, new failures. Drop fulfilling others' expectations, and drop asking others to fulfill yours. Remember: if you suffer, you suffer because of you; if others suffer, they suffer because of them. Nobody suffers because of others – remember that deeply. Only then will you be able to be really sincere to your inner self; and that sincerity is religiousness.

Hindus have called this *Rit*. Jesus calls it the kingdom of God. Chuang Tzu calls it Tao. Whatsoever the word used, it means to stay close to one's unconsciousness, and to flow with it without any conditions. It means to flow unconditionally with the unconscious wherever it leads, and to trust it.

This is what trust is. It is not a belief in a God, not a belief in a heaven or hell, not a belief in concepts, theories or philosophies. Trust means trusting nature from whence you came and to which, finally, you return. Trusting that nature, you will return fulfilled, and each moment of your life will be a new and deeper fulfillment. Otherwise each new act is a new failure.

If his acts are done in public, in broad daylight, he
will be punished by men. If they are done in private
and in secret, they will be punished by spirits.

Don't demonstrate yourself. If you demonstrate in public, in broad daylight, you will be punished by man. This has to be understood: when you become a demonstrator, a showman, when your life becomes a circus, an exhibition, people will appreciate you because you are falling victim to their whims, to their expectations. They will applaud you, but this is not going to last very long. Sooner or later they will start feeling your lies, because how long can you carry a lie? It shows, and when they start feeling your lies they will punish you.

Look at Richard Nixon: that happens to everybody who becomes a showman. First they applaud you. Now you have become a victim. Just to get their applause you will lie more and more. You will start fulfilling their expectations and you will become more and more unreal. This is a vicious circle. And the more unreal you become, the more they will be able to see that you are lying. Then they will start punishing you.

Whenever others appreciate you, beware; you are moving on a dangerous path. Sooner or later they will punish you. When people talk about your success, beware; now failure is not far off. When they put you on the throne, escape, because sooner or later they will throw you off. But you are so foolish and stupid that you never see the fact that somebody else was there on the throne before you. They put him there, and now for you they have thrown him off. Now they are garlanding and welcoming you, but sooner or later they will find another showman and they will throw you out. This happens to everybody who lives through public opinion. Don't ask for any success in the outside world and you will not have any failure. Don't ask people to respect you, then there will be no insult.

Chuang Tzu says: Be the last, so nobody can push you further back. Don't move to the front of the queue because then everybody will be your enemy and sooner or later they will punish you. Everything has its opposite with it: if they appreciate you they will punish you, if they respect you they will insult you.

What is the mechanism of it? When somebody respects you, he feels insulted deep down – deep down he has become inferior to you. So how can he forgive? He cannot. Someday the accounts will have to be put right. When he bowed down and touched your feet, that very moment a deep wound happened within him: he was lower than you. Now he will have to prove that he is not. Someday he will prove that he is higher than you.

Try to understand the inner mechanism: accounts have to be settled, you cannot go on with an imbalance. Whenever you appreciate somebody, at that very moment, if you are alert, you can find inside that you would also like to insult him. Only a time gap is needed. Sooner or later it will come up. A man who is wise never asks for your appreciation. When you come with garlands for him, he says, 'Stop here and now, because later I will have to pay.'

If his acts are done in public, in broad daylight, he will be punished by men. If they are done in private and in secret, they will be punished by spirits.

It may be that you are not doing your showmanship in public but in private. People have become so false that even in their bathroom when they are alone, they are liars. Even there they are not real and authentic. Lies have become so ingrained that you cannot easily put them aside – they follow you. Even in your dreams you lie – even in your dreams. Lies have become so deep-rooted that even there they follow you. If you want to kill your father, you will kill your uncle in your dream. This is how lies follow. Your uncle has not done anything to you but he is the nearest, and he looks just like your father. Even in your dream it is difficult to kill your father. That is why dreams become complex and Freuds and Jungs are needed to interpret them. You bring up the uncle, and Freud will read the father. The uncle is just the symbol – nearest to the father.

If you do your acts in private, then by nature itself you will be punished. Showmanship has to be punished. That is what Chuang Tzu means by the spirit: he means by nature itself you will be punished.

If you don't want to be punished then don't be a showman. Remain natural, whatsoever others say. Just because they say such and such, don't change yourself. Even if they say you are rebellious, criminal, bad, evil, let them think it. Even if they put you on the cross let them do it, but you remain true to yourself. When Jesus was crucified he could have escaped. Pontius Pilate was ready to forgive him but Jesus had to ask for it. He would not ask because he was authentically true towards his own nature.

When Socrates was punished by Athens there was a condition. They said, 'If you will promise the court that you will not talk around the town, and you will not discuss things and philosophies, if you will keep silent, then we can forgive you.'

Socrates laughed and said, 'That is impossible because I cannot be untrue to my own true nature. That is how I am. I will continue my business of talking. You can kill me, that is for you to decide.' He accepted poison but he would not accept silence; he would not accept having to keep quiet.

Be true to yourself, and don't look at what others are saying. This is the only way to reach to the divine, because it is the only way to be natural.

Let each one understand the meaning of sincerity and guard against display.

He will be at peace with men and spirits and will act rightly, unseen, in his own solitude, in the tower of his spirit.

He will be at peace with men and spirits ... If you are not in any way interested in showing who you are, you will be at peace with nature and people. Even if they kill you, you will be at peace. Jesus was at peace when he was crucified. Socrates was as peaceful as ever even when the poison was given. You will be at peace. What does it matter what they do? It does not touch you, you remain aloof, detached in your tower of the spirit. In your inner nature you are protected – nothing reaches and penetrates you.

He will be at peace with men and spirits and will act rightly, unseen, in his own solitude, in the tower of his spirit.

And when Chuang Tzu says he will act rightly, he does not mean right against wrong. No. He does not mean the opposite of wrong, he means the natural. The natural is right; the easy is right; to be yourself is right. To be yourself is all that you can really be. Anything else is to go astray.

CHAPTER 3

FLIGHT FROM THE SHADOW

There was a man who was so disturbed by the sight of his own shadow and so displeased with his own footsteps, that he determined to get rid of both.
The method he hit upon was to run away from them. So he got up and ran.
But every time he put his foot down there was another step, while his shadow kept up with him without the slightest difficulty.

He attributed his failure to the fact that he was not running fast enough. So he ran faster and faster, without stopping, until he finally dropped dead.
He failed to realize that if he merely stepped into the shade, his shadow would vanish, and if he sat down and stayed still, there would be no more footsteps.

Man creates his own confusion just because he goes on rejecting himself, condemning himself, not accepting himself. Then a chain of confusion, inner chaos and misery is created. Why don't you accept yourself as you are? What is wrong? The whole existence accepts you as you are, but you don't.

You have some ideal to achieve. That ideal is always in the future – it has to be, no ideal can be in the present. And the future is nowhere; it is not yet born. Because of the ideal you live in the future which is nothing but a dream; because of the ideal you cannot live here and now; because of the ideal you condemn yourself.

All ideologies, all ideals, are condemnatory because then an image is created in the mind, and when you go on comparing yourself with that image you will always feel that something is lacking, something is missing. Nothing is lacking and nothing is missing. You are perfect as far as there is any possibility of perfection.

Try to understand this, because only then will you be able to understand Chuang Tzu's parable. It is one of the most beautiful parables that anybody has ever talked about, and it goes very deep into the very mechanism of the human mind. Why do you go on carrying ideals in the mind? Why are you not enough as you are? Just at this moment, why are you not like gods? Who is interfering? Who is blocking your path? This very moment, why can't you enjoy and be blissful? Where is the block? The block comes through the ideal.

How can you enjoy? You are filled with so much anger; first the anger has to go. How can you be blissful? You are filled with so much sexuality; first the sex has to go. How can you be like gods celebrating this very moment? You are filled with so much greed, passion, anger; first they have to go. Then you will be like gods.

This is how the ideal is created, and because of the ideal, you become condemned. Compare yourself with the ideal and you will never be perfect, it is impossible. If you say 'if', then bliss is impossible because that if is the greatest disturbance.

If you say, 'When these conditions are fulfilled then I will be blissful,' then these conditions are never going to be fulfilled. And secondly, even if these conditions are fulfilled, by that time you will have lost the very capacity to celebrate and enjoy. And moreover, when these conditions are fulfilled – if ever, because they cannot be fulfilled – your mind will create further ideals.

This is how you have been missing life for lives together. You create an ideal and then you want to be that ideal; then you feel condemned and inferior. Because of your dreaming mind your reality is condemned. Dreams have been disturbing you.

I tell you just the opposite: Be like gods this very moment. Let there be anger, let there be sex, let there be greed – you celebrate life, and by and by you will feel more celebration, less anger; more blissfulness, less greed; more joy, less sex. Then you have hit upon the right path. It is not otherwise. When a person can celebrate life in its totality, all that is wrong disappears; but if you try first to make arrangements for the wrong to disappear, it never disappears. It is just like fighting with darkness. Your house is filled with darkness and you ask, 'How can I light a candle? Before I light a candle this darkness has to be thrown out.'

This is what you have been doing. You say that first greed must go then there will be *samadhi,* ecstasy. You are foolish! You are saying that first the darkness must go then you can light a candle – as if darkness can hinder you! Darkness is a nonentity, it is nothing, it has no solidity to it. It is just an absence, not a presence; it is just the absence of light. Light the light and darkness disappears. Celebrate, become a blissful flame, and all that is wrong disappears. Anger, greed, sex, or whatsoever else you name, are not solid; they are just the absence of a blissful, ecstatic life.

Because you cannot enjoy, you are angry – it is not that

somebody creates your anger. Because you cannot enjoy, you are in so much misery, that is why you are angry. Others are only excuses. Because you cannot celebrate, love cannot happen to you – hence sex. That is settling for shadows. And then the mind says: 'First destroy these and then there will be the descendence of God.' It is one of the most patent stupidities of humanity, the most ancient. And it follows everybody.

It is difficult for you to think that at this very moment you are gods, but I ask you: What is lacking? What is missing? You are alive, breathing, conscious – what else do you need? This very moment be like gods. Even if you feel that it is just an 'as if', don't bother. Even if you feel 'I am just presuming that I am like a god,' presume, don't bother. Start with the 'as if', and soon the reality will follow, because in reality you are. And once you start existing as a god, all misery, all confusion, all darkness disappears. Become a light, and this becoming has no conditions to be fulfilled.

Now I will enter this beautiful parable:

There was a man who was so disturbed by the sight of his own shadow and so displeased with his own footsteps, that he determined to get rid of both.

Remember: you are this man, this man exists in everybody. This is how you have been behaving. This is also your logic – flight from the shadow. This man was so much disturbed by the sight of his own shadow. Why? What is wrong with a shadow? Why should you be disturbed by a shadow? Because you may have heard – dreamers have said – that gods have no shadows. When they walk no shadow is created. This man was disturbed because of these gods.

It is said that in heaven the sun rises and gods walk but they don't have any shadows, they are transparent. But I tell you, this is just a dream.

Nowhere does anything exist, can anything exist, without a

shadow. If it is, then a shadow will be created; if it is not, only then the shadow can disappear.

To *be* means to create a shadow. Your anger, your sex, your greed – all are shadows. But remember, they are shadows. They are, in a sense, and still they are not: that is the meaning of a shadow. It is nonsubstantial. A shadow is just an absence. You stand, the sun's rays fall on you, and because of you, a few rays cannot pass. Then the figure is created, the figure of the shadow. It is just an absence. You obstruct the sun, that is why the shadow is created.

The shadow is not substantial, *you* are substantial. You are substantial: that is why the shadow is created. If you were like a ghost then there would be no shadow. And the angels in heaven are nothing but ghosts, ghosts dreamed up by you and your ideologists, men who create ideals. This man was disturbed because he had heard that you become a god only when the shadow disappears.

There was a man who was so disturbed
by the sight of his own shadow
and so displeased with his own footsteps,
that he determined to get rid of both.

What are your disturbances? If you go deep, you will find nothing but the sound of your footsteps. Why are you so disturbed by the sound of your footsteps? You are substantial so there must be a little sound – one has to accept this.

But the man had heard the story that gods have no shadows, and when they walk no sound of footsteps is created. These gods can be nothing but dream objects: they exist only in the mind. This heaven exists nowhere. Whenever something exists sound is created around it – footsteps, shadows. This is how things are, you cannot do anything about it; this is how nature is. If you try to do something about it you will go wrong; if you try to do something about it your whole life will be wasted, and in the end you will feel that you have not reached anywhere. The shadow remains, the footsteps make sounds, and death is knocking at the door.

Before death knocks, accept yourself – and then a miracle happens. That miracle is that when you accept yourself, you don't run away from yourself.

Right now, each one of you is running away from himself. Even if you come to me, you come to me as part of your escape from yourself. That is why you cannot reach me; that is the gap. If you have come to me as an escape from yourself you cannot come to me, because my whole effort is to help you not to escape from yourself. Don't try to escape from yourself, you cannot be anybody else. You have a definite destiny and individuality.

Just as your thumb makes a sign, a print, unique and individual – that type of thumb has never existed before and will never exist again. It belongs only to you, there will never be another like it – the same is the case with your being also. You have a being unique and individual, incomparable. It has never been before, it will never be again; only you have got it. Celebrate it! Something unique has happened to everyone; God has given a unique gift to everyone, and you condemn it. You want something better! You try to be wiser than existence, you try to be wiser than Tao – then you go wrong.

Remember: the part can never be wiser than the whole, and whatsoever the whole is doing is the final thing, you cannot change it. You can make an effort to do so and waste your life, but nothing will be achieved through it.

The whole is vast, you are just an atomic cell. The ocean is vast, you are just a drop in it. The whole ocean is salty, and you are trying to be sweet. It is impossible! But the ego wants to do the impossible, the difficult, that which cannot be done. And Chuang Tzu says: Easy is right. Why can't you be easy and accepting? Why not say yes to the shadow? The moment you say yes you forget it, it disappears, from the mind at least, even if it remains with the body.

But what is the problem? How does a shadow create a problem?

Why make a problem out of it? As you are right now, you make a problem out of everything. This man was puzzled, disturbed, by the sight of his own shadow. He would have liked to be a god, he would have liked to be shadowless.

But you are already like a god and you cannot be anything that you are not already. How can you be? You can only be that which you are; all becoming is just moving towards the being which is already there. You may wander, and knock on others' doors, but this is just playing hide-and-seek with yourself. It is up to you how much you knock on others' doors and how much you wander here and there. Finally you will come to your own and to the realization that your own has always been there. Nobody can take it away. Nature, the Tao, cannot be taken away from you.

This man was disturbed because of his shadow. The method he hit upon was to run away from it. That is the method everybody hits upon. It seems that the mind has a vicious logic.

For example, if you feel angry, what will you do? The mind will say: 'Don't be angry, take a vow.' What will you do? You will suppress it, and the more you suppress, the more the anger will move to the very roots of your being. Then you will not be sometimes angry and sometimes not angry; if you have suppressed too much you will be continuously angry, it will become your blood, it will be a poison all over. It will spread into all your relationships. Even if you are in love with someone, the anger will be there and the love will become violent. Even if you try to help somebody, in that help there will be poison because the poison is in you. And all your acts will carry it, they will reflect you. When you feel this again, the mind will say: 'You have not been suppressing enough, suppress more.' But anger is there because of suppression, and the mind says: 'Suppress it more!' Then there will be more anger.

Your mind is sexual because of suppression and the mind says: 'Suppress it more, find new methods and ways and means to suppress it more so *brahmacharya* will flower.' But it cannot flower that way. Through suppression sex not only goes into the body, it goes into the mind, it becomes cerebral. Then a person goes on thinking about it, again and again; hence so much pornographic literature in the world.

Why do people like to see pictures of naked women? Are women not enough? They are, they are more than enough! So what is the need? The picture is always more sexual than a real woman. A real woman has a body and a shadow, and her footsteps will be there, and sound will be created. A photograph is a dream: it is absolutely mental, cerebral, and it has no shadow.

A real woman will perspire and there will be a smell of the body; a picture never perspires, and there is no smell of the body. A real woman will be angry; a picture is never angry. A real woman will age, will become old; a picture always remains young and fresh. A picture is just mental. Those who suppress sex in the body become mentally sexual. Then their mind moves in sexuality, and then it is a disease.

If you feel hungry it is okay, eat. But if you think about food continuously then it is an obsession and a disease. When you feel hungry it is okay if you eat and are finished with it. But you are never finished with anything, and everything goes into the mind.

Mulla Nasruddin's wife was ill and she had been operated on. She had come back home from the hospital a few days before, so I asked, 'How is your wife? Has she recovered from the operation?'

He said, 'No, she is still talking about it.'

If you are thinking about something, talking about something, it is there. And now it is more dangerous because the body will recover, but the mind can go on and on and on – ad infinitum. The body may recover, but the mind will never recover.

If you suppress hunger in the body, it goes into the mind. The problem has not been thrown out, it has been pushed in. Suppress anything and it goes to the roots. Then the mind will say that if you are not succeeding, something is wrong, you are not making enough effort. Make more effort.

The method he hit upon was to run away from them.

Mind has only two alternatives: fight or flight. Whenever there is a problem, the mind says either fight it, or escape from it. And both are wrong. If you fight, you remain with the problem. If you fight, the problem will be there continuously. If you fight, you are divided, because the problem is not outside – the problem is inside.

For example, if there is anger and you fight, what will happen? Half of your being will be with the anger, and half with this idea of fight. It is as if both your hands are fighting each other. Who is going to win? You will be simply dissipating energy. No one is going to win. You can fool yourself that you have now got your anger suppressed, now you are sitting on your anger, but then you will have to sit on it continuously; not even a single moment's holiday is allowed. If you forget about it for a single moment, you will lose your whole victory.

So people who have suppressed something are always sitting on those suppressed things and they are always afraid, they cannot relax. Why has relaxation become so difficult? Why can't you sleep? Why can't you relax? Why can't you be in a let-go? Because you have suppressed so many things. You are afraid that if you relax, they will come up. Your so-called religious people cannot relax. They are tense, and the tension is because of this: they have suppressed something, and you say relax. They know that if they relax the enemy will come up; they cannot relax. They are afraid to go to sleep.

Go to your *mahatmas*: they are more afraid of sleep than anything. And they think in their minds that someday they will be capable of not sleeping at all. They go on cutting their sleep from eight hours to six, from six to five, from five to three, to two. And if an old monk, a *sannyasin*, can sleep for only two hours a day, this is thought to be something of an achievement. This is foolish. This is not an achievement. And this is not what Krishna means when he says in the Gita that when the world sleeps, the yogi is awake. This is not the meaning. The meaning is that the body is relaxed, the body goes into sleep, but the inner consciousness remains alert even in sleep. That is something absolutely different, it has nothing to do with ordinary sleep.

Really, a yogi sleeps better than you. He will do, because he can relax, he is not afraid. But these so-called religious people will be afraid, because in their dreams all that they have suppressed will come up. Mahatma Gandhi has written in his autobiography, 'I have become a victor of sex as far as my waking hours are concerned, but in sleep, sexual dreams still persist.' They will persist, because a suppressed thing will come up in the dreams. Why in the dream? Because now you are asleep, the censor is relaxed, and the fighter is no longer there – he is sleeping. The enemy will bubble up.

The mind thinks: 'Either fight' – if you fight then you suppress – 'or escape.' But to where will you escape? Even if you go to the Himalayas the anger will follow you, it is your shadow; the sex will follow you, it is your shadow. Wherever you go, your shadow will be with you.

The method he hit upon was to run away from them.
So he got up and ran.

But every time he put his foot down there was another
step, while his shadow kept up with him without the
slightest difficulty.

He was surprised! He was running so fast, but there was no difficulty for the shadow. The shadow was following easily, not even perspiring, not breathing hard. There was no difficulty on the part of the shadow because a shadow is not substantial; a shadow is nobody. The man may have been perspiring, he may have had difficulty breathing, but the shadow was always in step with him. The shadow cannot leave you in this way. Neither fight nor flight will help. Where will you go? Wherever you go, you will carry yourself with you and your shadow will be there.

He attributed his failure to the fact that he was not running fast enough.

So he ran faster and faster, without stopping, until he finally dropped dead.

One has to understand the logic of the mind. If you don't understand you will be a victim of it. The mind has a vicious logic, it is a vicious circle – it is circular. If you listen to it, then every step will lead you more and more into the circle. This man is perfectly logical. You cannot find any fault, any flaw, in his logic. There is no loophole, he is as perfect a logician as any Aristotle. He says that if the shadow is following him, it shows that he is not running fast enough. He must run faster and faster, then the moment will come when the shadow will not be able to follow him. But the shadow is yours, and the shadow is nobody. It is not somebody else following you; if it were, then the logic would have been right.

Remember: when there is somebody else the mind is always right; when you are alone, the mind is always wrong. In society, with others, the mind is almost always right; with yourself, in isolation, the mind is always wrong. Why? Because mind is just an instrument to exist with others, it is just a technique to help you to be with others, it has nothing to do with yourself. Mind is needed because of society. If a child is born and he is not exposed to any society then the mind will not develop, there will be no mind. It has happened many times.

It happened near Calcutta, thirty or forty years ago, that a girl was taken by wolves who took care of her, and she grew. She was fourteen when she was caught again by society. But she was just a wolf child, no human mind at all. She would run on all fours, and she was very dangerous – she needed to eat raw meat. And she was very strong: even eight strong men were not enough to control her. She had a wolf mind. She had to grow up with wolves, a society of wolves, so she had to grow a wolf mind. It was impossible to train her to stand on two feet. She would try two or three steps, and again she would fall down and be on all fours. But she could run so fast on all fours that nobody could follow her.

Again, just ten years ago, a boy was found in Uttar Pradesh, near Lucknow. The same incident had happened – wolves seem to be very loving to children. They raised the child, a boy. When he was caught he was about twelve. This time the doctors tried hard. They hospitalized the boy, they massaged him, they gave him medicines and everything. Within six months the child was dead, because they tried to make him a human being and his whole being refused. When they got hold of him he was so healthy – no human being was ever so healthy. He was wild, he was a wolf; and when they hospitalized him and started treating him he became ill. Within six months they killed him. They were trying to create a human mind, but it was impossible. They only succeeded in training him to say one word, his name. They named him Ram. In six months, that was their only success. If you asked him, 'What is your name?' the wolf child would say, 'Ram.' That was all.

A mind is a social function. A wolf needs a mind for a society of wolves; a man needs a mind for a society of men. And because of this there exist many types of human minds, because there are so many societies on the earth.

A Hindu has a different mind from a Mohammedan; a Christian has a different mind from an aboriginal; a Russian has a different mind from an American. They see differently, their perspective is different, their interpretation is different. The same thing is seen absolutely differently. Why? Because to exist in a particular society you need a particular mind. In Russia, if you believe in God you are thought to be crazy. In India, if you don't believe in a god you are thought to be crazy.

Once it happened that I was conducting a meditation camp and two dogs were watching people doing Dynamic Meditation with chaotic expressions. And then I heard one dog say to the other, 'When I do this, my master gives me worm pills! He thinks I am crazy!'

Wherever you go in the world, be alert! Don't do Dynamic Meditation in front of others – they will think you have gone crazy.

Everybody has settled for a mind, and every mind is a fragment. One has to throw away this mind – only then the cosmic mind, the universal mind, happens to you.

This fragmentary mind is just a method, just a function for society. You need language to talk to others, you need mind to relate to others. Remember: mind is almost always right when you are using it with others, and it is almost always wrong when you start using it with yourself.

The man running from his shadow was right. If somebody else had been following him then he would have been right, absolutely right: he was not running fast enough and that was why the other was following. But he was wrong, because there was nobody else. The mind was useless. Mind for others – meditation for yourself. Mind for others – no mind for yourself. That is the whole emphasis of Chuang Tzu, or Zen, or Sufis, or Hassids, of all those who know; of Buddha, Jesus, Mohammed, of all those who have known. The whole emphasis is: mind for others, no mind for yourself.

This man got into trouble because he used the mind for himself, and the mind has its own pattern. The mind said, 'Faster, faster! If you go fast enough, this shadow will not be able to follow you.'

He attributed his failure to the fact that he was not

running fast enough.

The failure was there in the first place because he was running. But the mind cannot say that, the mind has not been fed for it. It is a computer – you have to feed it, it is a mechanism. It cannot give you anything new, it can only give you whatsoever you have fed into it. The mind cannot give you anything new; whatsoever it gives you is borrowed. And if you are addicted to listening to it you will always be in trouble when you turn towards yourself. When there is a conversion, a turning towards the source, then you will be in difficulty. Then this mind is absolutely useless – not only useless, it is a positive hindrance, it is harmful. So drop it.

I have heard:

It happened that one day Mulla Nasruddin's son came home from his progressive school and brought a book on sexology. The mother was very much disturbed but she waited for Mulla Nasruddin to come. Something had to be done; this progressive school was going too far! When Mulla Nasruddin came his wife showed him the book.

Nasruddin went upstairs to find out where his son was. He found him in his room, kissing the maidservant. So Nasruddin said, 'Son, when you are finished with your homework, come down.'

But this is logical! Logic has its own steps, and each step follows another; there is no end to it.

This man followed the mind, so he ran faster and faster without stopping, until he finally dropped dead. Faster and faster without stopping – then only death can occur.

Have you ever observed that life has not occurred to you yet? Have you observed that there has never been a single moment of life as such happening to you? You have not experienced a single moment of the bliss that Chuang Tzu and Buddha talk about. And what is going to happen to you? Nothing is going to happen to you except death. And the nearer you come to death, the faster you run, because you think that if you go faster you will escape.

Where are you going so fast? Man and man's mind have always been mad about speed, as if we are going somewhere and speed is needed. So we go on becoming more and more speedy. Where are you going? Finally, whether you go slow or fast, you reach death.

There is a Sufi story:

A king dreamed that his death was coming. In the dream he saw a shadow standing, so he asked, 'Who are you?'

The shadow said, 'I am your death, and tomorrow, by the time the sun sets, I will be coming to you.'

The king wanted to ask if there was any way to escape, but he couldn't because he became so afraid that the dream was broken, and the shadow disappeared. He was perspiring and trembling.

In the middle of the night he called all his wise men and said, 'Find out the meaning of this dream.' And as you know, you cannot find more foolish people than wise men. They ran to their houses and brought their scriptures. They were big, big volumes. And they started to consult and debate and discuss and fight with each other and argue.

Listening to their talk the king became more and more confused. They were not agreeing on any point; they belonged to different sects, as wise men always do. They don't belong to themselves, they belong to some dead tradition. One was a Hindu, another was a Mohammedan, another was a Christian. They had brought their scriptures with them and they tried and tried. And as they got into discussion they became mad, and argued over and over again. The king was very much disturbed because the sun was rising, and when the sun rises, it is not long until the sun will set, because rising is really setting – it has already started. The journey has started and within twelve hours the sun will set.

He tried to interrupt them, but they said, 'Don't interrupt, this is a serious question.' Then one old man, who had served the king for his whole life, came near and whispered in his ear, 'It is better that you escape, because these people will never come to any conclusion. Wise men have never reached any conclusion. They will discuss and debate, and their death will come, but the conclusion will not come. My suggestion is that when death has warned you, it is better that you escape from this palace at least! Go anywhere, and go fast!'

This advice appealed to him, it was absolutely right. When man cannot do anything, he thinks of flight, escape. The king had a very fast horse, he got onto it and escaped. He had told the wise men, 'If I come back alive and you have decided, tell me – but right now, I am going.'

He was very happy, and faster and faster he went, because it was a life and death problem. Again and again he looked back to see if the shadow was coming, but there was no shadow. He was happy, death was not there, and he was escaping. By the time the sun was setting, he was hundreds and hundreds of miles away from the capital. Under a big banyan tree he stopped, got down from his horse, thanked it and said, 'It is you, you who have saved me.'

Suddenly, as he was talking to and thanking the horse, he felt the same hand that he had felt in the dream. He looked back. The same shadow was there, and Death said, 'I would also like to thank your horse, he is really fast. I have been waiting under this banyan tree all day and I was worried about whether you would be able to reach it or not, the distance was so great. But this horse is really something: you have arrived at exactly the moment you were needed here.'

Where are you going? Where will you reach? All this flight and escape will bring you under the banyan tree. And as you are thanking your horse or your car, you will feel the hand of Death on your shoulder. Death will say, 'I have been waiting here for you for a long time. You have come.'

And everybody comes at the right moment, not a single moment is lost. Everybody reaches there right on time, nobody is ever late. I have heard that a few people have arrived before their time but I have never heard of anybody reaching there late. Some people reach there before their time because of their doctors.

He attributed his failure to the fact that he was not running fast enough. So he ran faster and faster, without stopping, until he finally dropped dead.

He failed to realize that if he merely stepped into the shade, his shadow would vanish …

Easy it was – the easiest! If you just move into the shade where the sun is not, the shadow disappears, because a shadow is created by the sun. It is the absence of the sun's rays. If you are under a tree in the shade, the shadow disappears.

He failed to realize that if he merely stepped into the shade, his shadow would vanish …

That shade is called silence, that shade is called inner peace. Don't listen to the mind, just step into the shade, into the inner silence where no rays of the sun enter. You remain on the periphery, that is the problem. There you are in the light of the outside world, and shadow is created. Close your eyes, move into the shade. The moment you close your eyes the sun is no longer there.

Hence all meditations are done with closed eyes – you are moving into your own shade. Inside there is no sun and no shadow; outside is society, and outside are all types of shadows. Have you ever realized that your anger, your sex, your greed, your ambition, are all part of the society? If you really move in and leave the society out, where is anger? Where is sex? But remember, in the beginning when you close your eyes, they are not really closed. You carry images from the outside inside and you will find the same society reflected. But if you continue simply moving, moving, moving inside, sooner or later the society will be left out. You are in, society is out – you have moved from the periphery to the center.

In this center there is a silence: no anger, and no anti-anger; no sex, and also no *brahmacharya*; no greed, no nongreed; no violence, no nonviolence – because those are all outside. The opposites are also outside, remember. Inside you are neither, not this nor that. You are simply a being, pure. This is what I mean, being like a god – a pure being with no opposites hanging around, no fighting, no 'flighting'… Simply being. You have moved into the shade.

He failed to realize that if he only moved into the shade then his shadow would vanish, and if he sat down and stayed still, there could be no more footsteps – it was really so easy. But that which is easy is so difficult for the mind, because mind always finds it easier to run, to fight, because then there is something to do. If you say to the mind, 'Don't do anything,' that is the most difficult thing. The mind will ask, 'Give me a mantra at least, so that with closed eyes I can say *Aum, Aum; Ram, Ram …*' Something to do, because how can we remain without doing anything, without something to run after, to chase?

Mind is activity, and being is absolute inactivity. Mind is running; being is sitting. The periphery is moving; the center is not moving. Look at a bullock cart moving – the wheel is moving, but the center around which the whole wheel moves is static, absolutely static, nonmoving. Your being is eternally unmoving, and your periphery is continuously moving. This is the point to remember in Dervish dancing. When you do it, let the body become the periphery – the body moves, and you are eternally unmoving. Become a wheel. The body becomes the wheel, the periphery, and you are the center. Soon you will realize that although the body goes on moving faster and faster and faster, inside you can feel that you are not moving; and the faster the body moves the better, because then the contrast is created. Suddenly, the body and you are separate.

But you move with the body continuously so there is no separation. Go and sit. Simply sitting is enough, not doing anything. Simply close your eyes and sit, and sit, and sit, and allow everything to settle. It will take time, because you have been unsettled for so many lives. You have been trying to create all sorts of disturbances. It will take time, but only time. You need not do anything; you simply look and sit, look and sit … Zen people call it *zazen*. *Zazen* means just sitting, not doing anything.

This is what Chuang Tzu says:

He failed to realize that if he merely stepped into the shade, his shadow would vanish,
and if he sat down and stayed still, there would be no more footsteps.

There was no need to fight, and there was no need to escape. The only thing needed was just to move into the shade and sit still. And this is to be done during your whole life. Don't fight with anything and don't try to escape from anything. Let things take their own course. You simply close your eyes and move inside to the center where no sunray has ever penetrated – there is no shadow. And really, that is the meaning of the myth that gods have no shadows. Not that there are gods somewhere who have no shadows, but the god that is within you has no shadow because no outside penetrates there. It cannot penetrate, it is always under the shade. That shade Chuang Tzu calls Tao, your innermost nature – utterly innermost, absolutely innermost.

So what is to be done? One, don't listen to the mind. It is a good tool for the outside but it is absolutely a barrier for the inside. Logic is good for people, it is not good for yourself. On the contrary, faith is better, because faith is illogical. Faith is dangerous in society because it will cheat you. There logic is needed, doubt is needed. In tackling things, logic and doubt are needed. Science depends on doubt and religion depends on faith, *shraddha*. Just sit, with a deep trust that your inner nature will take over. It always takes over, you have only to wait; patience only is needed. And whatsoever your mind says, simply don't listen to it, because mind says: 'Drop it!'

And mind will go on saying things because you have always listened to it, you have given it so much significance. Even where it is absolutely useless it will go on suggesting and advising.

I have heard that a bank was trying to decide if they should have computers and automatic mechanisms installed in their head-quarters. So an efficiency expert was called in to do some research work: which people were needed and which people were not needed, which people could be disposed of.

The efficiency expert asked a clerk, 'What do you do here?'

The clerk said, 'Nothing.'

Then he asked an executive: 'What do you do here?'

The executive said, 'Nothing.'

Triumphantly, very happy, the efficiency expert turned to the directors and said, 'I told you, there is much duplication. Two people doing nothing – there is much duplication!'

An efficiency expert is an efficiency expert – he uses logic, he has been trained. If two persons are doing the same thing then there is duplication, and if two persons are not doing anything then too there is duplication and one can be disposed of. One has to be retained to do nothing.

Listen to the mind for the outside world, don't listen to the mind for the inside – simply put it aside. There is no need to fight with it, because if you fight with it, it may influence you. You simply put it aside – that's what faith is.

Faith is not a fight with the mind. If you fight, then the enemy impresses you, and remember, even friends don't have such an impact as enemies have. If you fight with someone continuously you will be influenced by them, because you will have to use the same techniques to fight them. Ultimately, enemies become similar. It is very difficult to be aloof and detached from the enemy; the enemy influences you. And those who start fighting with the mind become great philosophers. They may talk about anti-mind, but their whole talk is of the mind. They may say, 'Be against the mind,' but whatsoever they say is coming from the mind, even their enmity. And you have to remain with your enemy. And by and by enemies settle terms, and they become the same.

It happened in the Second World War: Adolf Hitler almost completely turned the whole world Nazi, Fascist. Even his enemies, those who were fighting against Fascism, also became Fascist; they had to. One interesting incident happened: Adolf Hitler was almost mad, and he wouldn't listen to the military experts. He thought himself to be the greatest military genius ever born; so the whole war was to be conducted according to his whims. That's why in the beginning he continued to win, because the French generals, English generals, American generals and Russian generals, could not understand what was going to happen. They could have understood if the war was being run by military generals, they have the same minds. Then they could have known what the next move would be. But here was a madman who didn't believe in any military training, who didn't believe in any military tactics or strategy, who would simply decide. And what was his way of deciding? He had astrologers to decide!

And you may be surprised that when Churchill came to know, he also had to appoint an astrologer. And Churchill thought that this was foolish – because he was an army man! It was foolish to decide how the war should be run by using astrologers! But if the enemy is doing it, what can you do? And the moment he appointed astrologers he started to win, because now they were the same.

Always remember: don't fight with the mind, otherwise you will have to yield to the terms. If you want to convince the mind, you have to be argumentative – and that is the whole point. If you have to convince the mind you have to use words – that is the whole problem.

Simply put it aside. This putting aside is *shraddha*. It is not against mind, it is beyond mind; it is simply putting it aside. Just as when you go out you use your shoes, and when you come in you put them aside – there is no fight, nothing. You don't say to the shoes, 'Now I am going in and you are not needed so I will put you aside.' You simply put them aside; they are not needed.

Just like this: Easy is right – there is no fight. Easy is right – there is no struggle and conflict. You simply put mind aside, move into the inner shade and sit; then no footsteps are heard, and no shadow follows you. You become god-like. And you can become only that which you are already. So I tell you, you are god-like, you are gods. Don't settle for less than that.

And don't create any ideal, otherwise you will create conflict and condemnation, escaping and fighting – and your whole life becomes a riddle. Life is a mystery, not a riddle. It has to be lived, not solved.

CHAPTER 4

FIGHTING COCK

Chi Hsing Tzu was a trainer of fighting cocks for King Hsuan.

He was training a fine bird. The king kept asking if the bird was ready for combat.

'Not yet,' said the trainer. 'He is full of fire. He is ready to pick a fight with every other bird. He is vain and confident of his own strength.'

After ten days he answered again, 'Not yet. He flares up when he hears another bird crow.'

After ten more days, 'Not yet. He still gets that angry look and ruffles his feathers.'

Again ten days. The trainer said, 'Now he is nearly ready. When another bird crows, his eye does not even flicker. He stands immobile like a block of wood. He is a mature fighter. Other birds will take one look at him and run.'

The human mind always ends with the ego – that is its final growth. So first try to understand how the human mind becomes the ego.

The ego is the barrier: the more you are, the less the divine can be; the less you are, the more available you are for the divine. If you are totally empty the divine becomes the guest; and he can become the guest only when you are totally empty, when not even a fragment of you is left. Then you become the host and he becomes the guest. When you are not, you are the host; when you are, all your prayers are in vain, all your invitations false. When you are, you have not called him yet because your call can only be authentic when you are not. It is the silent thirst of an empty being, a silent prayer without any words of a mind which is no more, of an ego which is dissolved.

Once it happened that Mulla Nasruddin came to me, very much disturbed, sad, perplexed, and he said: 'I am in deep trouble. A problem has arisen – and I am not a blind believer, I am a rational man.'

So I asked him, 'What is the problem?'

He said, 'Just this morning I saw a mouse sitting on the Koran, the Holy Koran! So I am disturbed: if the Koran cannot protect itself against an ordinary mouse, how can it protect me? My whole faith is shattered, my whole being is troubled. Now I cannot believe in the Koran anymore. What should I do?'

So I told him, 'This is the logical step. Now you start believing in the mouse, because you have seen with your own eyes that the mouse is stronger than the Holy Koran.'

And, of course, strength is the only criterion for the mind; power is what the mind is in search of – Friedrich Nietzsche is right.

I told Mulla Nasruddin, 'Man is nothing but a will to power. And now you have seen with your own eyes that a mouse is more powerful than the Holy Koran.'

He was convinced. Of course there was no way to escape from logic, so he started worshipping the mouse. But soon he was in trouble because one day he saw a cat jump on the mouse. But this time he didn't come to ask me; now he had the key in his own hand – he started to worship the cat. Soon he was in trouble again. A dog chased the cat and the cat was trembling, so he started to worship the dog. But then again he was in trouble.

One day his wife beat the dog to death. Then he came again. He said, 'Now this is too much. I can worship a mouse, a cat, a dog, but not my own wife.'

So I told him, 'Nasruddin, you are a rational man, and this is how reason moves. You cannot go back, you have to accept it.'

So he said, 'Then I will do one thing. I will take a picture of her without anybody knowing and I will go inside my room, lock the door from the inside, and worship her. But please don't tell her.'

So he started to worship her in secrecy and privacy. Things were going well. Then one day Mulla Nasrudin's wife came running to me, and she said, 'Something has been wrong for many days. We thought that he had gone a little crazy because he had been worshipping a mouse, then he was worshipping a cat, then a dog, and for a few days he has been doing something secret inside his room. He locks it and allows nobody in. But today, just out of curiosity, I looked through the keyhole, and it is too much to bear!'

I asked, 'What was he doing?'

She said, 'You come and see.'

So I had to go and look through the keyhole! He was standing naked before a mirror worshipping himself! So I knocked on the door, and he came out and said, 'This is the logical conclusion. This morning I got angry and beat my wife, and I thought, "I am more powerful than her." So now I am worshipping myself.'

This is how mind goes on moving towards the ego – the final goal is 'I'. And if you listen to the mind this goal is bound to come sooner or later: you will have to worship yourself. And I am not kidding. This is how the whole of humanity has come to worship. All gods have been thrown aside, all the temples have become useless, and man worships himself. How does it happen?

If you listen to the mind it will convince you, by subtle arguments, that you are the center of the world, you are the most significant being in the world, you are the most superior – you are God. This egoistical attitude is bound to come; it is a logical, final step. And the mind will raise doubts about everything but it will never raise any doubt about your ego.

Whenever the mind feels that it has to surrender, it will raise doubts. It will say: 'What are you doing? Surrendering to a master? Surrendering to a God? Surrendering in a temple, or in a church? Surrendering in prayer and love? Surrendering in sex? What are you doing? You are losing yourself. Be alert and control yourself, otherwise you will be lost.'

Whenever there is something where you can let go of yourself, the mind resists. That is why the mind is against love – because love is a surrendering. In love the ego cannot exist. That is why the mind is against a master, a guru, because the ego has to be surrendered; otherwise the master cannot function. That is why the mind is against God, because if there is a God then you can never be the most superior; then the ego will always remain inferior, then you can never be enthroned upon the highest conceivable pedestal – so you cannot allow God.

Nietzsche said: It is impossible for me to allow there to be a God, because then what will happen to me? Then where am I? If God is, then I am nowhere; so I will choose myself, not God. That is why he said: God is dead and man is now free, absolutely free. Nietzsche set the trend for this century; he was the prophet of this century. He is at the base of you all, whether you know him or not; he is deep down in everybody who has been born in the twentieth century. Within you God is dead, only the ego is alive.

And remember: they cannot both exist together.

In the Old Testament there is a beautiful sentence. The sentence is, 'You cannot see God alive.' The meaning is the same: when you see God you have to die, you cannot see God alive. When you die, only then can you see God because you are the barrier, you are the wall. Ego or God, that is how things are going to be; you cannot manage both. And if you try to manage both, you will manage the ego and God will be dead – within you. In existence, God cannot be dead; but within you, God will be dead. He will not be there. You have pushed him out because you are too filled with yourself. You are too much. And the ego is not porous; it has no space for anybody else. It is very jealous, it is absolutely jealous. It will not allow anybody else to enter into the inner sanctum of your being. It wants to be the most superior ruler.

The mind is always against surrendering. That is why, as the mind has become more prominent, all dimensions of surrender have disappeared. This century suffers because this century cannot surrender. This is the problem. This is the basic crux of the modern mind – and you go on asking: How can I love? The mind cannot love. The mind can go to war, that is easy, but the mind cannot move into love – that is impossible – because in war the mind can exist, it can function well; but in love, mind has to surrender.

Love means giving power to the other over yourself. And you are afraid: it means the other becomes so important, so much more impor-tant than you that if a crisis comes you would sacrifice yourself for your lover. The lover is enthroned – you are just a servant, you are just a shadow. This is difficult for the mind. That is why love is not possible and even sex becomes impossible. Because even in sex a moment comes when you have to lose yourself – only then can the orgasm happen, only then can the whole body be filled with a new energy, with new vibrations, with bio-electricity. It can become a vibrant, radiant flow – you lose yourself – but even that is not possible.

Ejaculation is not orgasm, it is just the physical part of it.

Orgasm is psychic, it is spiritual. Ejaculation is just futile; it can relieve the body, that's all. It works as a safety valve: when there is too much energy you can release it through ejaculation, but that is not the real thing. The real thing is when you come to a peak of vibrancy, you come to a peak of ecstasy, and from that peak everything relaxes, your whole being relaxes. First, the whole being vibrates with a new music – it is in tune with the cosmos, the ego is not there, you are just energy; there is nobody inside, just energy moving like a river in flood – and then the flood goes, the river relaxes, and you are in tune with the whole cosmos – then it is orgasm. Orgasm is an inner phenomenon.

But orgasm has become impossible, and because of the lack of orgasm ninety percent of people are neurotic in a subtle way. This is because you have lost the easiest approach to the divine. You have lost the natural possibility of being one, even for moments, with the whole. And the whole rejuvenates, the whole gives you life and energy, the whole refreshes you. And the old is destroyed by the orgasm – your whole energy becomes new, fresh and young. Otherwise, you go on becoming dull and dead. But this has become impossible because of the ego. The problem is the same, whether it is in the dimension of sex, or of love, or of prayer, or of meditation, the problem is the same. You have to surrender, and the ego cannot surrender, it can only fight.

Why is the ego always ready to fight? Every moment you are ready to jump upon someone, to find an excuse to fight, argue, and be angry. Why is the ego always in search of a fight? Because fight is the fuel: through fight it feels powerful; through fight it exists. Ego is the deepest violence, and if you want to strengthen the ego you have to go on fighting continuously. For twenty-four hours a day you have to fight with something or other. But an enemy must be there so that you can have the challenge, the conflict, and you can maintain the ego.

Ego needs constant war. Why? Firstly, through war it accumulates energy. Secondly, ego is always afraid, that is why it is always ready to fight – there is fear. Ego can never be fearless, never. Why? Because it is a false thing, it is not natural, it is not part of the Tao. It is an artificial human device; you have to manage it and maintain it continuously. If for even a single moment you don't manage it, it will disappear – that is the fear. So you are constantly alert.

If for even twenty-four hours you live an egoless existence, you will be surprised, amazed, mystified. What happened to that ego which you have been carrying for so many lives? Even within twenty-four hours it will simply disappear because it needs a constant refueling, again and again. It is not a natural phenomenon; it has no perpetual energy in it.

Existence goes on perpetually, eternally; it has something eternal, inexhaustible. This tree may die, but immediately another tree will replace it; the energy moves into another. Your body may fall, but the energy moves into another body. You have deep down, like everything else in existence, some eternal energy which cannot be exhausted. You need fuel for the body. If you don't eat and don't drink you will die. If you don't eat, then within three months you will die; if you don't drink, within three weeks you will die; if you don't breathe, within three minutes you will die. Constant fuel is needed for the body because the body is not an eternal phenomenon.

But for consciousness no fuel is needed. When this body dies your consciousness moves into another womb. Consciousness is perpetual movement. It is nonending energy – no beginning, no end. It never started and it will never end. That is why when you become one with consciousness there is no fear. Fear disappears only when you have hit upon the eternal source, the immortal, which cannot die – the deathless.

And the ego is very fragile; every moment it is on the verge of dying. And anybody can kill it, just a gesture can kill it, just a look. Somebody looks at you, and the ego is troubled. That man seems to be an enemy. A gesture of enmity and you feel a trembling because the ego is fragile. It is a false, artificial thing, it has to be maintained. That is why there is so much fear, and amidst this fear, this oceanic fear, you manage to create a few islands of bravery. Otherwise, it would be too difficult.

You think yourself brave – even a coward, the most cowardly man, thinks himself brave – because that too is a very complex problem. The ego is afraid, fearful, inside, because death can happen at any moment. In love, death can happen; in prayer, death can happen to the ego; in any deep relationship the ego will have to die. Even if you look at a rose without thinking, the ego will have to die. Even a rose can kill it; it is so fragile, just flimsy, a dreamlike thing – nothing substantial about it. So afraid, and deep down continuously thinking of death, still you go on thinking yourself to be brave. That is how this bravery, this fearlessness, this 'I am not a coward,' helps your ego. If you come to know that the ego is a coward, that 'I am a coward' – if you really realize and become aware that this ego is fear and nothing else – you will not maintain it. You will drop it. Why carry a disease? But the disease is hidden and you think it is not a disease; rather, it is the only health.

It happened that Mulla Nasruddin got married. He went to the hills for his honeymoon. The very first night, at midnight, somebody knocked on the door. Nasruddin got up and opened the door. There was a man with a pistol in his hand, a robber. He came in. But he forgot about robbery when he saw Mulla Nasruddin's wife, a beautiful young girl. He forgot all about robbery. And he said to Mulla Nasruddin, 'You stand in that corner.'

Then he drew a circle around him, and told him, 'Don't step out of it – one step and you are no more.' Then he kissed Nasruddin's wife and made love to her.

When he had gone, the wife said, 'What sort of man are you?

– standing there in the circle and watching another man make love to your wife!'

Nasruddin said, 'I am not a coward!' And triumphantly he continued, 'Whenever the man turned his back towards me I would step out of the circle, and not just once, three times!'

This is how the ego goes on maintaining itself, just stepping out of the circle. When the back is turned, when death is not looking at you, then you step. And not only once, thrice! And you feel good. And I tell you that everybody is standing in a corner with a circle around him. You stand inside the circle and sometimes you step out just to feel that you are not a coward. But the ego *is* a coward, it cannot be otherwise. You cannot see a fearless man with an ego – it is impossible, it is not in the way of nature.

Why is it impossible? How can the ego be fearless? It cannot be eternal, it cannot be immortal, death is bound to happen. The ego is a created phenomenon, created by you; it is going to disappear. And when death is there – a certainty – how can you be fearless? Sometimes you may step out of the circle, that is all. But with ego there can be no fearlessness. So remember three words: one is 'coward', another is 'brave', and the third is 'fearlessness'. Cowardice is part of the ego, the deeper part, the real thing; and bravery is stepping out of the circle thrice. It is also part of the cowardice but hidden, decorated. It is a wound with flowers upon it, a wound hidden by flowers. Bravery is nothing other than cowardice decorated and refined; inside every brave man you will find a coward. Even your Napoleons, Hitlers and Alexanders are cowards. Their bravery is nothing but stepping out of the circle thrice – inside you will find the same trembling coward. Just to hide that coward, you project bravery – bravery is a trick. And now psychologists also know about it.

Religion has always been aware that to hide something you project the opposite. If you are a fool, you will try to project some wisdom around you to hide the fact. If you are ugly then you will beautify your body, your face, your hair, to somehow hide the fact that you are ugly. With clothes and ornaments you will try to hide it. If you are inferior inside, you will project superiority, just to show others that 'I am not inferior.' If you feel a nobodiness – and everybody feels it because with the ego, everybody is a nobody – then you will try to project, and enforce and emphasize that you are somebody.

Cowardice and bravery are two aspects of the same coin: fear is in both, they are two faces of fear. One is simple and direct, another is cunning and hidden – a brave man is a cunning coward.

I have heard:

Once it happened that a soldier fighting on the front got very scared, so he started to run towards the rear. An officer stopped him and asked, 'What are you doing? Where are you going? The fight is on! Are you a coward?'

But the man was so scared, he didn't bother to answer; he continued running. The officer followed him, got hold of him and said, 'Where are you running? Why are you not answering? Do you know who I am? I am your general!'

The soldier said, 'My God, am I that far back?'

Your generals, your leaders – they are always at the back. They never get killed, they are never in trouble, they are perfect cowards posing as if they are the bravest. Others die for them and they remain at the back. Your Napoleons, your Hitlers, your Alexanders are all cowards projecting, creating a phenomenon that is just the opposite of their inner feeling. This has to be remembered; only then can you remember a third possibility: fearlessness. A man who is fearless is neither a coward nor brave, he is neither. He cannot be, because he is simply fearless. A Mahavira, a Buddha, a Chuang Tzu, a Jesus – they are not brave men, not at all, because they are not cowards. You can be brave only if you are a coward! You can step out of the circle thrice only if you are standing in the circle; otherwise how can you step out of it? If you never agreed to stand in the circle, how can you step out thrice and show your bravery?

A fearless man is one who has come to know the deathless within himself, one who has come to understand the inner, the immortal, the innermost eternal. Then there is no fear, and then there is no bravery either, because bravery is just a cover-up. This man is neither a fool nor is he wise, because wisdom is simply nothing but a cover-up. And this man is not divided into opposites: this man is a unity, he is one, he is a unique phenomenon; that is why you cannot define him. It is impossible to define a buddha. How will you define him? Will you call him a coward? You cannot! Will you call him brave? You cannot! Will you call him a fool? You cannot! Will you call him wise? No! Because wisdom is the opposite of foolishness and bravery is the opposite of cowardice.

What will you call a buddha? Whatsoever you call a buddha will be wrong. You have to be simply silent before a buddha. Will you call him a sinner or a saint? No, he is neither. How can you be a saint without sin inside? Sainthood is nothing but a decoration, a cover-up. This is the problem. Whenever a buddha appears, this is the problem: we cannot define him, we cannot put him into any category. You cannot label him, there is no way you can put him anywhere. Either he belongs to everywhere or he belongs to nowhere. He transcends all categories. Pigeonholes are not for him. The whole language drops before a buddha, the mind becomes silent. You cannot say anything which can be relevant. He is fearless, he is mindless; you cannot call him a fool or a wise man because the mind is needed for both.

And now enter this beautiful story of Chuang Tzu: it is one of his most beautiful parables.

Chi Hsing Tzu was a trainer of fighting cocks for King Hsuan. He was training a fine bird. The king kept asking if the bird was ready for combat.

This man, Chi Hsing, was not only a trainer, he was a man of Tao. In China, in Japan, in the Far East, they have used all sorts of things as stepping boards for meditation. All sorts of things: archery, painting, swordsmanship, even training cocks and birds to fight. Name any dimension of life and they have used it for an inner training. This man, Chi Hsing, was asked by the king to train a cock for him. The king was interested in combat, in competition, and of course he was also interested in his cock winning the competition.

Even through cocks our egos fight. We use everything for the ego; even games become adulterated by it. Then you are not interested in the game, you are only interested in how to win it – that is the difference between play and a game. In play you are interested in the play itself – children's play. Then play is beautiful, and if your whole life can become a play it will become a beautiful thing. In a game you are not interested in the play itself, you are interested in the end result. You are interested in how to win, and when you are interested in how to win, you have destroyed the game. Now it is no longer play, it has become a business.

From the very first, remember that this man, Chi Hsing, had one type of interest in training the cock, and the king had another: he was interested in combat, and the trainer was interested in something else.

Chi Hsing was training a fine bird.

The king kept asking if the bird was ready for combat. 'Not yet,' said the trainer, 'He is full of fire.'

Look ... the king would have said: 'If he is full of fire, that is what we need, because when you fight with somebody and you are full of fire there is more possibility of winning.' The king must have been puzzled. What type of trainer is this man? He says, 'Not yet, because he is still full of fire.'

'He is ready to pick a fight with every other bird.'

He is constantly ready to fight – that means he is afraid, so he is not ready. When you are afraid, how can you be ready to fight? Look at the different minds: the logic of the mind will say that if you are full of fire and ready to fight with everybody, then you can become a great warrior – you are already. Why are you waiting? What are you waiting for? If the fire is ready, fight! Because if you wait too long the fire may go; if you wait too long the energy may subside.

But with a no-mind it is absolutely different, the gestalt is different. The man of no-mind says: 'Because he is still ready to fight at every moment, he is not yet ready.' Why? Because when you are ready to fight at every moment you are a coward. Fight is a cover-up. You want to prove that you are a brave man. The very wanting, the very desire to prove, means that you are not. A man who is really wise will never in any way be searching for opportunities to prove that he is wise. A fool is always in search of a way to prove that he is wise. A man who is really in love, who has become love, will not try to prove that he is in love.

When you are not in love you try to prove in many, many ways that you are in love. You bring presents, you go on talking about love, but all your efforts say just the opposite. If you really love a person you will not even mention the fact that you love them. What is the need? If the other cannot understand your love without words, the love is not worth anything. If you have to say it, it means that something is false.

Ask a Dale Carnegie and he will say that even if you don't feel it, every morning tell your wife again and again that you love her. Whenever you have an opportunity in the day, don't forget to repeat it. When you go to sleep, repeat it again, make it a mantra. And he is right – as you are, he is right, because your wife will depend on words. You also depend on words. That is why whenever two people fall in love, in the beginning they talk so much about love. They are so poetic, and because they are courting each other there is much romance and dreaming. By and by it subsides, because you cannot continue the same thing again and again, it looks foolish. And the moment it starts looking foolish, they start feeling that something has gone wrong. Now there is no love because the love depended only on words. In the very beginning it was not there; you talked about it, but it was not there. Your talk was a cover-up.

Remember this word cover-up. In your whole life you are doing that in every dimension. And Dale Carnegie looks right, he appeals. His books are being sold all over the world – millions of copies, second only to the Bible. But I tell you: beware of Dale Carnegies because they are the persons who are making you more and more false. Then you cannot be authentic. There is no need to say, 'Love,' or, 'I love you.' Let your whole being say it. If you love, it will say it – words are not needed at all. The way that you say it will express it; the way that you move will express it; the way that you look will express it. Your whole being will express it.

Love is such a vital phenomenon that you cannot hide it. Has anybody ever been capable of hiding his love? Nobody can hide it; it is such a fire inside – it glows. Whenever somebody falls in love you can see from his face, from his eyes, that he is no longer the same person – something has transformed him. A fire has happened, a new fragrance has come into his being. He walks with a dancing step; he talks, and his very talk has a poetic flavor to it. And not only with his beloved – when you are in love your whole being is transformed. Even talking to a stranger on the street, you are different. And if the stranger has known love in his life he knows that this man is in love.

You cannot hide love, it is almost impossible. Nobody has ever been successful in hiding love. But when it is not, then you have to project it, then you have to pretend it.

A small boy was visiting a zoo and there was a deer park, full of deer. He asked the keeper, 'What are these animals called?'

The keeper replied, 'The same thing that your mother calls your father in the morning when they get up.'

The boy said, 'Don't tell me that these are skunks!'

Something goes sour; something becomes like a wound when it is false; something becomes ugly. There is no ugliness except falseness, but you hide it with the opposite.

'Not yet,' said the trainer. 'He is full of fire.'

That shows that he is afraid, otherwise why is he full of fire? To whom are you showing your fire? What is the need? Fear inside, fire outside: that is the projection.

'He is ready to pick a fight with every other bird.'

Unnecessarily. Whosoever comes on his path, he is ready.

'He is vain and confident of his own strength.'

Not yet. He is not ready. When you think you are confident of your strength, remember well, you are hiding something from yourself. What do you mean when you say, 'I am confident'? If you are really confident the word is meaningless. You are not confident, you are pretending. And not only to others! You are repeating to yourself, 'I am confident.' You are creating an auto-hypnosis. If you repeat it long enough you may start feeling it, but that feeling will have no inner energy in it.

Everybody keeps on repeating to himself, 'I am confident.' Why? What are you hiding? If this confidence that you talk about is really there then there is no need to say anything about it. A really confident man is not even aware of it. This has to be understood:

whenever something is false you are aware of it, self-conscious. When something is real, you simply forget it. Do you remember that you are breathing? If something goes wrong, yes. If it is hard and there is something wrong with your lungs and you have a cold or asthma, then you remember that you are breathing. But when everything goes okay, you are not conscious. *When the shoe fits, the foot is forgotten.* When you are really confident, confidence is forgotten.

People come to me and they say that they have absolute confidence in me. What is this 'absolute'? What are you covering up? Is confidence not enough? What is *absolute* confidence? It is not absolute, that is why you say it. You say, 'I love you totally.' What is this total? Have you ever heard about any love which is not total? Love is total. Why do you repeat the same word again? Inside you know it is not total, and if you don't say it who else will say it? Nobody can know it without your saying, because if it was total, everybody would know.

A total love is a transfiguration; a total love is a death and a new life; a total love needs nobody to say anything about it.

I have heard about a great connoisseur: he was a wine taster. A friend invited him to his house because he had some very, very old valuable wines and he wanted to show this man his collection. He wanted this man's appreciation. He gave him one of his most valuable wines. The man tasted it but remained silent. He didn't say anything, not even that it was good. The friend felt hurt. Then he gave him a very rough, ordinary wine. He tasted it and said, 'Very, very good, fine!'

The friend was puzzled. He said, 'I am puzzled. I gave you one of the rarest, most valuable wines, and you remained silent, yet to this ordinary, not even costly, rough wine you say, "Very, very good!"'

The connoisseur said, 'For the first, nobody is required to say anything. It speaks for itself. But for the second, somebody is needed to praise it, otherwise it will feel hurt!'

When you say 'absolute' confidence you know that it is not absolute; that is why you are saying it, although you may not be conscious of it. Be conscious and use words carefully.

> *'Not yet,' said the trainer. 'He is full of fire. He is*
> *ready to pick a fight with every other bird.*

> *He is vain and confident of his own strength.'*

And you can observe this in your own life also. This is happening all around. You are ready to fight with everybody – just waiting for the opportunity, just for some excuse. Someone treads on your toe and a fight starts. Why are you so ready? Because you are troubled inside, you know you are nobody, so if someone treads on your toe immediately you say, 'Do you know who I am?' And you yourself don't know.

> *After ten days, he answered again, 'Not yet. He flares*
> *up when he hears another bird crow.'*

The king went on insisting because the day for the competition was coming nearer and nearer, and the king's cock must win. And this man went on delaying – the excuses that he was giving looked just absurd.

Whenever there is a man of Tao his statements will look absurd. They are, because they don't fit in with your mind.

He says again after ten days: *'Not yet. He flares up when he hears another bird crow.'* He is still immature, childish. This is not the way of a warrior, this is the way of a coward. This is not the way of a fearless man, a fearless cock, no! It is not the way of those who are fearless.

When anybody – when any bird is crowing, why do you feel that it is meant for you? Why do you feel that the challenge is for you? Why do you take the whole world as your enemy? If you take the whole world as your enemy, it means that somewhere, deep down, you have not hit upon the source. Otherwise the whole world would be felt as friendly; friendliness would be the main note. If enemies happen that would be an exception. Now enmity is the main note and if friends happen that is an exception. And you can never know, and you can never even believe in a friend, because you know enmity so much.

It happened that Mulla Nasruddin was made a Justice of the Peace. It has to be done because there are mischievous people. If they are very, very mischievous, you make them governors. If they are even more mischievous, you send them abroad as ambassadors. If they are just ordinarily mischievous, local, then you make them Justices of the Peace. They have to be given something to do so that they don't make too much mischief.

Mulla Nasruddin is a mischievous person, but not very big; if you will allow me to say so, a very small VIP, not a big gun – just a local gun. So they made him a JP – Justice of the Peace. He changed his drawing room into a court, engaged a clerk and a watchman, got up in the early morning, waited and waited, but nobody turned up. By the evening he was very depressed and he said to the clerk, 'Not a single case! No murder, no robbery, no crime committed in the town. If things continue in this way then it will be a very boring job. I was very excited, but not even a traffic offense! Nothing has turned up.'

Said the clerk, 'Don't be so depressed, Mulla. Just trust in human nature. Something is bound to happen sooner or later. I still have enough trust in human nature.'

What type of human nature is this clerk talking about? He says that he still has enough trust, something is bound to happen. 'Just you wait, things will happen.'

Your courts, your judges, your governments depend on you, on your nature. This whole nonsense is run because of you, and the basis of it is that you are always ready to fight. If the society really becomes more and more natural, the government will disappear. It is a disease. The courts will disappear – they are not good signs. The policeman is there because the criminal is there, and the whole structure exists just because of one thing: because you are always ready to fight, to flare up. Because of your ego the government exists, the court exists, the magistrate exists. If ego is dropped the whole of politics disappears. All politics exist because of the ego.

'Not yet. He flares up when he hears another bird crow.'

After ten more days, 'Not yet. He still gets that angry look and ruffles his feathers.'

He is getting silent, growing, becoming more and more mature – but not yet. As yet, *'He still gets that angry look and ruffles his feathers.'* Deep down in the unconscious he is still ready to fight. On the surface he is getting calm and quiet, but if a cock passes he still gets that angry look. Now it is not conscious, now it is unconscious; but he is growing, moving. Now the fight has dropped from his conscious mind but from the unconscious it has not dropped – not yet.

Again ten days. The trainer said, 'Now he is nearly ready.'

Not yet perfectly ready, but nearly ready.

'When another bird crows, his eye does not even flicker. He stands immobile like a block of wood. He is a mature fighter. Other birds will take one look at him and run.'

There is no need for him to fight. When the fighter is mature, there is no need to fight. When the warrior is really there, fearless, what is the need to fight? His very presence will be enough: other birds will run. And this happened. This bird was put into combat; he just stood there. The other birds came with much bravery, they stepped out of the circle, they were filled with ego, arrogant and vain – but then they looked at this bird. This bird looked abnormal, not of this world at all. He was standing just like a buddha. They tried to make him angry but not even his eyes would flicker. They jumped, they crowed, but to no effect. Then they trembled: this bird is not natural, this bird is a stranger, he does not belong to us.

They simply got the message that this bird was neither cowardly nor brave; he was simply fearless, and whenever there is a fearless being the other has to run. The training is the same for a Zen warrior, for a samurai – the same. He has to fight but with no anger. This seems difficult, because you even love with anger; yet he has to fight without anger.

There is a Sufi story:

It happened in the life of Omar, a great Mohammedan Caliph. He was fighting with an enemy for thirty years. The enemy was very strong and the fight continued – a lifetime of war. In the end, it happened one day that the opportunity came.

The enemy fell off his horse and Omar jumped on him with his spear. In just one second the spear would have pierced the heart of the man and everything would have been finished. But in that small gap the enemy did one thing: he spat on Omar's face – and the spear stopped.

Omar touched his face, got up and told the enemy, 'Tomorrow we start again.'

The enemy was puzzled. He said, 'What is the matter? I have been waiting for this for thirty years, and you have been waiting for this for thirty years. I have been waiting, hoping that someday or other I would be on your chest with my spear and the thing would be finished. That opportunity never came to me, but it came your way. You could have finished me in a single moment. What is the matter with you?'

Said Omar, 'This has not been an ordinary war. I have taken a vow, a Sufi vow, that I will fight without anger. For thirty years I was fighting without anger. But just for a moment anger came. When you spat, just for a moment I felt angry and it became personal. I wanted to kill you – the ego came in.

Up to now for thirty years that was not a problem at all, we were fighting for a cause. You were not my enemy, it was not personal in any way. I was not in any way interested in killing you; I just wanted the cause to win. But just now, for a moment, I forgot about the cause. You were my enemy and I wanted to kill you. That is why I cannot kill you. So, tomorrow we start again.'

But the war never started again because the enemy became a friend. He said, 'Now teach me. Be my master and let me be your disciple. I would also like to fight without anger.'

The whole secret is to fight without the ego, and if you can fight without the ego then you will be capable of doing everything without the ego. Because fight is the climax of the ego: if you can do that then you can do everything. Right now you cannot even love without ego.

So this is the training of a samurai, of a Zen warrior – to fight without the ego just like this cock. *'Now he is nearly ready.'* But remember the words 'nearly ready'. Why not perfect? Because the Tao says the perfect cannot exist in this world, only the nearly perfect. The moment you are perfect, you disappear. Perfection cannot exist in matter, in the material. Matter itself gives a little imperfection of its own. You cannot be in the body and be perfect – a little will always be missing – and that little which is missing is the link.

That is why you can be in the body. Once you are perfect you disappear, you die. But a perfect man never dies; he simply disappears. You depart, but a perfect man disappears. Departure means that arrival will happen immediately, because departure is just a part – the beginning of arrival. Arrival is the beginning of departure. You depart from this world to arrive again. A perfect man simply disappears because he is so perfect that matter cannot hold him; he is so perfect that the body cannot contain him; he is so perfect that in this imperfect world he cannot have any form. He becomes formless.

That is why the trainer said, *'Now he is nearly ready.'* And you cannot imagine how he can be any readier. This seems to be the last thing. *'When another bird crows, his eye does not even flicker.'* What more perfection? *'He stands immobile like a block of wood.'* What further perfection is possible? *'He is a mature fighter. Other birds will take one look at him and run.'*

What further perfection is possible? It is possible. Because he may be standing immobile, just like a block of wood; his eyes may be static, with not even a flicker; the other birds may run and he may win the combat – but he still is. That is why he is not perfect: he still *is*.

And everything that he is doing is being done through effort: that is why he is imperfect. He has been trained to do this and now he is ready. He will perform, but deep inside he is the old cock. A slight tremor will be there. It cannot be detected, nobody can detect it; from the outside he is a perfect saint, but inside he is still the old cock, deep down at the center he is still the same. And this is the problem. You can practice religion and you can practice it so much that you become almost perfect. But almost perfect is still imperfect, and you have to be absolutely perfect.

What is absolute perfection? When the training, the effort, is dropped. *Easy is right*. And this cock is still with effort; he is doing it. He is immobile, but deep down it is not a nondoing. He is doing it. He has been trained, disciplined.

Religion is not a discipline, it is not something to practice. It is something to flow into, to let go in. It is something not to be forced. You are not to begin from the outside and force it; you have to help it from the inside and let it flow, overflow, to the outside. It should be spontaneous.

So what is to be done? If you wait for the spontaneous it doesn't seem to come. If you practice you may become just like this cock: good for the combat, good for the other, but for yourself you remain the old.

That is what has happened to many so-called saints. You go to them – their saintliness is still with effort. They are maintaining it. And whenever you maintain something it is not authentic, because the against, the opposite, is still lying there somewhere in the unconscious. It can uncoil at any moment; and if you relax it will uncoil.

Once it happened that a Sufi was brought to me. For thirty years he had been practicing, and he had really practiced, there was no doubt about it. He was almost perfect, just like this cock. He had many disciples and they told me that wherever he looks – in the trees, in the rocks, in the stars – he sees Allah, the divine, everywhere.

The Sufi came to stay with me for three days. He chanted continuously – the Sufis call it *Gigra* – the name of Allah. Even when taking his bath he would go on chanting. I asked him, 'Why? If you are now able to see Allah everywhere, why go on chanting his name? What are you practicing for? If Allah is everywhere and the divine is everywhere, to whom are you calling? And who is this chanter inside? Drop it! For the three days that you are here with me drop all your practice.'

He could see the point – he was a humble man. He could see the point that if you are still practicing then it has not been achieved. He said, 'I have absolute confidence that it has been achieved.'

So I said, 'Then you drop it.'

The moment he said 'absolute confidence' it was clear that he would be in difficulty if he dropped it. He dropped it, he had to, and for three days I watched him.

On the third day, at four o'clock in the morning, he came running into my room, started shaking me and said, 'What have you done? Everything is lost! Now I cannot see God: things have started to appear again. A tree is a tree, a stone is a stone. What have you done? You have killed me. You have destroyed my thirty years' effort. You are not a friend, you are an enemy!'

So I told him, 'Be a little more silent and sit by my side, and let us see what has happened. I am not your enemy. Because even if you continue this practice for thirty lives, nothing is going to happen. You will always be almost ready. Any time you stop this practice, the old will be back. It has not disappeared, it is only hiding, and you are pushing it in. Your practice is nothing but pushing it in. You stop the practice and it uncoils. It is like a spring: you go on pushing it and you think everything is okay; you take your hand off and the spring opens and uncoils and everything is back as it was. So don't be angry and don't feel at a loss. This is a great realization. Now don't practice, just look at the tree! You need not project God into it.'

This is the difference between an authentic and an unauthentic religious man. Look at the tree, don't impose God on it. If you say it is God and go on repeating it you will be almost at the point where it will start looking like God. But that God is false. You have imposed it, it is a projection. Look at the tree and be silent. No need to project your God on the tree: the tree is God enough, it doesn't need your God to be imposed on it.

You just be silent with the tree, and by and by, as you become more and more silent, you will see that with your silence the tree is transforming. And one day you will realize that everything is divine; and nobody can take that divineness away from you. It is not a practiced thing, it has happened. The real happens not through words but through silence.

And this trainer said that now he was nearly ready – because he had practiced, had been forced. This is how many so-called saints are 'completely' ready, trained. They are good for demonstration, but, deep down, good for nothing. A real sage is one who lives spontaneously. All his experience is without any projection of the mind.

So what is to be done? In the beginning you will have to practice, otherwise the spontaneous may not come. And you have forced it to such hidden depths, it may not bubble up, it may not pop up into your consciousness. So what is to be done? Practice first, and practice so totally that you also come to the point where I can say to you, 'Now you are nearly ready.'

Then the next step is to drop all practice, and just watch what is happening. If you drop the practice, then everything old will start coming again. Now just be a witness and watch it. If you can watch, it will exhaust itself – no need to do anything. ·

Your practice is just to push the coil to the very end – push the spring to the very end. What happens? You try it with a spring – you push it to the very end and then let it go. It will not only uncoil, it will jump. This happens if you practice with your whole being as much as possible – you can never be really whole, but as much as possible.

Your mind, just like a spring, is pushed against a wall and you go on pushing and pushing and pushing. All these meditations that I tell you to do are just pushing the mind to the wall, to the very end. And the moment I see that now there is no more ahead, the spring cannot be pushed any more, any further, you are almost ready, I will say, 'Drop!' The spring will not only uncoil, it will jump out of you! And once the mind jumps out of you, you are freed from it. Then no practice is needed. Then there is just moment-to-moment living, celebrating; then moment-to-moment thanksgiving; then moment-to-moment bliss and ecstasy.

CHAPTER 5

MONKEY MOUNTAIN

The Prince of Wu took a boat to Monkey Mountain.
As soon as the monkeys saw him they all fled in panic
and hid in the treetops.
One monkey, however, remained, completely
unconcerned, swinging from branch to branch – an
extraordinary display.
The prince shot an arrow at the monkey, but the
monkey dexterously caught the arrow in mid-flight.
At this the prince ordered his attendants to make a
concerted attack. In an instant the monkey was shot full
of arrows and fell dead.

Then the prince turned to his companion Yen Pu'i,
'You see what happened? This animal advertised his
cleverness. He trusted in his own skill. He thought no
one could touch him. Remember that! Do not rely on
distinction and talent when you deal with men!'
When they returned home, Yen Pu'i became a disciple of
a sage to get rid of everything that made him
outstanding.
He renounced every pleasure. He learned to hide every
distinction.

Soon no one in the kingdom knew what to make of him.
Thus they held him in awe.

This story carries one of the most secret keys of Tao. Tao says
that whatsoever is beautiful in you, hide it, never act it out;
whatsoever is truthful in you, valuable, hide it, because whenever
a truth is hidden in the heart, it grows like a seed hidden in the
earth. Don't throw it out. If you throw a seed on the street for
everybody to see it will die, and die to no purpose. It will simply die,
there will be no rebirth.

Treat all that is beautiful, good and true, just like a seed. Give
it some soil, a hidden place in the heart – don't display it. But just
the opposite is done by everybody: whatsoever is wrong, you hide
it; you don't want it to be known by others. Whatsoever is ugly you
hide and whatsoever is beautiful, even if it is not, you try to
advertise it, you magnify it, you display it. Hence the misery –
because the ugly grows and the beautiful is lost. The untrue grows,
it becomes a seed, and the truth is thrown away. The precious is
thrown and the rubbish grows; you become like weeds. No flower
comes to your life because you have never done the right thing –
hidden the seed of the flower within. This opposite is the path,
and I say this is one of the most secret keys of Tao.

A man of Tao remains ordinary, absolutely ordinary. Nobody
knows who he is, nobody knows what he carries within him, what
treasure. He never advertises, he never tries to display. But why
do we advertise? Because of the ego. You are not satisfied with
yourself, you are satisfied only when others appreciate you.
Kohinoor is not enough. You may have a valuable stone, but it
is not enough; others must appreciate it. Others' opinion is more
valuable, not your being. You look into others' eyes as if they are

mirrors and if they appreciate you, applaud you, you feel good.

Ego is a false phenomenon. It is the accumulation of others' opinions, it is not a knowledge of the self. This self, the so-called self which is really the ego, is nothing but the accumulation of reflections – and then there is always fear. Others may change their mind, you are always dependent on them. If they say you are good you have to follow their rules to remain good, you have to follow them to remain good in their eyes, because once they change their opinion you will no longer be good. You have no direct approach to your being, it is via others. So you not only advertise, you magnify, you falsify. You may have a little truth, a little beauty, but you magnify it and it becomes ridiculous.

I remember – and I will never forget it – the first time Mulla Nasruddin was introduced to me. A mutual friend introduced us. The friend said, among other things, that Mulla Nasruddin was a great writer. And he smiled knowingly. So I asked Mulla Nasruddin, 'What have you written?'

He said, 'I have just finished *Hamlet*.'

I couldn't believe my ears, so I asked him, 'Have you ever heard of a guy known as William Shakespeare?'

Mulla Nasruddin said, 'This is strange, because before, when I wrote *Macbeth*, somebody asked the same thing.' And he asked, 'Who is this man William Shakespeare? It seems that he keeps on copying me. Whatsoever I write, he also writes.'

You think that everybody is copying you and the reality is that you go on copying everybody else. You are a carbon copy, you are not a real person, because a real person never needs any display.

I have heard:

It happened once at a hill station, on the lawn of a big hotel, that three elderly women were playing cards. A fourth approached and she asked if she could join them. They said, 'Of course, you are welcome, but there are a few rules.' And they handed her a printed card, with four rules on it. The first was: Never talk about mink coats, because we all have them. Second: Never talk about your grandchildren, because we are all grandmothers. Third: Never talk about jewelry, because we all have precious jewelry purchased from the best of places. And fourth: Never talk about sex – what was, was!

But everybody wants to talk about himself: his mink coats, his jewelry, his children, his sex. And everybody bores everybody else. And if you tolerate bores, you tolerate them only because it is a mutual understanding: if he is boring you he will allow himself to be bored by you. You are just waiting – when he stops his display, you can start your own. And the whole of life becomes false, a continuous display. What do you achieve through it? Just a false feeling that you are important, extraordinary.

How can one become extraordinary by having mink coats? How can one become extraordinary by owning valuable jewelry? How can one become extraordinary by doing this or that? Extraordinariness is not concerned with what you do, it is concerned with what you are. And you are already extraordinary; everyone is unique, there is no need to prove it. If you try to prove it, you will just prove the opposite. If something is already the case, how can you prove it? If you try to prove it you simply show that you are not aware of the uniqueness that has already happened to you.

So if you want to prove something it shows that you are doubtful about it. You want to destroy your doubt through others' eyes, through their opinions. You are not really convinced that you are a beautiful person, you would like others to say that you are beautiful.

In a small village it was the custom of the village priest that whenever he married somebody he would kiss the bride – it was an old tradition. One woman who was going to be married was very concerned. She thought herself very beautiful, as every woman does. It is womanly, it is nothing new. Really, every woman thinks so – even the ugliest. She thought herself very beautiful, and she was very concerned and worried. She said again and again to the would-be husband, to the groom, 'Go and tell the priest that I don't want to be kissed after the marriage.'

Just before the marriage, she again asked the groom, 'Have you been to the priest and told him?'

The groom very sadly said, 'Yes.'

The bride asked, 'Why are you so sad?'

The groom said, 'I told the priest and he was very happy. He said, "In that case I will charge only half the usual fee."'

You may go on thinking yourself a beautiful person but nobody thinks that way about you because everybody is concerned with his own beauty, not with yours. And if anybody nods and says, 'Yes, you are beautiful,' he or she is just waiting for you to nod about his or her beauty. It is a mutual bargain: you fulfill my ego, I fulfill yours. I know well that you are not beautiful, you know well that I am not beautiful, but I fulfill your ego, so you fulfill mine.

And everybody seems to have such a need to feel unique. That means you have not come upon your own being which is unique without any need of proof. Proofs are needed only for lies – remember. That is why you cannot prove God – because he is the ultimate truth. Proofs are needed only for lies; truth needs no proof. It is – simply it is.

And I tell you that you *are* unique, extraordinary. Don't try to be so, it is ridiculous – you simply become a laughing stock and everybody smiles when you turn your back. If you are not convinced about your uniqueness who is going to be convinced about it? Conviction is beyond proof. And how does it come? It comes through self-knowledge.

So there are two ways: knowledge – direct, knowing oneself directly, immediately – this is the right way. And the wrong way is knowing oneself through others – what they say. And if you don't know yourself, how can they know you? They are very far away. You are the nearest person to know yourself. If you don't know your reality, how can others know?

But because we lack self-knowledge we need a substitute. Ego is the substitute, and ego is on constant display. You are just like a display window in a market. You have become a commodity, you have made yourself a commodity on display, always on display, always begging for somebody to say you are good, beautiful, you are saintly, you are great, extraordinary.

Tao is against this, because Tao says that this is how you waste your life. The same energy can move directly towards your being, and when the being is revealed it is extraordinary.

So a man who is in search of self-knowledge will remain ordinary in the eyes of others. He will not bother – he will hide himself, he will not display. He will not be on exhibition, he will not be a stage-show. He will remain silent, live silently, enjoy life silently. He would like nobody to bother about him, because whenever somebody bothers about you, thinks about you, it is going to be difficult and complex – self-knowledge becomes more and more difficult.

You have to go there alone; and if you are looking at the crowd, and if you think that the crowd has to follow you, you will never reach it. If you are an exhibitionist then you will remain a commodity, a thing. You can never become a person, because 'person' is hidden deep in the recesses of being. It is the deepest possibility in the whole of existence. You are the greatest abyss. Nobody else can go there with you. You will have to go alone. And if you are too concerned about others, what they say, what they think, you will remain on the periphery. That is one thing.

The second thing is: just to be on display you hide whatsoever is ugly. In clothes, in words, in gestures, in masks, in actions, you try to hide whatsoever is ugly and wrong. What are you doing? This wrong will become a seed inside and it will grow. And the more you push it in, the more you are throwing it towards the source of all energy; it will be strengthened. And the beautiful you throw out – it will never become a seed.

Just do the opposite. If you have something ugly, show it to others: it disperses. If you are an angry man, tell everybody, 'I am an angry man, don't love me, don't be a friend to me. I am a very bad man. I am ugly, I am immoral, I am greedy, I am sexual.' Say whatsoever is ugly about you, not only say it but authentically act it out. And you will be surprised that whenever something is thrown out, it disperses.

And hide the beautiful; let it go deeper so that it can get roots in your being, and it will grow. But you have been doing just the opposite.

Now, try to understand this story:

The Prince of Wu took a boat to Monkey Mountain.

Chuang Tzu always watched monkeys. He was deeply interested in them because they are the forefathers of man. And a monkey is hidden in you! This whole world is nothing but a monkey mountain; all around are monkeys. What is the characteristic of a monkey? What is the deepest character in the monkey? It is copying. Gurdjieff used to say that you cannot become a man unless you stop being a monkey – and he was right. Somebody asked him, 'What is the deepest characteristic of a monkey?' He said, 'Copying, imitation.'

The monkey is a perfect imitator. What have you been doing your whole life? Have you been a man or a monkey? You imitate, you just look around and you follow; following, you become false. You see somebody walking in a certain way, you try to walk that way; somebody is wearing a particular dress, you would like to have

that dress; somebody has got a car, you would like to have that car
– everything!

You never look at what your need is. And if you do look to your
need, life can become a blissful existence, because needs are not
much. Imitation will lead you on a path which reaches nowhere
in the end. Needs are not much, needs are always few; if you look
to your need, you can be satisfied. Contentment is easy, because
what is needed? Few are the needs. But if you imitate, then millions
of unnecessary needs crowd all around. And there is no end to
them, because there are millions of people and you would like to
imitate everybody. It becomes impossible; you start living
everybody's life and then you forget that you were here to do your
own thing, and you have become an imitator.

You are here to fulfill your own destiny and that destiny is
individual, it is nobody else's. This existence has given you birth
to fulfill a particular destiny which cannot be fulfilled by anybody
else. No Buddha can do it, no Jesus can do it, only you can do it.
And you are imitating. That is why Hindus say that unless you stop
imitation you will be thrown again and again into existence – that
is the theory of rebirth. You will be thrown in again and again unless
you fulfill your destiny; unless you flower, you will have to come
back. How can you flower if you imitate? You see a musician and
you want to be a musician; you see an actor and you want to be an
actor; you see a doctor and you want to be a doctor. You want to be
everything except yourself – and that is all that you can be, nothing
else. Nothing else is possible, and nobody else is like you, so
nobody can become your ideal.

Love a Buddha, Buddha is beautiful – but don't imitate, else
you will miss. Jesus is wonderful, but he is needed no more;
existence has fulfilled that destiny, that work is complete. He has
come to a flowering. That is why whenever a person has flowered
he never comes back. Love Jesus, but don't be an imitator,
otherwise you will end up unfulfilled, in misery and anguish. You

cannot really follow anybody. You can take hints, but then you have to be very alert; hints should not become blind imitations.

. If you see a buddha, take how he has flowered as a hint. What are the methods? What has he been doing? Try to understand it, and let that understanding be absorbed. By and by you will start feeling your path. It will never be like the Buddha's, it can never be, it will be absolutely different. But absorbing Buddha will help. You will have to grow in your own way, but absorbing him will make you more understanding. That is the difference between an authentic disciple and a follower who is false.

A disciple is something completely different from a follower, and I would like to tell you to be my disciples but not my followers. What is discipline? Discipline is learning. The root word of discipline comes from learning. It is nothing to do with self-control, no. A disciple is one who is ready to learn; a disciple is one who is ready to absorb; a disciple is one who is open, receptive; a disciple is one who is ready to become a womb. He is not antagonistic, he is not fighting and arguing. He is trying to understand, and when you try to understand, the head stops functioning. Because the head can do two things: it can either fight or it can follow. It can either be a blind follower or a blind enemy, but it can never be a disciple.

A disciple is totally different because he is not head-oriented; a disciple is heart-oriented. He loves the master, absorbs him, and then goes on his own way.

It is a very indirect, very delicate thing. It is not direct. You cannot just look at the master and do whatsoever he is doing – then you will become a follower. You cannot learn the words and start repeating them – then you will become a follower, then the effort has been in the head, and the head is the problem.

Whenever you are not fighting and not in search of somebody to imitate, your consciousness falls from the head to the heart. Then you are open, then you are simply in love. That is what is meant by *shraddha*, faith, trust. It is neither belief nor disbelief.

Don't think that trust or faith is belief, it is not. Belief is in the head, disbelief is in the head; trust is in the heart. It has nothing to do with belief or disbelief. Believing or not believing is not a concern at all; you simply love. You see a rose flower. Do you believe in it or do you disbelieve in it? You don't do anything, you simply look at it. Nobody is a follower, nobody is against. The sun rises in the morning. What do you do? Are you a believer or a disbeliever? Do you close your eyes because you are a disbeliever, or do you follow the path of the sun the whole day because you are a follower? Either way you will go mad. You simply enjoy, you absorb the morning, the freshness of it, the youngness, the newness – with the sun everything is becoming alive. You enjoy the very life and become more alive through it. You look at a rose and something of the rose reaches to your heart. Outside the rose is flowering, inside, the heart starts flowering. You reach a master, a Buddha or a Jesus, a Chuang Tzu. What do you do? Do exactly as you would do with a rose or with a sunrise: no need to follow, no need not to follow – just absorb.

Jesus' last words to his disciples were, 'Eat me, let me be your drink and your food, let me flow in your blood, absorb me.' When he says 'Eat me,' that means absorb me, digest me; don't follow outwardly, digest me, and then you will have your own inner light.

A real master never gives you rules, he gives you the eye. He never shows you the path, never says this is the path, follow. He simply gives you the light and says: Now take the light and go into the darkness, this light will show your path. A false master always gives you a map: This is the map. Don't go astray, follow this map. He never gives you the light. If you have the light then there is no need for the map; you will find your path.

And everybody's path is going to be different because everybody *is* different. Let this understanding go deep into your heart: there are not two persons similar, there cannot be. Existence is not repetitive, existence is not yet exhausted; existence goes on flowering in new uniquenesses. Everybody is extraordinary, no need to prove it. If you want to prove it, you will become a monkey, not a man. Stop copying.

It is easy to copy, difficult to understand. That is why one copies, because it is so easy – just a rule has to be followed. You need not have any understanding about it. A clear-cut rule is given and you follow it. People come to me and they say, 'Give us clear-cut rules, so that we can follow.' They are saying, 'We are not going to grow, we are not going to be-come mature ourselves. You simply give us clear-cut rules: what to eat, what not to eat, when to get up early in the morning and when to go to bed. Just give us clear-cut rules so that we can follow.' You want to become a monkey, not a man.

A man will never ask for clear-cut rules, he will ask for under-standing so he can find his own way, so he can move in the wide world. He need not have a map with him, no need for any compass. Just your inner light will show your path.

And there is beauty because there is freedom. When there is no freedom, there is no beauty. Bondage, slavery, is the ugliest thing in the world.

> *The Prince of Wu took a boat to Monkey Mountain.*
> *As soon as the monkeys saw him, they all fled in*
> *panic and hid in the treetops.*

> *One monkey, however, remained, completely*
> *unconcerned, swinging from branch to branch – an*
> *extraordinary display.*

That monkey must have been a leader of the monkeys, a president, a prime minister. When all ordinary mortals flee, how can a leader? How can a leader, a great leader, follow ordinary monkeys? He had to show himself – his toughness. Otherwise, in the eyes of the monkeys, his prestige would be gone. It was not a show for the prince, it was a show for the other monkeys. If you want to remain a leader you have to be tough. If you want to remain a leader you have to go on display.

All the political leaders are always on display. You never know their real faces – nobody does. Not even their wives and children know their real faces. They have become so efficient that nobody knows who they are; they always go on just showing off. It is said that if a politician says yes to something, it means perhaps; if he says perhaps, it means no; and if he says no, he is not a politician at all. Whatsoever a politician says, he never means it; whatsoever he means he never says it. And through a politician you can understand yourself because he is just a magnified picture of you. The leader is just a magnified picture of the follower and it is always easy to see things in a magnified picture. With a magnifying glass you can see.

It is good to try to understand leaders of men because they are the great monkeys. And you think you are following them? Basically, deep down, they are following you. A leader is always a follower of his own followers because he always has to look where you are going, what you are doing. He must know beforehand where the wind is blowing so that he can be just ahead.

Once Mulla Nasruddin was going somewhere on his donkey, and the donkey was going fast. A friend asked, 'Where are you going, Nasruddin?'

Nasruddin said, 'To tell you the truth, I don't know. Don't ask me. Ask this donkey.'

The man was puzzled so he said, 'What do you mean?'

Mulla Nasruddin said, 'You are a friend, so I must be truthful and frank. This donkey is adamant and stubborn, as all donkeys are, and he creates difficulties. When I pass through a market or a town, if I insist that we should go this way, he insists on going the other; and then in the marketplace it becomes ridiculous, I become a laughing stock. People say that not even your donkey follows you! So I have made it a rule that wherever he goes, I go with him. Everyone thinks that the donkey is following me but that is not true. But the donkey feels happy and my prestige is safe.'

Every great leader goes on just following his followers. He goes on seeing where the wind is blowing and he must always be ahead. That is the secret of being a great leader: you must be able to know what the people want. You must give them a slogan before they become aware of what they want; then they follow you.

This monkey must have been a leader. It had to be shown that he was not afraid, even of a great prince. Other monkeys had fled, poor ordinary monkeys, but he was no ordinary monkey, he was a king himself. He must stand out, he must remain there; that is how he will get more prestige in the eyes of the monkeys.

One monkey, however, remained, completely unconcerned, swinging from branch to branch – an extraordinary display.

The prince shot an arrow at the monkey.

And your princes are also not very different. This was insulting to the prince, this monkey was being insulting. It was natural that all the monkeys had taken flight. But now a great prince … and here was just an ordinary monkey trying to display, showing that he is tough. No, this could not be allowed because the prince had his own followers. The prince had to look to other men, to what they would think if even a monkey did not bother, was unconcerned with the prince. The monkey had to be killed. The logic remains the same whether you are a man or a monkey.

The prince shot an arrow at the monkey, but the monkey dexterously caught the arrow in mid-flight.

At this the prince ordered his attendants to make a concerted attack.

Because this monkey seemed to be much too arrogant, very egoistic. Look ... the prince can see the ego of the monkey but he cannot see his own ego. And this is happening all over the world. In every relationship you can always see the ego of the other, but you cannot see your own – and the other one goes on seeing your ego.

This is a story written by a man; just think if a monkey had written the story, it would have been absolutely different. Just think, a Chuang Tzu amongst monkeys writing this story... Then he would have written that the prince was very arrogant, stubborn and unnecessarily violent – because the monkey was not doing anything wrong, he was just enjoying himself. Why should the prince be offended? Why should he have felt that this monkey had to be killed? That prince must have been a very, very egoistic person. He tried to kill, and the monkey was simply defending himself, nothing else.

If you look at the story from the standpoint of a monkey it will be totally different, but the base is the same and this always happens. A man of wisdom always looks at every problem from the other's point of view also. You cannot be wise if you have only one point of view. Sometimes try to stand in others' shoes and just look from there.

Many couples come to me, wife and husband, and there are great problems – the greatest! – because that is the basic unit of life. Much tension, much ego, much falsity goes on and on and on, and it becomes a hell. Couples come to me and I always suggest that for one day they try the other's role: let the wife become the husband and the husband become the wife. For twenty-four hours try the other's role and then it will be very easy to understand the other. Even in a one-hour dialogue play the other's role and reply from the other's point of view, and you will feel very relaxed.

One must be flexible enough to see what the other is feeling at that moment. The husband comes home and he says something and he feels very innocent, but the wife feels offended. He can't understand what is happening, he has not said anything. Just meditate a little, be in the wife's place, think that you are the wife and the husband comes in and says the same sentence. How would you feel? Immediately you will be able to understand why the wife is feeling that way. And if you can understand the other, you will be able to understand yourself more. The other always sees that you are an egoist. You never see it, you are blind to yourself.

The prince was also blind. He could see that this monkey was trying to display but he couldn't see why he himself was feeling offended. Let him display – monkeys are monkeys, let him enjoy; he is not doing any wrong to anybody, just jumping from one branch to another, swaying, playing a game. Let him play. Why was the prince so concerned? He felt that he was being insulted, that this monkey was trying to say, 'You are nothing, I am unconcerned. You may be a prince of men but monkeys don't bother about you. And I also am a prince and you are nothing before me. Can you sway like me from one branch to another?'

It is said that when Darwin discovered that man evolved from monkeys, somebody retorted, 'First also ask the monkeys.' I am also of the opinion that if we ask the monkeys they would not say that man is an evolution. He is a fall – a fall from the monkeys. Look … monkeys are stronger than you, they can do a few things that you cannot do. They are much happier than you, they enjoy life more than you. So what have you gained through your evolution, your mechanical gadgets, your weapons, your atomic bombs? Why do you think it is an evolution, a growth, a development? Ask the monkeys, they will laugh and they will say that you are fools. You cannot even walk on all fours. You cannot climb a tree like a monkey.

The monkey and the prince are both in the same boat.

The prince shot an arrow at the monkey, but the monkey dexterously caught the arrow in mid-flight.

The prince is more violent than the monkey because the monkey's display is simply to ask, 'Why should you kill me?'

But man is more violent than any animal.

There is a zoo in Tokyo – if you ever go to Tokyo, don't miss the zoo. Go there! All sorts of wild animals are there, hundreds of cages, and there is a last cage on which there is a notice board: 'The Most Dangerous Animal of All'. But the cage is vacant, empty. If you look – and you will look! – for the most dangerous animal of all, you will find him, because there is a mirror.

The monkey was innocent in his ego. Animals have their egos but they are still innocent, not so violent. But man is violent, man seems to be the only violent animal. Tigers kill, lions kill, but just to eat, never otherwise. Man kills not only to eat, he enjoys killing. Hunting is a game for him. He will simply kill to kill – and no animal in the world kills his own brothers and sisters, no! A lion will not kill another lion, a monkey will not kill another monkey like himself.

Man is the only animal which kills other men. There is an inbuilt protection in every animal; zoologists say that every animal carries an inbuilt mechanism not to kill the same species. But it seems that something has gone wrong with man: he kills his own species. There is nothing like war in the animal world, although individuals fight.

Animals have more understanding. If two dogs fight, sooner or later, within minutes, they come to an understanding. Man never comes to an understanding; unless he kills, there seems to be no solution. Even dogs are more intelligent. If two dogs bark, show their teeth, jump at each other, that is just a show, they are trying to feel the pulse, who is the stronger. It is a mock fight. They have not yet started and when one feels that he is not so strong then he knows it is futile to fight. He simply shows with his tail – stop! And then the thing is finished, they have come to an understanding. A hierarchy is established – the stronger will of course win, so why go through a fight unnecessarily?

Only man is foolish, the most foolish animal, because he will never believe that the weaker will be defeated and that the stronger will be victorious. It is ordinary arithmetic that the stronger will win, so why fight? There is no need. Hitler can bark at Stalin, Stalin can bark at Hitler, and they can both call their mathematician and count who has the most airplanes, the most bombs. Within minutes the thing can be settled – then you just show by your tail. No need to go to war, because a war will only prove what can already be done on a table – that is, who is the strongest. Why such a wastage, such a wastage of human beings?

But no, it is impossible. Human beings are such egoists that even the weaker thinks that somehow he is going to win. No animal deceives himself so much. Mock fights are there just to judge who is stronger, then it is finished. You will say of a dog who puts his tail down that he is a coward. No, he is not – he is simply intelligent. He is weak, so what is the need to get into a fight? It is proved, and it is proved innocently without any bloodshed. The same thing is going to be proved even through a fight. Why go to war unnecessarily? This is more economical.

At this the prince ordered his attendants to make a concerted attack.

Look at the foolishness! Just to kill a monkey a concerted attack is needed – many men attacking the monkey from all sides.

In an instant the monkey was shot full of arrows and fell dead.

And the prince must have felt very good, he had done something. But look at the foolishness – a concerted attack by so many people, and with the prince there must have been at least a hundred attendants. A hundred men killing a monkey and then feeling good, victorious! The monkeys must be laughing at what you have done.

... the monkey was shot full of arrows and fell dead.

Then the prince turned to his companion Yen Pu'i ...

And look how even in our foolishness we prove that we ... are wise! This prince had killed unnecessarily and in no way could this be called a victory. Just to kill one monkey took a concerted attack of a hundred persons with arrows; and the monkey was without any weapon, naked, with no protection.

Is it a victory? It is not a victory at all, it is not even diplomacy. Even ordinarily, if we fight a warrior, we give a weapon to the other. He must have a sword, he must have the same protection. They were all protected, but an unprotected innocent animal had been killed.

The prince is foolish, but look at his advice. Even from our foolishness we go on feeling that we are wise. What did he say? He said to his companion, Yen Pu'i:

... 'You see what happened? This animal advertised his cleverness, he trusted in his own skill.

He thought no one could touch him. Remember that! Do not rely on distinction and talent when you deal with men!'

This is one of the subtle things to be understood. We are always wise if we have to advise others, but when we are in the same trap, with the same problem, the same crisis, we are not so wise. If somebody else comes to you with a problem you will give him good advice; and the advice may be right, but if you have the same problem you will not be able to give yourself the same advice. Why?

Because when it is somebody else's problem you are detached.

This prince told his companion:

> ... 'You see what happened? This animal advertised
> his cleverness, he trusted in his own skill.
>
> He thought no one could touch him. Remember that!
> Do not rely on distinction and talent when you deal
> with men!'

He could see the foolishness of the monkey, but he could not see the foolishness of what he had done. And, as I feel, he had done a more foolish thing than the monkey.

He had also advertised his skill, he had also shown his talent, and not only with men but with monkeys too. He displayed who he was: he was not an ordinary man, he was an extraordinary prince. He was no ordinary mortal. And then he gave this advice to his friend: *'Do not rely on distinction and talent when you deal with men.'* But the advice is right.

And it happened, as it happens many times, that the friend took the advice and it transformed his whole being. The prince remained the same. So if you can learn, you can learn from fools also. If you cannot learn, even a buddha is useless, you will not learn. And sometimes it happens that the people who advise you remain the same. If you can learn you can transform yourself.

Sometimes teachers are left behind and disciples move fast and reach the goal. Because you can give good advice to others it doesn't mean that you have attained that truth.

This is good. The advice is beautiful and Tao says the same thing. Tao has the same teaching but not with the same mind as the prince. Chuang Tzu has put the teaching in the prince's mouth, but the prince is just like a scholar, a pundit, who knows the words but who has not lived it through. It is not a live experience, it is just a doctrine. The prince must have heard it from somewhere, from some Taoist source, because this is one of their keys.

> ... 'You see what happened? This animal advertised
> his cleverness, he trusted in his own skill. He thought
> no one could touch him. Remember that!'

Don't display, don't exhibit; otherwise you will cause unnecessary troubles, you will invite unnecessary problems. You may even get so involved in it that it may prove your death.

> 'Do not rely on distinction and talent when you deal
> with men.'

This advice came from the mouth of the prince. The friend was really a wise man because he wasn't concerned whether the prince himself followed what he was saying. And it should happen in life that you are not concerned; you should simply take the advice and become changed ... but you are concerned.

What is the use of thinking about the bottles? Just take the content. What is the use of asking about the container? Just taste the contents, and if the contents are good, forget the container. This prince was in the same position as the monkey, even worse, but he uttered one of the secrets of Taoist teachings. He may have read about it, he may have been taught it, and suddenly the situation provoked his knowledge. So he said to the companion, 'Don't display! Don't become an exhibitionist, otherwise you will be in trouble. And *Don't rely on distinction and talent when you deal with men.*' Why? Because every man is an egoist. If you depend on your talent you will be in trouble because you will create enemies. If you depend on distinction you will be in trouble because all around you there will be enemies. Nobody wants you to be superior to them.

Once Mulla Nasruddin came to me, very excited. He said, 'Now you have to help me.'

I asked him, 'What is the matter?'

He said, 'I feel terrible, it is awful. Recently I have been developing an inferiority complex. Help me! Do something!'

So I said, 'Tell me something more about it. Why are you developing an inferiority complex?'

He said, 'Recently I have been feeling that everybody is as good as I am.'

Whenever you show your talent you are showing that the other is not as good, and the other will be offended. Remember, the prince is offended just by a monkey swaying in the trees!

If you show your distinction, if you say that you are something, if you try to prove your talent in subtle ways, everybody will be offended. And they cannot forgive you; they will take their revenge. With every man of distinction the masses take revenge. It may be that Jesus was crucified because the masses could not tolerate his superiority – and he *was* superior. They could not tolerate this man of quality. He was extraordinary, they had to kill him.

Athens could not tolerate Socrates. He was rare – one of the most unique minds ever born, so penetrating that there is no comparison. Athens could not tolerate him, everybody felt offended.

Chuang Tzu says: Don't rely on talent when you deal with men. Remain hidden!

It has to be remembered that a Taoist master has never been crucified or poisoned. Never! Because they never rely on talent. They never say that they are distinct from you. They never say that they are higher than you, more divine than you, holier than you. No, they never say anything. They behave in such a way that everybody around them will feel that they are superior to them.

Chuang Tzu himself lived such an ordinary life and such a beautiful life that nobody even suspected that here was a man of very extraordinary dimensions. He would pass through villages, and the villages would not even become aware that Chuang Tzu had passed.

Once it happened that the emperor heard about Chuang Tzu from some source, and the rumor was that he was a very wise man. So he sent his prime minister in search of him. But where to find him? He had no home, no address – he was a wanderer. Chuang Tzu used to say that if you stay in one place it is difficult to hide, people will start suspecting. Because you have something, they will suspect, and by and by they will become aware. So before they become aware leave them, otherwise you will be in trouble. So he was a constant wanderer – no address, no home. Where to find him?

But they tried – when the emperor orders, it has to be tried. They asked many Taoist teachers, 'Where can we find Chuang Tzu?'

They said, 'Very difficult, nobody knows. He moves like the wind, unknown, like a cloud, whereabouts unknown. But you go, and if some villager says that there is a man here who is absolutely ordinary, then catch that man, he may be Chuang Tzu.'

And they found him in that way. In a village some people reported, 'Yes, there is a man who has just come to this village, absolutely ordinary. You cannot find a more ordinary man than he.' When asked where he was, they said, 'He is fishing on the bank of the river.'

They went there and said to Chuang Tzu, 'The emperor has inquired about you, and we have been searching for you. Would you like to come to the court? Would you like to become a member of the court – advisor to the king?'

Chuang Tzu said, 'Wait, and let me think.'

And the next day, when they came to ask him, he was not found in that village; he had escaped. People had suspected, they had come to know.

A man of Tao moves absolutely without identity. Why? Because if you show talent then people cannot forgive you. People can forgive fools, but they cannot forgive wise men. That is why Jesus was crucified, Socrates was poisoned. You feel so utterly inferior before a Jesus or a Socrates, how can you forgive them? It is natural, you will make a concerted attack. You will all make a concerted attack to kill that man. Then you will feel that a burden has been thrown off. A Jesus is so superb – if he just stands by your side you feel inferior; he has to hide himself. This teaching is very basic.

The prince told these words to his companion, Yen Pu'i.

When they returned home, Yen Pu'i became a disciple of a sage to get rid of everything that made him outstanding.He renounced every pleasure. He learned to hide every distinction.

Soon no one in the kingdom knew what to make of him. Thus they held him in awe.

Many things: this man, Yen Pu'i, was really a wise man. He didn't bother about who had given the message to him. He didn't bother about the vehicle, he simply took the message.

Remember this: you always bother about the vehicle. If I say something to you, you start wondering about me: whether this man is reliable, whether this man has attained what he says. First you would like to be convinced about me, but that is impossible. Notice what I am saying, look at that – forget me completely. It is my business whether I have attained or not, it is none of your business. Why are you concerned about it? Whatsoever I am saying, if you feel the fragrance of it, try it; try the medicine, not the doctor. Don't be concerned with the doctor, be concerned with the medicine – because finally it is the medicine that is going to cure you. And it is possible to find the right medicine even from a quack doctor.

The opposite is also possible: it is possible to find the wrong medicine from a right doctor. The real thing is the medicine.

This man, Yen Pu'i, must have been a very wise and intelligent man; otherwise he would have thought, 'This fool, this fool of a prince! He is giving me advice and he himself lives with distinction, lives an exhibitionist's life.'

Nobody lives like kings – they are always on display, on the throne. And they want to make it clear to everybody that nobody is like them. They create a distance between ordinary mortals and themselves – a gap. You cannot go and put your hand on a king's shoulder. No! He will feel offended: 'What are you doing? Are you saying that you are similar to me?' You will be killed!

It is said that Hitler never allowed anybody to put a hand on his shoulder. Never! Not a single friend. Nobody was allowed to use his name, Hitler; he was to be called *Fuehrer*. Nobody was allowed to use his proper name because that would show friendship. He never loved any woman, because it is very difficult to love a woman and not to make her equal to you – it is impossible. And women are so intelligent and cunning; if you love them they will not only try to be equal, they will try to be superior – and they can prove it. He never loved a woman. He had some relationships, but never a love relationship – just sexual. And he would treat the woman just like a servant – not only a servant, but a slave.

He lived with a woman for many years, and one day a small incident happened. The woman wanted to go and see her mother – her mother was ill and in hospital – and Hitler said no. He was very dictatorial; if he said no, he meant it. The woman thought that she wouldn't discuss the matter anymore; when Hitler went to the office she could go just for a few minutes and see her mother and come back. There was no problem. Hitler went to the office.

The woman went to see her mother and came back before Hitler returned. At the gate he inquired if his girlfriend had been out. She had been out. He inquired if she had been to the hospital.

Then he went in and without asking anything, he killed her, shot her dead immediately.

What type of love is it when only slaves can be tolerated? Love makes you equal. An egoistic person cannot love because love equalizes. There are only two forces that equalize: one is love, the other is death. When you love a person you have become equal to that person. And if you really love, in that moment of love you will feel that the whole existence is equal: nobody is inferior and nobody is superior. Everybody is unique, different, but nobody is inferior, nobody is superior.

In love you feel a communion with the whole existence; everything becomes equal, equally valuable. And death is a great equalizer. When you die all distinctions drop, and a dead Hitler is just like a dead dog – no difference. Can you see any difference between a dead dog and a dead Hitler, or even a dead Buddha? No distinction can be made, the body is just the same: dust unto dust. And those who can love can become, and feel, an equality with the whole existence – even with rocks.

If you are in love you will feel a vibration that everything is equal, even a rock is equal with you. Then there is no death because then you cannot die – you have felt such a unity with existence. This unity will continue. The form will disappear, the body will be no longer there, but the innermost unity will remain. In new waves you will arise, in new trees you will flower, in new beings you will dance, but you will continue.

This is one of the most paradoxical things – that you are unique and yet one with existence. This paradox cannot be explained; you have to experience it. You are unique and yet one with existence.

When they returned home, Yen Pu'i became a disciple of a sage ...

He didn't bother whether the prince had taken his own advice to his heart or not. The prince continued the same, in the old way, but

Yen Pu'i changed his whole existence. He became a disciple of a sage. And if you want to change your life you have to become a disciple, because alone it is really difficult, alone it is almost impossible. You need the help of someone who has known. You need to trust in someone who has gone ahead of you.

Discipline means to learn from someone, to surrender to someone, to be receptive to someone; not to follow and imitate, but just to absorb his understanding so your own inner flame is lit; just to come to a lighted flame so that your own flame is lit. Then you can move on your own, then you have become a universe unto yourself. But before that it is difficult to find, difficult to move, difficult to reach the right path.

Near a sage many things become possible, many impossible things become possible, because a sage is the only miracle in the world. He lives in the body and he is no longer the body; he is here with you and no longer with you; he touches you and yet a vast, infinite distance exists between you and him. A sage is the only miracle. If you live around him, just silently, just absorbing, drinking his wine, soon you will feel the miracle and that it has started to change you.

It is just like when you are ill, you go to Switzerland. What can Switzerland do? But the whole climate is healthy; in that healthy climate your disease cannot persist. Your disease needs support and there is no support for it, so it drops; without support it drops.

Near a sage, you have changed your climate. You live with people who are ignorant just like you, you live in a certain climate, a milieu. Then you come near a sage – you have changed the climate; you have come to the Himalayas, to the Alps, to Switzerland. Now the climate is different, now he is not going to support your illnesses. He will by and by take away all supports. Without the supports the illness fails. And when there is no illness, your own health flowers.

All that needs to be done is to remove the illnesses – health is already there, it is not to be given to you. Only remove the illness, and health flowers. Near a sage, the climate changes. But you have to be open. If you go to Switzerland and you have iron, steel armor around you, you will not be changed because your steel armor will carry its own climate within. Go to a sage without any armor, without any defense – that is what the meaning of surrender is.

> *When they returned home, Yen Pu'i became a disciple*
> *of a sage to get rid of everything that made him*
> *outstanding.*

Look … all that we do in our life is learn how to become outstanding: how to be first in the class, first in the university, how to get the gold medal, how to be a Nobel prizewinner, how to be outstanding in some way or other – anything will do.

Once Mulla Nasruddin knocked at the door of the manager of a great circus, and he said:

'You have to look at me, I have a terrific act! I am a dwarf.'

The manager looked at Nasruddin. He was six feet two inches tall, and he was saying, 'I am a dwarf!'

So the manager said, 'What are you saying? You seem to me six feet two inches tall!'

Nasruddin said, 'Yes, that is right. I am the longest, tallest dwarf in the world.'

The mind goes on finding ways and means to be outstanding. If you cannot be anything else, at least you can be the tallest dwarf – but be something, somebody! The whole education, culture, civilization teaches you to be outstanding, and Tao says: Don't be outstanding, drop all that is outstanding; just be ordinary, just be simple. *Easy is right;* to be ordinary is to be right, because to be ordinary you will be easy. If you want to be extraordinary, outstanding, you will always remain uneasy and tense because you have to prove something. You have to convince others, and your whole life will remain always indecisive. With indecision there will be a wavering inside, a trembling.

> ... *Yen Pu'i became a disciple of a sage to get rid of everything that made him outstanding. He renounced every pleasure. He learned to hide every distinction.*

> *Soon no one in the kingdom knew what to make of him. Thus they held him in awe.*

And Tao says that when nobody knows what to make of you – you are so ordinary that nobody knows what to make of you, nobody knows any use for you, you cannot be used, you are so ordinary, without any talent – then, they say, the real mystery reveals itself through you. Then you become a real mystery. When you cannot be used you become godlike. What is the meaning? Whenever you are used, you become a thing; whenever you cannot be used, you become a person.

A person is not a utility, a thing is a utility. If somebody asks you who you are you say, 'I am a doctor.' What do you mean? It means that society is using you as a doctor. It is a function, not a personality. It is not your person, not your being, it is a utility – society is using you as a doctor. Somebody is a carpenter, somebody else is a shoemaker. Is this your being, or just a utility in society? Society is using you as a thing, and the more valuable your use, the more society will value you.

But if you drop all talents, if you become just ordinary and nobody knows what to do with you, nobody can use you, you have gone beyond society. Now you are no longer a thing, you have become a person. And this does not mean that you will not do anything – you will, but nobody will use you. You will 'do' on your own; it will be your flowering.

A rose flowers, not for those who will pass, not for those who will see, not for those who will smell the fragrance. No! It flowers on its own. A man of Tao flowers on his own. He is like a rose, he is not a utility. And a man who has not known his innermost being is always like a thing, always on display in the window of a shop; always waiting for somebody to come and use him with all his certificates, distinctions, talents; always crying, 'Come and use me, make me a thing. I am a most valuable thing, you will never get anything better than me. Come and use me!' This is your whole cry. And if this is your cry, you will become a thing.

A man of Tao drops all distinctions, he burns all certificates, he destroys all bridges; he remains in himself, he becomes a flower. And this flowering is purposeless – it has no utility. Many are benefited by it, but it is not for them, it is for one's own self. He has attained his own destiny. Then there is fulfillment.

As a thing you will remain unfulfilled because you have to be a person, an authentic person. You have not to be a thing, not to be a husband, because to be a husband is a thing; you have not to be a wife, because to be a wife is to be a utility. Just be a flower, then you can love. But there is no need to be a husband, no need to be a wife. You can share, but there is no need to advertise. A flower flowers; it does not need any advertisement. If somebody partakes of its pleasure and happiness, it is okay; if nobody passes by the spot, it is also okay.

When you flower for yourself, everything is okay, nothing is wrong. When you are for somebody else, just waiting in a showcase – labeled, priced, catalogued, advertised – you will never reach to a fulfillment, because a thing is dead; only a person is alive. Be alive, and be a person. And this you can never be if you go on copying. If you remain on the monkey mountain you will never be the real, you will continue to be the false. Drop all falsities, exhibitions, displays. Just be yourself, ordinary and unique, and fulfill your destiny. Nobody else can do it for you. You can absorb me, you cannot follow me. I never followed anybody, I had my own path. You will have your own path. You will move on a path on which nobody has ever moved and nobody will move on it ever again.

In the spiritual world no footprints are left. It is just like the sky: a bird flies – no footprints are left, nobody can follow. Just take a delight in me, be happy with me and you will absorb. And that will become a light within you and that will show you the path. But don't copy, don't believe or disbelieve, don't be head-oriented.

Don't be a monkey. Be a man.

CHAPTER 6

SYMPHONY FOR A SEABIRD

You cannot put a big load in a small bag, nor can you,
with a short rope, draw water from a deep well.
Have you not heard how a bird from the sea was blown
inshore and landed outside the capital of Lu?
The prince ordered a solemn reception, offered wine to
the seabird in the Sacred Precinct, called for musicians
to play the compositions of Shun, slaughtered cattle to
nourish it.
Dazed with symphonies, the unhappy seabird died of
despair.
How should you treat a bird? As yourself, or as a bird?
Ought not a bird to nest in deep woodland or fly over
meadow and marsh?
Ought it not to swim on river and pond, feed on eels
and fish, fly in formation with other waterfowl,
and rest in the reeds?

Bad enough for a seabird to be surrounded by men
and frightened by their voices! That was not enough!
They killed it with music!
Water is for fish, and air for men.
Natures differ, and needs with them.

*Hence the wise men of old did not lay down
one measure for all.*

There is no human nature as such – there are just human
natures. Each individual is a universe unto himself, you
cannot make any general rules. All general rules go false. This has
to be remembered very deeply, because on this path there is every
possibility that you may start following rules, and once you become
the victim of rules you will never come to know who you are.

You can know yourself only in total freedom – and rules are
prisons. They are prisons because no one else can make rules for
you; he may have discovered the truth through these rules, but
they were for him. Nature differs – they helped him but they will
not help you; on the contrary, they will hinder you.

So let understanding be the only rule. Learn, grow in understanding, but don't follow rules. Rules are dead, understanding is
alive; rules will become an imprisonment, understanding will give
you the infinite sky.

And every man is burdened with rules, every religion becomes
nothing but rules. Because Jesus attained, because Buddha
attained, their lives became a rule for everybody else to follow. But
nobody else is a Gautam Buddha, nobody else is a Jesus Christ;
so at the most you can become a decorated carbon copy, but you
will never be your authentic self. If you follow Jesus too much you
will become a Christian but never a Christ, and that is the danger.
To become a Christian and to miss Christ is not worth it. You can
become Christ, but then Jesus cannot be your rule, only your own
understanding will be the law.

Jesus followed nobody. He had a master, John the Baptist, but he never followed any rule. He felt the master, he remained with the master, he looked at the flame of the master, he absorbed the master, he was baptized by the master – but he never followed any rules. Other followers of John turned against Jesus. They said, 'This man has betrayed you. He is going on his own, he is not following the rules strictly.'

No man of understanding can follow rules strictly. Only people who are dead can follow rules strictly because no rule is for you; you are your own rule. Understand, learn from others just to find your own rule, but remember, never impose that rule on anybody else – that is violence. Your so-called *mahatmas* go on enforcing rules on others because through rules they kill and destroy, and they enjoy violence. Their violence is very subtle; they don't kill you directly, they kill you very indirectly. If somebody attacks you directly you can defend yourself. When somebody attacks you indirectly – for your own sake – you become completely a victim, you cannot even defend yourself.

Many gurus are nothing but violence, but their violence is subtle. So whenever you come near a man who wants to impose his rules on your life, wants to give you a fixed frame, wants to give you a window to look at the truth through, escape from him, there is danger. A real master will not give you a window to look at the truth through, he will bring you out under the sky. He will not give you a pattern to live by, he will simply give you the feeling, the understanding, and understanding will help you to move. Understanding is free and your own.

Remember: because you don't want to understand, because understanding is difficult and arduous, because understanding needs courage and understanding needs transformation, you simply become victims of those who want to give you rules. But rules are substitutes, you can get them easily. You can easily make your life a disciplined life, but this will be a false thing. You may be acting, pretending, but this cannot be real.

There is a Jewish story I would like to tell you. Jesus must have heard it because it is older than Jesus and everybody knew the story in those days. He must have heard it from his mother, Mary, or from his father, Joseph. The story is beautiful, you may also have heard it. The story is this:

There was a so-called wise man, almost a rabbi ... I say almost because although he was a rabbi, to be a real rabbi is difficult. To be a real rabbi means you are enlightened. In fact he was just a priest, he had not known anything. But people knew about him, that he was a wise man. He was coming back from a nearby village to his home.

As he was passing, he saw a man carrying a beautiful bird. He purchased the bird and started thinking to himself, 'Back home I am going to eat this bird, this bird is beautiful.'

Suddenly the bird said, 'Don't think such thoughts!'

The rabbi became scared! He said, 'What, have I heard you speak?'

The bird said, 'Yes, and I am no ordinary bird. I am also almost a rabbi in the world of birds. And I can give you three pieces of advice if you promise to release me and make me free.'

The rabbi said to himself, 'This bird speaks. He must be someone who knows.'

This is how we decide: if somebody can speak he must know! Speaking is so easy, knowing is so difficult – they are not related to each other at all. You can speak without knowing, you can know without speaking. There is no relationship. But to us a speaker becomes a knower.

The rabbi said, 'Okay, you give me three pieces of advice and I will set you free.'

Said the bird, 'First piece of advice: Never believe in any absurdity, whosoever should be saying it. It may be a great man, renowned all over the world, with prestige, power, authority – but if he is saying something absurd, don't believe it.'

The rabbi said, 'Right!'

The bird said, 'This is my second piece of advice: Whatsoever you do, never try the impossible, because then you will be a failure. So always know your limit. One who knows his limitations is wise, one who goes beyond his limit becomes a fool.'

The rabbi nodded and said, 'Right!'

'And,' said the bird, 'this is my third piece of advice: If you do something good, never repent; only repent that which is bad.'

The advice was wonderful, beautiful, so the bird was set free. Happy, the rabbi started walking towards his home and he thought in his mind, 'Good material for a sermon! In the synagogue next week when I am going to speak I will give these three pieces of advice. And I am going to write them on the wall of my house and I will write them on my desk so I can remember them. These three rules can change a man.'

Then, suddenly, he saw the bird sitting on a tree and the bird started laughing so loudly that the rabbi said, 'What is the matter?' The bird said, 'You fool! I have got a very precious diamond in my belly. Had you killed me you would have become the richest man in the world.'

The rabbi repented in his heart, 'I am really foolish. What have I done? I believed this bird.' He threw down the books that he was carrying and started climbing the tree. He was an old man and he had never climbed a tree in his life. And the higher he climbed, the higher the bird would fly to another branch. Finally the bird reached the very top and the old rabbi also – and then the bird flew away. Just at the moment when he was going to catch the bird, it flew. He missed his step and fell down from the tree. Blood began to flow. Both legs were fractured – he was almost dead.

The bird came again to a lower branch and said, 'Now, first you believed me, that a bird can have a precious diamond in his belly. You fool! Have you ever heard such an absurdity? And then you tried the impossible – you have never climbed a tree. And when a bird is free, how can you catch him with bare hands, you fool? And you repented in your heart, feeling that you had done wrong when you had done a good deed, you had made a bird free! Now go home and write your rules and next week go to the synagogue and preach them.'

But this is what all preachers are doing. Understanding is lacking; they only carry rules – rules are dead things. Understanding has no weight, you need not carry it – it carries you, it becomes your wings. It is not a weight at all, you need not even remember it. If you understand a thing you need not remember it, it becomes your blood, your bones – it is *you*. Whatsoever you do will be done through that understanding; it is an unconscious phenomenon.

Rules are conscious, understanding is unconscious, and Chuang Tzu is always in favor of the unconscious. The whole tradition of Tao is for the unconscious. Don't force rules, just try to understand things. If you force rules upon yourself you will not become enlightened, you will remain ignorant inside, just decorated from without.

Jesus used to say, 'I look at you and I feel that you are like graves, whitewashed – inside dead, outside a whitewashed wall.' It may look beautiful and clean, all your rules can give you an outer cleanliness, but inside you remain the old fool. And remember, only fools follow rules; a wise man tries to understand and forget the rules. A wise man is free to move; a man who has rules cannot move, he always has to follow the rule. And life changes every moment – from moment to moment it goes on changing, it does not wait for you or your rules. Every moment is new. And if the rule is old, you will always miss your step and you will always be a misfit. Whenever there is a man who follows rules he will always be a misfit everywhere, because life goes on flowing and you are stuck with the rule.

As I see within you, you are all stuck with rules. In your childhood, rules were given to you and you are stuck there. Since then you have never moved. You may have been jogging on the same spot but you have not moved. You may become old – seventy years old – but deep down you remain stuck. The whole effort towards enlightenment is how to get unstuck, how to move, how to become a flow again and not be frozen. Don't be like ice – frozen; become like water, a river flowing. Rules will never allow you that. Remember that life goes on renewing itself and only understanding can respond.

Mulla Nasruddin was always talking in negative terms so I told him, 'Be more positive. Why look at life with such a negative eye? Then you will find only thorns and no flowers.'

So he said, 'Okay, now I will make it a rule always to be positive.'

The next day his wife went shopping in the market and she told him to look after the children. When she came back she immediately felt that something had gone wrong. The whole house was sad, children were not running here and there – no noise. She became apprehensive. And then she looked at Nasruddin who was sitting at the door and immediately she felt that something really had gone wrong.

Afraid, she said, 'Nasruddin, don't tell me anything bad, just tell me the good news.'

Nasruddin said, 'I have taken a vow not to be negative at all so you need not remind me. You know our seven children? Six of them didn't fall under a bus!'

This is how he had become positive! You can change the words, but deep down you remain the same. You can change the behavior, but deep down you remain the same. The real thing is how to change your being – not your behavior, not your words, not your clothes – how to change your being. A man of rules changes himself on the periphery. A man of understanding changes himself, then the periphery changes automatically. When the center changes, the periphery changes automatically; it has to change. But when the periphery changes there is no necessity for the center to change with it.

What can rules do? They can tell you what to do and what not to do, but they cannot change you, they can only change your actions, and actions are not you. Actions come from you, but you are deeper than your actions. Rules can change your behavior – behavior means your relationship with others – but they cannot change you. Only in your total aloneness are you your being, not in relationship.

And then Chuang Tzu says that natures differ.

One man came to me. He had been doing *shirshasana* – a yoga posture – standing on his head, the head-stand posture. It is written in the books that it is very beneficial, and because it is very beneficial he had been doing it for very long periods. Now he was in such an inner turmoil that he was almost going mad. So he asked me what had gone wrong. He was a man of rules, he followed Patanjali word for word: diet, sleep time, exactly as they should be. He was a very regulated man. So he could not think what had gone wrong. I asked him to tell me his whole routine. He did *shirshasana* for one hour in the morning, and one hour at night. And he was waiting, expecting that at any moment enlightenment would happen. It had not happened; instead he was going mad, he was crazy!

Shirshasana suits certain people. And the more idiotic a person is, the more it suits him. To a man of intelligence it is dangerous; the higher the intelligence, the more dangerous. Because it is not just a posture, it changes your whole body chemistry.

Man has attained intelligence but no animal has. Why? Because man stands on two legs – that is the whole point. If a child continued to walk on all fours, he would never become a man. He would never attain that intelligence. When your spine is parallel to the earth blood flows equally all over the body; it goes to the legs in the same amount as it goes to the head. Then the head cannot develop subtle nerves – it cannot develop a subtle nervous system. Your brain mechanism is subtle, very subtle, the most subtle thing in the world.

Your head weighs only one and a half kilos. Even if it is the head of an Einstein, a great genius's head, it still weighs only one and a half kilos. In this small head there are seventy million cells. Each cell can carry millions of bits of information. And the cell is so subtle that if the blood flows too fast the cell dies. Blood must not move into the head too much, otherwise it washes away the subtle mechanism. So if someone is stupid, idiotic, imbecilic, *shirshasana* is the best thing, because it cannot do any harm and he will feel very good. It will not do any harm and he will feel very good because the blood will flow to the head in a flood, and when the flood recedes, everything will relax. He will feel very good, just as when you take a bath you feel very good. But if you are very intelligent then it is dangerous. Then you will get stuck in it, your subtle mechanism will be destroyed. You may feel good physically, but mentally it will prove destructive. So if a very intelligent person does it he may go mad; if an unintelligent person does it he may become more healthy.

And then there is the question of time: how much? For a few seconds even for an intelligent man it may be good, just a few seconds, just a flood and then back; then nothing is destroyed, everything just becomes more alive in the brain. But that has to be decided by a master, not by you – you cannot do it through books. Only a living master can decide how many seconds will be enough for you, otherwise you will be moving in danger. But the human mind is childish.

If something goes wrong with your watch, the first inclination is to open it to see what has gone wrong and to do something. Please don't do anything, otherwise many more things will go wrong. Because a watch is a subtle mechanism and only somebody who knows should open it. You will not be repairing it; you may do so much harm that it will become almost impossible to repair. And a watch is nothing – before a brain a watch is nothing.

Don't do anything through books; books cannot be helpful. Somebody is needed who can look through your mind, and through the whole brain system, who can feel how your inner brain is functioning; only he can decide how many seconds and whether it will be good or not. And this is just an example. Many people go on trying things through books. Life is very complex; books can only give you dead rules, and if you follow them you are moving into a dangerous zone. It is better not to do anything than to do something wrong. It is better to remain ordinary, remain in an ordinary life. If you cannot find a living master, if you cannot trust in somebody, then don't do it. At least you will remain sane; otherwise, you can go insane.

The inner system of your bio-energy is very complex – the whole universe is nothing compared to it. The whole universe moves on very simple lines.

Man is the most complex being; that is why no lion can go mad but man is always on the verge. Almost any moment you can go mad. It is such a complex phenomenon that one should move in it with great alertness. And understanding is needed, not rules. Through books, scriptures, rules, you can have knowledge but not understanding. Each person is different: man is different from woman, each individual is different from the other. Not only that, every day you are different from the day before. Yesterday you were one person, today you are somebody else, tomorrow you will be somebody else again. A very, very deep understanding is needed; rules cannot be the substitute.

Now we will enter the sutra: Symphony For A Seabird.

You cannot put a big load in a small bag, nor can you,
with a short rope, draw water from a deep well.

But this is what everybody is doing: trying to put a big load in a small bag. You never bother about the bag or what your capacity is.

The first thing is to know your limitations, then think about your achievement. What is your capacity? What are you capable of? What is your intrinsic capacity? Nobody bothers about it. If a man who has no musical ear goes on trying to become a musician his whole life will be wasted, because a musician is born, not made.

A man who has no feeling goes on trying to become a poet or a painter. If a man who has no eyes tries to become a painter he is going to be a failure, because a painter has a different type of eye – almost the third eye. When you look at the trees you see one green; when a painter looks he sees thousands of greens, not one. Each tree has a greenery of its own. And he *feels* color; color has a vibration for him; the whole world is nothing but color.

Hindus say that the whole world is sound. It so happens that those few people who wrote the Upanishads were poets, musicians; they had an ear for sound. Then the whole universe turned into a sound – *omkar, anahata*. A man who has never been in love with music goes on trying with the mantra *aum* – nothing happens. He goes on repeating it inside – nothing happens. He goes to this master and that and never thinks about his own capacity.

If you have a musical ear, if you have a heart which can understand music – not only understand but feel – then a mantra will be helpful. Because then you can become one with the inner sounds, then you can move with those sounds to more and more subtle layers. Then a moment comes when all sounds stop and only the universal sound remains. That is *aum*. That is why Hindus say that the whole world consists of sound. This is not true, this is not an absolute truth; this is the truth of the musician.

Remember: there are no absolute truths, every truth is individual – it is *your* truth. There is no truth as an objectivity. Your truth may not be a truth to me, my truth may not be a truth to you, because truth is not objective. I am there, involved in it; my truth means me, your truth means you.

When Buddha reaches, when Jesus or Chuang Tzu reaches, they have reached the same universal source, but their interpretations differ. A Buddha is not a musician at all; he finds no sound there. He is not a painter; he finds no color there. He is a very silent man – silence is his music. That is why he finds a formless void – *shunya* – everything empty. That is his truth. He has come to the same source. The source is one, but the people who come are different. They look, they see, they feel in different ways. That is why there are so many philosophies, so many religions.

When Meera comes to the same source she starts dancing. You cannot conceive of Buddha dancing, you cannot conceive of Jesus dancing! Meera starts dancing – she has come to the beloved. The heart of a woman, the feeling of love – then the source becomes the beloved. She has come to her lover. The source is the same, the truth ultimately is the same, but the moment someone says it, it is different. And remember, nobody's truth can be yours; you have to uncover it.

The first thing is to remember your capacity, but you are so confused you cannot feel what your capacity is. Hence the need of a master who can take your pulse with his hand and who can feel what your capacity is. You may go on making much effort in a wrong direction but the outcome will be nothing. You can reach only in a certain way; you can reach only through you.

You cannot put a big load in a small bag, nor can you, with a short rope, draw water from a deep well.

Know your capacity – that is the first point. If you rightly know your capacity, then the first step has been taken and the last is not very far away. If the first is wrong, then you may walk and walk for lives together and you will not reach anywhere.

Have you not heard how a bird from the sea was

blown inshore and landed outside the capital of Lu?

A beautiful parable – a bird from the sea landed outside the capital of Lu, a beautiful bird.

The prince ordered a solemn reception … because a prince is a prince, and he thought that a king among birds had come, and just as other princes have to be received, so this bird which was so beautiful had to be received with equal honor. But how to receive a bird? The prince had his own ways…

> *The prince ordered a solemn reception, offered wine to the seabird in the Sacred Precinct, called for musicians to play the compositions of Shun, slaughtered cattle to nourish it.*
> *Dazed with symphonies, the unhappy seabird died of despair.*

Although everything was done to receive the guest, nobody bothered who the guest was. The guest was received according to the host, not according to the guest – and that killed the poor bird. Many of you are simply dead because of the host. Nobody looks at you.

A child is born and the parents start thinking what to make of him. Even before he is born they start thinking.

I was staying in the home of a friend. The friend is a professor in a university, and his wife is also a professor. Both are very intelligent persons with gold medals and certificates and PhDs. I saw their daughter – they have only one daughter – playing on the piano, weeping and crying. So I asked her mother, 'What is the matter?'

The mother said, 'I always wanted to be a musician and my parents wouldn't allow it. This is not going to happen again to my daughter – she *has* to be a musician. I have suffered so much because my parents wouldn't allow me, they forced me to be a professor. I am not going to force my daughter to be a professor, she is going to be a musician!' And the daughter was crying and weeping!

You are so confused because of others: your mother wants you to be one thing, your father something else. It is bound to be so because they never agree; fathers and mothers, they never agree!

Mulla Nasruddin's son told me, 'I would like to be a doctor but my mother insists that I have to be an engineer. So what can I do?'

I said, 'You do one thing. You spread the rumor that your father wants you to be an engineer.' So now he is a doctor!

They are always opposed, father and mother, and their opposition goes deep within you, it becomes an inner conflict. Your father and your mother may be dead, no longer in this world, but they are within your unconscious – still fighting. They will never leave you in peace. Whatsoever you do, your father says do it, then your mother says don't. Your inner conflict is your parents' conflict. And then there are uncles and brothers and sisters and many relatives, and you are alone amidst so many well-wishers. And they all want you to be something according to them. They destroy you. And then the whole of your life becomes a confusion – you don't know what you want to be, you don't know where you want to go, you don't know what you are doing and why you are doing it. Then you feel miserable. Misery comes if you cannot grow to be a natural being; if you cannot grow according to yourself.

This happened to that seabird and this has happened to all seabirds – you are all seabirds. One day you landed in a womb in the capital of Lu; you were received with great pomp and show. Astrologers decided what was to be done, musicians welcomed you with their music, parents with their love. And all together they have made you just insane and nothing else.

A wise man receives you not according to him, he receives you according to you. The seabird was killed by the musicians and their beautiful symphonies. And the prince was doing everything right: this was how a guest had to be received.

How should you treat a bird? As yourself, or as a bird?

Always give the opportunity to the other to be himself – that is what understanding is, that is what love is. Don't force yourself on others. Your wishes may be good, but the result will be bad. A good wish is not enough in itself; it may turn poisonous. The real point is not your good wish. The real point is to give freedom to the other to be himself or herself. Allow your wife to be herself; allow your husband to be himself; allow your child to be himself – don't force.

We are all seabirds, unknown to each other, strangers. Nobody knows who you are. At the most, all we can do is to help you to be whatsoever you are going to be. And the future is unknown; it cannot be forced. And there is no way to know it, no astrology will help; these are all foolish methods. People depend on them because people are stupid. Astrologers continue to exist because we go on wanting to know about the future so that we can plan. Life cannot be planned; it is an unplanned flood. And it is good that it is unplanned.

If it is planned then everything will be dead and boring. It is good that nobody is able to predict the future, it is good that the future remains unknown, unpredictable, because there lies the whole freedom. If the future becomes known then there is no freedom left, then you will move like a predictable mechanism. But that is what we want, or that is what we try to do.

If you are a little understanding, give others around you freedom to be themselves and don't allow anybody to interfere with your freedom. Don't make anybody a slave to you and don't become a slave to anybody. This is what *sannyas* is. This is my meaning of *sannyas*. It is a man who has decided not to enslave anybody and not to be enslaved by anybody; a man who has decided to remain authentically true to himself; and wheresoever this truth leads, he is ready to go.

This is courage – because it may lead you into insecurity and you would like to be more secure; so you will listen to others and their well-wishing and then their symphonies will kill you. They have already killed you. Why do you listen to others? Because you feel that they know more.

I heard one small child asking his elder brother something. The small one was five and the elder was ten. The junior was saying to the senior, 'You go to mother and ask for her permission so that we can go to the theater.'

So the senior said, 'But why not you? Why don't you go?'

The junior said, 'You have known her longer than me.'

This is the whole problem: you listen to your mother because she has known this world longer than you. You listen to your father because he has known this world longer than you. But do you think that just by being here a long time anybody knows anything? Do you think time gives understanding? Do you think seniority is wisdom? Then go to the government offices and look at the senior people there. Seniority may be wisdom in a government office but it is not in life.

Life is not understood through time, it is understood through meditation. It is a going inwards. Time is an outer movement; time is on the periphery. A man can live for a thousand years and remain stupid. Actually he will become more stupid because he will grow. And if you have a seed of stupidity in you, within a thousand years you will become such a vast tree that millions of stupid people can rest under you. Whatsoever you have, grows; nothing is static, everything is growing. So a stupid person becomes more stupid, a wise person becomes more wise – but time has nothing to do with understanding.

Understanding is not temporal, it is not more experience. It is not the quantity of experience that makes you wise, it is the quality. A single experience can give you more wisdom, if you bring the quality of awareness to it, than you may gain in many lives. A man may have made love to many women, thousands of women, thousands of times. Do you think he knows what love is? There is quantity! You ask a Byron, a Don Juan – there is quantity! Don Juans keep records, they go on counting how many women they have conquered. There is quantity, but have they known love? One single love can give you wisdom if you bring quality to it. The quality has to be brought by you. What is that quality? That quality is awareness. If you make love to a single woman for a single time, with your total being, fully alert, you have come to know what love is. Otherwise you can go on and on and on, it becomes a repetition. And then you need not do anything, the wheel repeats by itself, it becomes automatic.

Wisdom is something that happens when you bring awareness to any experience. The meeting of awareness and experience is wisdom. Experience plus awareness is wisdom. With experience plus more experience plus more experience quantity is gained, but there is no quality … which would make you free and knowing.

Whenever a child is born, if the mother loves the child, if the father loves the child, they will not force themselves on him because they will know at least this much: they have been failures. So why give the same pattern to this child? Why destroy another life again? But look at the stupidity. They would like the child to follow their path. And they have not reached anywhere, and they know deep down that they are empty, hollow, but again they are forcing a child to move on the same path, to reach the same hollowness in the end. Why? Because it feels good to the ego to know that 'My child is following me.'

You may not have reached anywhere, but if your son is following you it gives you a good feeling as if you have attained; the son is following you. And if you are not satisfied by a son, then you can gather followers, disciples. And there are many who are always ready to fall into anybody's trap, because people are so unfulfilled that they are ready to follow anybody's advice. And the problem is that because of others' advice they are unfulfilled – and they go on asking for it again and again.

Mind is a vicious thing. You are so empty and hollow because you have been following others' advice; yet again you are searching for others to advise you. When will you become aware that basically you are missing because you have not followed your inner voice?

So a master cannot give you rules. If a master gives you rules, know well he is a pseudo master. Escape from him! A master can only give you understanding, and show you how to understand yourself – then rules will come but they will come out of your understanding.

> *How should you treat a bird? As yourself, or as a bird?*
> *Ought not a bird to nest in deep woodland or fly over*
> *meadow and marsh?*
> *Ought it not to swim on river and pond, feed on eels*
> *and fish, fly in formation with other waterfowl, and*
> *rest in the reeds?*
>
> *Bad enough for a seabird to be surrounded by men*
> *and frightened by their voices. That was not enough!*
> *They killed it with music.*

Everybody is being killed by music. That music comes out of good wishing, the well-wishers, the do-gooders. The whole thing seems to be so absurd and insane. If you plant one thousand trees and only one comes to flower and nine hundred and ninety-nine die, will anybody call you a gardener? Will anybody give you any credit for the one tree that has flowered? They will say it must have flowered in spite of you because you killed nine hundred and ninety-nine. You cannot take credit for the one, it must have escaped somehow! It must have escaped your skill, your experience, your wisdom.

In millions of men, one becomes a buddha and flowers. What is happening? Why do many trees have to live without flowers? And look at a tree when there are no flowers and flowers never come. What sadness settles on the tree! It cannot laugh, it cannot sing, it cannot dance. Flowers are needed to dance. How can you dance? Even if I say to you, 'Dance!' how can you dance? Because dance is an overflowing delight, such an overflowing that every cell of the body starts dancing; you become a dancing cosmos. But how can you? The energy is not flowing, there is no energy coming. You are somehow carrying yourself, dragging yourself. How can you dance? Flowers come when the tree has so much that it can give. Flowers are a gift, they are a sharing. The tree is saying to the whole universe: I am more than I need. It is a song. The tree is saying: Now I move into the world of luxury, my needs are fulfilled. The tree has more than it needs – then flowering happens.

And you are so discontented, you don't have even as much as you need. How can you dance? How can you sing? How can you meditate?

Meditation is the ultimate flowering, the ecstasy that comes only when you are overflowing in a flood, when you have so much energy that you cannot sit, you can only dance; when you have so much energy that you cannot do anything but share and invite guests to share your energy and your delight, your singing and your dancing.

What has happened to man? What has man done to man that nobody flowers? And if Buddha flowers, remember well, it is not because of you, it is in spite of you. It is in spite of Buddha's father and mother, in spite of his teachers.

It happened that one of my university teachers came to see me. He said, 'You must remember that I was your teacher.'

So I told him, 'Yes, I remember. How can I forget? It is in spite of you that I am whatsoever I am. You could not succeed with me.

You tried and I will always feel thankful towards you that you failed. You couldn't succeed!'

He really loved me and he tried in every way to force me into the academic world. He loved me so much and he cared so much about me that whenever there would be an examination, in the morning he would come with his car and take me to the examination hall, because he was always afraid that I may not go or that I may be meditating. Before examinations he would come to tell me, 'Read this, read this, read this. This is coming up … because I set the paper.' And again and again he would remind me, 'Have you read that or not? Know well: I am the paper-setter and that is coming up.' He was always afraid that I wouldn't listen to him.

He loved me. Your parents also loved you, your teachers also loved you, but they are unconscious, they don't know what they are doing. Even though they love you something goes wrong, and that something is that they try to give you something according to themselves. He wanted me to become a great university professor, somewhere in some great university, head of a department, or a dean or a vice-chancellor.

He imagined these things and I always laughed and asked him, 'What will I gain through this? What have you gained? You are a head of the department, a dean with so many degrees – Honorary Doctor of Literature, and this and that – what have you gained?'

And he would smile knowingly and say, 'You just wait and do whatsoever I am saying.' Because at this question, 'What have you gained?' he would always feel a little perplexed, confused. What could he say?

He had not gained anything and now he was nearing death. He would have liked his ambition to move through me. He would have liked me to carry his ambition.

A father dies unfulfilled, but he hopes that at least his son will reach the goal. And this is how it goes on and on, and nobody reaches. Love is not enough; awareness is needed. If love is there without awareness it becomes an imprisonment, and if love is there with awareness it becomes a freedom. It helps you to be yourself.

> *Bad enough for a seabird to be surrounded by men and frightened by their voices. That was not enough! They killed it with music.*

> *Water is for fish and air for men. Natures differ, and needs with them.*

> *Hence the wise men of old did not lay down one measure for all.*

You cannot be treated as things. Things can be similar; souls cannot be. You can have one million Ford cars just the same. You can replace one Ford car with another Ford car and there will be no trouble, but you cannot replace a human being. When a human being disappears, that place that he occupied will always remain forever and forever unoccupied. Nobody can occupy it, it is impossible to occupy it, because nobody can be exactly the same as that man was. Everybody is unique so no rules can be laid down.

The wise men of old … but if you go to the wise men of today you will find rules and regulations and everything – a framework. They will make you a soldier but not a *sannyasin*. A soldier is a dead man because his whole function is to bring death into the world. He cannot be allowed to be very alive, otherwise how will he bring death? Death can only come through a dead man. He has to kill. And before he kills others he has to be killed completely himself, through rules.

So the whole army training is to kill the aliveness of the person, the consciousness of the person – to make him an automaton. So they go on saying to him, 'Right turn, left turn, right turn, left turn,' for years together, every day for hours! What nonsense is going on? Why 'right turn', why 'left turn'? But there is a point to it – they want to make you an automaton. 'Right turn' – and every day for hours you are doing it. It becomes a bodily phenomenon. When they say, 'Right turn!' you need not think about it, the body simply moves. When they say, 'Left turn!' the body simply moves. Now you are a mechanism. And when they say, 'About turn!' you shoot; the body moves, the consciousness does not interfere.

The whole point of army training all over the world is to cut consciousness from your actions so that the actions become automatic – you become more efficient, skilled. Because consciousness is always a trouble … If you are killing a person and you think, you will miss. You may think, 'Why kill this man? He has not done anything to me. I don't even know who he is, he is a stranger.' If you think, you will also have the feeling that you have a mother at home, a wife, a small child, who are waiting for you, and the same is going to be the case with the other. A mother must be waiting somewhere, a wife praying that her husband will come back, a child hoping that his father will be back. Why kill this man and kill those hopes of a child, of a wife, of a mother, of a father, brother, friends? Why kill this man? And he has not done anything wrong to you; it's just that two politicians have gone mad. They can go and fight with each other and decide the matter. Why decide through others?

If you are alert, aware, it will be impossible for you to shoot and kill. So the whole training of the army is to divide awareness and action, to cut and create a gap. So awareness continues on its own, and action continues on its own, and they become parallel; they never meet.

Just the opposite is the training of a *sannyasin*: it is how to destroy the gap that exists between consciousness and action – how to bring them together. They should not be parallel lines, they should become one whole. It is how to be conscious in each of your actions, how not to be an automaton. And when all your automatism disappears you have become enlightened; then you are a buddha.

Through rules this cannot be done. Through rules you can be made a soldier but you cannot be made a *sannyasin*. All rules have to be dropped; understanding has to be gained. But remember, dropping the rules does not mean that you become anti-social. Dropping the rules only means that because you exist in the society you follow certain rules, but they are just rules of the game – nothing else.

If you play cards then you have rules: a certain card is the king, another card is the queen. You know that this is foolishness – no card is the king, no card is the queen; but if you want to play the game, certain rules have to be followed. They are rules of the game, nothing is ultimate about them. You have to follow the traffic rules.

Remember: the whole of morality is nothing but traffic rules. You live in a society; you are not alone there, there are many others. Certain rules have to be followed, but they are not ultimate, they have nothing of ultimacy in them. They are just like walking on the left. In America you walk on the right – no problem. If the rule is followed, keep to the right, it is okay. If the rule is followed, keep to the left, it is also okay. Both are the same but one has to be followed. If you have both the rules then there will be traffic jams and there will be difficulty – unnecessary difficulty.

When you live with others, life has to follow certain rules. Those rules are neither religious, nor moral, nor divine; they are just man-made. One has to be aware of this, one has to know their relativity; they are formal.

You need not break all the rules, there is no need, because then you will be in unnecessary trouble, and rather than becoming a *sannyasin* you will become a criminal. Remember that! A *sannyasin* is not a soldier, a *sannyasin* is not a criminal; a *sannyasin* knows that rules are just a game. He is not against them, he transcends them, he goes beyond them, he keeps himself free of them. He follows them for others but he doesn't become an automaton. He remains conscious and fully alert.

Consciousness is the goal. That is why Chuang Tzu says:

Hence the wise men of old did not lay down one
measure for all.

They have not laid down any measures really. They have attempted, through many ways and means, to awaken you. You are so fast asleep – I can hear your snoring! How to awaken you? How to shock you towards awareness? And when you are awake, no rules are needed. Still you follow rules but you know no rules are needed. You don't become a criminal, you transcend and become a *sannyasin*.

CHAPTER 7

AUTUMN FLOODS

Chuang Tzu told the story of the autumn floods:
The autumn floods had come. Thousands of wild
torrents poured furiously into the Yellow River. It surged
and flooded its banks until, looking across, you could
not tell an ox from a horse on the other side.
Then the River God laughed, delighted to think that all
the beauty in the world had fallen into his keeping.
So downhill he swung, until he came to the ocean.
There he looked out over the waves toward the empty
horizon in the east, and his face fell.
Gazing out at the far horizon, he came to his senses and
murmured to the Ocean God, 'Well, the proverb is right:
"He who has got himself a hundred ideas thinks he
knows more than anybody else." Such a one am I. Only
now do I see what they mean by expanse!'
The Ocean God replied, 'Can you talk about the sea to
a frog in a well? Can you talk about ice to a dragonfly?
And can you talk about the way of life to a doctor of
philosophy?'

Life is experience and not theory. It needs no explanation. It is there in all its glory, just to be lived, enjoyed, delighted in. It is not a riddle, it is a mystery. A riddle is something which can be solved, a mystery is something which can never be solved. A mystery is something you can become one with; you can dissolve into it, you can melt into it – you yourself can become mysterious. This is the difference between philosophy and religion. Philosophy thinks that life is a riddle; you have to solve it, find explanations, theories, doctrines. Philosophy thinks that there is going to be some answer, that life is a question mark and one has to work hard at it. Of course, if you take life as a question mark, your effort becomes intellectual. The very assumption that life is a question leads you into more and more intellectual efforts, and in search of an answer you decide upon theories.

Religion says that to take life as a question is basically false. It is not a question – it is there, with no question mark. It is there as an open secret; it is an invitation. You have to become a guest, you have to move into it. It is ready and welcoming – don't fight with it! It is not a question, don't try to solve it! It is not a riddle. Come and become one with it, and you will know it. The knowing will come from your totality, not from the intellect. Intellect is a partial effort, and life needs you to be totally with it, to flow with it, so one with it that you cannot feel what is what, you cannot feel where you end and where life begins. The whole of life becomes you, the whole of you becomes life. This is what salvation is. It is not a solution, it is a salvation.

This is what Hindus have called *moksha*: it is not a theory, a conclusion, it is a totally different way to live with existence. It is not head-oriented. Really, you become headless, you lose all distinctions; the periphery dissolves – you are just like a drop in the ocean. You lose your boundaries and you gain the cosmic boundaries which are infinite.

The first thing to understand is not to take life as a question. Once you take it as a question you will be in trouble; you will have already moved on a wrong path – it will be a cul-de-sac. Somewhere, in some theory, you will be stuck. Everybody is stuck somewhere in a theory, and then it is very difficult to drop the theory. You cling to it because the question scares you. At least a theory is some consolation, at least you feel that you know. You don't know! Mind cannot know, mind can only theorize. It can go on spinning words faster and faster; it can play with words, arrange them, but they are all interpretations – not the real, just your interpretation of it.

It is just like a map. You see the map of India? You can go on carrying that map with you, you can go on thinking that you are carrying India in your pocket, but the map is not the country. You can have a theory about a rose, about what a rose is. You can even have a photograph of a rose, but that photograph is just a photograph, it carries nothing of the living phenomenon that a rose is.

Look at a child – he is still without a mind. He opens his eyes and just looks at the world. Bring a rose to him. He does not know the name, he cannot label it, he cannot categorize it, he cannot say what it is. Still the rose is there – the colors flood the child, the beauty of the rose surrounds him, the fragrance reaches to his very heart. He does not know what it is but he passes through a living moment. You tell the child, 'This is a rose,' and the experience will never again be the same; never again will the child be able to experience the mystery of the rose. Now, whenever a rose comes before him he will say, 'This is a rose.' Now he will carry the word. You have made him poor – and he was very rich. The whole rose was there, and he could only live it; there was no other way to describe it, to define it.

A rose is a rose is a rose. You cannot say what it is, this or that. The child was silent, there was no functioning of the mind; the mind was not there, there was no barrier. The heart of the rose melted into the heart of the child, the heart of the child melted into the heart of the rose. The child could not even say where he ended and the rose began, where the rose ended and he began – there were no boundaries. They became one in that moment of awe. For a single moment they were not two – oneness happened.

But you have told him: 'This is a rose.' Now the experience will never be there again. The moment the rose is there, immediately the mind will say, 'This is a rose.' The mystery is lost; now there is an answer, now the child knows. What absurdity! Now you will say the child is growing in knowledge, but just the opposite is the case. Before you told him what was what, he knew; but he knew with his totality. It was not knowledge, it was experiencing. But then you thought he was ignorant. Now you think he knows because he carries a word in his mind.

The word 'rose' is not rose, the word 'god' is not God, the word 'love' is not love. But we go on accumulating these words. And then there are clever minds who arrange these words into interpretations, theories and arguments. And the more argumentative, the more theoretical you become, the further you move from the rose. Then even echoes become impossible: nothing comes to you, you never go to anything – you simply live in the mind, arranging words.

I have heard an anecdote:

Three Jews were going for a morning walk. They were friends, old friends, discussing many things. Then they saw the mayor's big car pass by and the mayor waved his hand and said, 'Hello!'

Now there was trouble. The first one said, 'Don't get so happy! He said hello to me – and he has to!'

The two asked, 'What do you mean?'

The first one said, 'I have taken ten thousand dollars from him. I borrowed the money, and for two years he has been waiting and waiting. He had to say hello to me!'

The other one said, 'You are wrong! The hello was said to me –

and he had to. The reason is that I have lent him ten thousand dollars. He owes money to me and he is always afraid of me. The moment he sees me he gets scared – he has to!'

The third laughed and the two others turned to him and said, 'What do you mean? Why are you laughing?'

He said, 'He had to say hello to me, not to you – there you are both wrong. He neither owes money to me nor do I owe money to him. Why shouldn't he give me a clean hello?'

Once you start looking at reality through the mind then everything becomes a problem; then the ego starts interpreting and then you have only interpretations. You may have proofs for them, and those proofs may look reasonable, but only to you, not to anybody else – because it is your ego that gives those interpretations. And you get more and more fixed in your interpretations because you have invested so much in them.

If somebody says something which goes against Christianity, a Christian feels hurt. If somebody says something against Hinduism, a Hindu feels hurt. Why? If you are really a truth seeker, as religious people say they are, why should you get hurt? You should inquire – he may be right. But the ego is involved. It is not a question of Hinduism being right or wrong, it is a question of *you* being right or wrong. How can you be wrong? If you are wrong, then your image starts shaking – you cannot be wrong. Then for small things, very small things, you start fighting and arguing. But the real fight, the basis of all fight, is that you are fighting against life. With your answers you are trying to conquer life; with your theories you are trying to manipulate life. And you think that if you know the theories then you will be the master.

Through knowledge you strengthen your ego. So if somebody says there is no knowledge through the mind, the ego simply becomes deaf. It never listens to it because it is dangerous. The mind says: 'This is also a theory.' The mind says: 'Even anti-philosophy is a philosophy, even Chuang Tzu is a philosopher.' Then everything is settled and you move again into your interpretations. But remember, Chuang Tzu is not a philosopher – neither am I.

Philosophy is an attitude towards life. 'Attitude' means a choice, and choice can only be fragmentary.

A mystic never chooses. He looks at the whole without any choice on his part; he does not become a chooser. If you choose, then there is a problem immediately because life is contradictory. Life exists through contradictions, and it is beautiful how life manages the impossible. The night and the day exist as neighbors, not neighbors really – the day melts into the night and becomes the night; the night melts again into the day and becomes the day. Love and hate exist together: the love melts and becomes the hate, the hate melts and becomes the love. Life and death exist together: life goes on melting into death and death goes on melting again into life. Existence is contradictory, but there is a deep harmony between the opposite polarities.

For the mind this looks impossible, this cannot be. How can opposites exist together? How can there be a harmony between life and death? How can there be a harmony between hate and love? The mind says: 'Love is never hate and hate is never love.' The mind says: 'A is A and B is B and A is never B.' Mind is logical and life is contradictory, that is why they never meet. So if you say that this man is good, you cannot believe that this man is also bad. But life is such: the sinner exists in the saint and the saint exists in the sinner. Only logic is clear-cut, with boundaries, definitions.

Life is not clear-cut, it moves into the opposite. Just look … you can be a saint this moment and a sinner the next. What is the problem for life? You can be a sinner this moment and the next moment you can rise above it and become a saint. What is the problem?

Look at the inside phenomenon: how things melt into the opposite, how opposites exist together. You are happy, happy like a flower, happy like a star, and suddenly you become sad. Look ... is this sadness something separate from your happiness? Or has the same energy become sadness? Who was happy and who is sad? Are there two persons within you or the same person having moods? And the same energy goes on moving: sometimes it is sad and sometimes it is happy. If you understand this then you don't create a contradiction between the two. And then your sadness has a flavor of happiness and your happiness has a depth of sadness also.

If a buddha is sad you will see a blissful feeling in his sadness, you will see an undercurrent of compassion. His sadness is beautiful. And if a buddha is happy, and if you look deep and observe him, you will feel that in his happiness there is a depth – just the same depth as there always is with sadness. His happiness is not shallow.

With you, the problem is that whenever you are happy you are shallow; but whenever you are sad you may be deeper, less shallow. That is why laughter has a ring of shallowness. If you laugh it seems you are laughing just on the periphery, but when you weep, you weep from the heart. It is easy to pretend laughter, it is very difficult to pretend tears. If they do not come it is impossible to bring them. You can force smiles, you cannot force tears. The more you force, the more you will feel they won't come, the more the eyes will be dry. Your sadness has a depth, your laughter has a shallowness.

But when Buddha laughs, he laughs as deeply as tears can go; and when he weeps, he weeps as beautifully as you smile. The contradictions have lost their contradictoriness, they have become one. That is why to understand Buddha is difficult – because he has become as contradictory as existence itself. He is an absurdity – now he is a mystery himself.

A religious person is in search of truth, a philosopher is in search of interpretations.

I have heard that once it happened in a men's club that three professors of philosophy were discussing, in a panel discussion, what is most beautiful in a woman.

The one philosopher said, 'It is the eyes – the eyes carry the whole of the woman, they are the most beautiful part in a feminine body.'

The second one said, 'I don't agree. The hair is the most beautiful part of a feminine face and body, it gives it the beauty and the mystery.'

And the third said, 'I don't agree with you. You are both wrong – it is the legs, the way a woman walks, the curves of her legs, just the marbleness of her legs, that gives her the whole feminine beauty.'

One woman, an old woman, who was listening very seriously to this discussion, elevated her nose and said, 'I must get out of here before one of you boys says the truth!'

A woman is not a philosopher, she has no theories – she *knows*. A religious person has an intuitive grasp – it is not intellect, it is his whole being. He feels rather than knows. And feeling hits the center. So remember one thing: through philosophy you will never reach the truth, you will just go about and about and about.

Omar Khayyam has said in his *Rubaiyat*, 'When I was young I frequented both doctor and saint. About and about they argued and I came out by the same door as I went in.' He visited so many philosophers, so many saints – but they talked about and about and he had to come back by the same door.

Nothing is gained, only life is wasted. The sooner you become alert, the better. The sooner you become aware and drop out of the trap of philosophy, the better, because life will not wait for you and your theories; it is moving fast. Soon death will happen and you will die with your theories in your hand; and they won't help, they are just dead ashes.

Chuang Tzu says: Live, don't think! That is all that those who have known have always said.

Live, don't think! Drop thinking and become a being – your totality is required. It is okay that for science you use your head, it is okay that you use your heart for art, but for religion *you* are required in your totality. If the head functions alone it produces dry theories; if the heart functions alone it creates fictions, dreams. Your totality is required. And when you function totally you reach the total that is the universe – you become the same, and only the similar can know it. If you become total in your small circle then the total of the vast circle, the *brahman*, is ready to receive you. This is one thing.

The second thing before we enter this parable is that mind is always conditioned. It cannot be unconditioned. Being is unconditioned, mind is a conditioning. Mind is always trained by the society in which you live, trained by the experiences through which you pass. So a frog has a frog mind – he lives in a well, that is his whole universe. And you also have a frog mind because you also live in a well: the well of the Hindu, the well of the Mohammedan, the well of the Christian or the Jew. And you have a boundary – it may be invisible, but then it is more dangerous because you can jump out of visible boundaries more easily. Invisible boundaries … you never feel that they are there so they just cling to you.

It is easier for a frog to come out of his well than for you to come out of your Hinduism, your Christianity: it is difficult, because the well is invisible. A frog lives in a fixed well – he can jump out of it. You live in a well that you carry around you; it is like a climate, always surrounding you; it is your invisible personality. Wherever you go you carry your well with you, you remain in it. Whatsoever you see, you see through it.

All interpretations come from conditioning – and only one who is unconditioned can know the real, can know the true. A Hindu cannot know God, a Christian cannot know, a Jew cannot know – because these are minds. Only someone who has come to realize that he is neither a Hindu, nor a Mohammedan, nor a Christian – only he can know.

An Indian cannot know the truth, a Japanese cannot know the truth, a Chinese person cannot know the truth, because truth has no boundaries. Nationalities create conditionings: they have to be dropped. One has to become absolutely naked before the truth, with no clothes, no conditionings; neither a Hindu, nor an Indian, nor a Mohammedan, nor a Chinese – just a being, a pure being with nothing to cling to. Then you are out of the well. And if you cling to the well, how can you reach the ocean? And if you carry the conditionings of the well, even if the ocean is there you won't believe it, you won't see it, because your eyes will be closed to this vastness. They can know only that which is narrow, like a well.

The third thing to be remembered is that mind always wants to live with inferiors, it is always afraid of the superior. So everybody goes on searching for the inferior – friends, wife, husband – just the inferior to you, so you can feel superior.

In India, they have a proverb that a camel never wants to come to the Himalayas. That is why he lives in deserts – there *he* is the Himalayas! If he comes near the Himalayas then what will happen to the ego? That's why you escape whenever there is any fear for the ego. If you come to a buddha you will escape, because a camel never wants to come to a Himalaya. You like your desert – at least you are somebody there. George Bernard Shaw is reported to have said, 'If I am not the first in heaven I would not like to go there. Even hell is preferable if I am first. If I am to be second in heaven, it is not for me.'

He is saying something about you. Just think: will you be at ease in heaven where you are not the first? And you cannot be, because Jesus will be there, Buddha will be there, they are already occupying the queue; you will be far behind. But in hell there is a possibility of your being first – and it is also easier. You can be in misery, but you would like to be the first, the foremost, somebody

– you would not like to be blissful and nobody. And this is the problem: only nobodies can be blissful; somebodies will always be in misery because the very feeling that 'I have to be somebody' creates misery. Then you are in competition and conflict, then there is continuous tension with everybody – everybody else is the enemy. And the mind always seeks the inferior, it surrounds itself with inferiors. Then you become the most supreme.

Look at this tendency. If it persists you will go on falling and falling and falling, and there is no end to it. Always seek the superior if you are really seeking the truth, because truth is the most superior. If you are seeking the inferior then finally you will end with some ultimate lie.

If you really want to go to the divine, then seek the superior, because the superior is the glimpse of it. Always seek the superior. But then you have to be humble, then you have to bow down, then you have to surrender. This is the problem for the ego, for the mind.

Mind tends to seek the inferior, that is why mind can never reach the most superior, the highest peak of life. Mind will finally reach hell. Mind *is* hell, and no-mind is heaven.

Now we will try to penetrate this beautiful parable:

The autumn floods had come. Thousands of wild torrents poured furiously into the Yellow River. It surged and flooded its banks until, looking across, you could not tell an ox from a horse on the other side.

Then the River God laughed, delighted to think that all the beauty in the world had fallen into his keeping. So downhill he swung, until he came to the ocean. There he looked out over the waves toward the empty horizon in the east, and his face fell.

Gazing out at the far horizon he came to his senses and murmured to the Ocean God, 'Well, the proverb

is right. "He who has got himself a hundred ideas
thinks he knows more than anybody else." Such a one
am I. Only now do I see what they mean by expanse!'

The Yellow River is one of the greatest rivers in the world, and one of the most dangerous. And of course, when the river is in flood, autumn flood, and thousands and thousands of torrents, streams, small rivers and rivulets, are falling into it and it is flooded, it becomes a small ocean in itself. And the River God thought, 'Now there is nobody comparable to me, and the whole beauty of the world has fallen into my keeping. Now I am vast, incomparably vast, there is nobody else who is so vast.'

This is what is happening to every ego. Every ego is the Yellow River. When you are a child it is a small current – just at the very source, not very big or vast. Then streams fall into it, you gather many experiences, much knowledge, certificates, money, wealth, prestige, respect – you go on gathering. Thousands of torrents fall in and the river goes on becoming vaster and vaster, bigger and bigger. This is the autumn flood that comes when you are young – then you think no one is comparable to you, you are incomparable. Then you are filled with the ego, puffed up. Everybody in his young age becomes puffed up – the autumn flood. And then he thinks, 'Now the beauty of the whole world has fallen into my keeping.' You ask any person. Whatsoever he says, don't listen. Just look at the way he says it. He may say that he is a humble man, but look in his eyes – he is saying, 'I am the most humble man, there is no comparison to me.' He may be saying that he is not so beautiful as others; but look, he is waiting for you to contradict, to say, 'No, you are wrong.' And if you nod and say, 'Yes, you are right,' you are creating one more enemy. He was being diplomatic. What he wanted to say was something else, but he wanted to hear it from you.

In youth, everyone is in a flood, and then the whole outlook is tinged and colored by the ego. Then you walk, then you talk, behave, relate, but everything is tinged, colored, by the ego. Much misery of course happens because you are thinking yourself to be that which you are not, and you are believing in the shadow. Soon the flood will recede – the autumn is not going to be forever. You will become old, torrents will not fall into you, streams will become dry, banks will appear, summer will come, and this vast-looking Yellow River will become just a tiny stream. You may become just a dry bed of sand and nothing else.

It happens in old age: then one feels very irritated, cheated – as if existence has been cheating you. Nobody has cheated you, you simply magnified yourself foolishly. Your own ego created the whole problem – now you feel cheated. You cannot find a man who is old and yet happy. If you can find one, live with him – he is a wise man. You can find happy young men, that is nothing. If you can find a happy old man, that is something. When the summer has come and the autumn flood is no more and an old man is happy, then he has known something else: he has found some eternal source.

When you are young you have a dance in your feet – that is nothing, it is just the flood. But when you are old and everything has been taken back – nobody even remembers you, nobody bothers about you; you are simply neglected, out of the way, thrown away like rubbish, garbage – and you are still happy …

Buddha has said that when you find an old man as happy as a youth, there is something there – bow down to him, listen and learn from him. In India, it was the tradition that whenever we found an old man happy, dancing, we would make him a master. He would move to the forest, he would create a small university around him – a *gurukul*, a household of the master – and disciples would start pouring in from all over the country.

In India we have never made a young man a teacher, only an old man can be a teacher – and that is right. Exceptions may happen, but generally it is right. Only an old man can be a teacher, one who has lived through all seasons of life, who is seasoned and still happy and blissful. To be in flood and happy is nothing special, it is ordinary, but to be happy and ecstatic when the stream is almost dry, when only sands are left, when one's whole body is just a ruin… To be alive at the peak of life and to dance is nothing. But when death comes near and you go dancing to meet it, then it is something. Then the rare has happened, the extraordinary has entered into the world of the ordinary; then the divine has penetrated.

If you are happy because you are young you will not be happy for long, soon your happiness will be shattered. And if you can become aware before it is shattered, it is good. This is the beauty: if you can become sad while you are young, you will be happy when you become old; otherwise you will become sad because now this is just a flood. If you look at it, it is not you; it is the thousand torrents falling into you that are giving you the impression that you are vast. Soon that which is given to you will be taken, and if you can be happy when everything is taken, only then is your happiness unshakable. Then your happiness has become bliss.

This is the difference between happiness and bliss: happiness depends on others – the thousand torrents falling in; bliss depends just on you, it is independent. It has no conditions to be fulfilled, it is unconditional. It is simply because of you; it has no causality, nothing causes it. If you are happy with your girlfriend, your boyfriend, your lover, then somebody is causing your happiness. Soon it will be taken away, because it is an autumn flood. Seasons will change, the wheel of life will go on moving – it will be taken away.

That which is caused cannot be forever; that which is uncaused can be forever – remember that always whenever you are happy. Remember: is it something uncaused or caused? If it is caused then it is better to be sad, because it is going to be taken away. It is already on the way, it has already left you – sooner or later you will realize it has gone, because causation is part of the world which is in a flux, this dream world that Hindus have called *maya,* this illusion which goes on moving like a dream. And if you believe in it, it becomes a nightmare. If you don't believe it, you can discard it – then you can look at the witness, which is uncaused.

The River God became swollen:

So downhill he swung, until he came to the ocean.

And someday or other you will come to the ocean. What is the ocean? Death is the ocean – vast. Life has a source to it, death has no source. Life has banks to it, sometimes flooded – then it looks vast; sometimes not flooded – then it becomes a tiny stream. But death has no banks to it – it is oceanic.

And just like every river has to come to the ocean, so every river of consciousness has to come to death. Wherever you are going, whatsoever path you choose, whichever direction, it makes no difference – you will reach the ocean. The ocean surrounds you in all directions. You will reach death, and near death all your dreams will be shattered – the whole ego will be shaken.

So downhill he swung, until he came to the ocean.
There he looked out over the waves toward the empty
horizon in the east, and his face fell.

That is how old men become sad. Their faces fall, happiness disappears; the zest, the enthusiasm, the dream, everything simply dies. They look and see nothing but a soulless ocean in which they are going to be merged and dissolved – they will be no more. Every river falling into the ocean feels the same. And every river, it is said, looks back to the days when she was something, looks back before she falls into the ocean, remembers the past, the floods, the autumn, the days when she was somebody. But you cannot go back! There is no possibility of going back in time. One has always to move further and further; and every river has to fall. It falls crying. Go to the ocean and sit near a river falling into the ocean – you will feel such sadness in the river.

Every old man, all old persons start looking backwards. Old people always go into memories, the days when they were something, somebody, the days when they were loved and respected and honored. They go on again and again. Just listen to old men and you feel they are very boring. Why do you feel they are boring? Why do you feel irritated? Because they go on repeating the same story of the old days. Always they start in the good old days. Why the good? Why aren't the days good now? No old man can believe that the days are good now – they were always in the past, the golden past, the good old days when things were like this and that. This is not a question of things, or economic situations or political situations – nothing. They were young and everything was good. They were flooded.

It happened that a chief justice of the Supreme Court of the United States went to visit Paris after he retired. He had been once before, thirty years before. His old wife was also with him. Looking at Paris for two or three days, he became very sad and he said, 'We were waiting for this, to come and see Paris, but nothing looks like it was before.'

The wife laughed and said, 'Everything is as it was before, only we are not young. Paris remains the same.'

But now other rivers are in autumn flood. Your summertime has come, and when you are old how can Paris be the same as when you were young? Paris is the symbolic city of young people indulging. There are cities for different seasons: Varanasi is the city of the old people, Paris is the city of the young people. Paris indulges, Varanasi renounces. In India, when people want to die they go to Varanasi to live there and to die there – it is the city of the old, the summertime. When you become old, the whole world seems to be old and dying. But the world remains the same, only you go on changing.

Look, and drop your mind. Then you are neither young nor old, then there are no seasons – because the innermost spirit has no seasons to it, no autumn, no summer, nothing. It remains the same, it is eternal. Otherwise, whenever your river comes to the ocean your face will fall, you will become sad – sad and burdened with old memories, thinking about the past because now there is no future. A child never thinks of the past because there is no past. A child is just fresh – a blank page; things are going to be written on it but as yet nothing is written. He cannot move backwards, he always thinks of the future.

Ask a child and he is always thinking of how to grow, how to grow soon and fast, how to become like Daddy – and he doesn't know what is happening to Daddy, in what trouble Daddy is – he doesn't know. He wants to become powerful, strong, tall, somebody, soon. He would like a miracle to happen – to go to sleep at night and in the morning to be old and grown up. Every child thinks of the future. Childhood thinks of the future, because for childhood there is expanse in the future. Seventy years to live – nothing lived before. There is no past; that is why a child has not much memory.

If a child becomes angry he forgets it immediately; immediately he can laugh, because there is not much past which can become a burden. He goes on forgetting the past because his whole energy is moving towards the future; he cannot look back, no child looks back. A young man in youth remains in the present. He is just in the middle, he lives here and now. No need to go to the past because the present is so beautiful, he is so flooded, the ego is so high; no need to go to the future because the future cannot be better than this.

There are old countries just like old men. For example, India is an old country; it always thinks of the past, ancient ages. There are young countries, for example America; it lives here and now, just this moment. There are young countries, for example China. China is a young country now – reborn, it looks to the future. Much is going to happen, soon the world will become a utopia. Countries move just like persons. Young men live in the present: everything is so good, nothing could be better. But this cannot continue forever. Soon the old days set in and the old man thinks of the past.

Mind is either in the past, or in the present, or in the future, because past, present and future are, all three of them, parts of mind. They are not tenses of time, but parts of mind. But when you drop the mind you are in eternity; it is neither past nor present nor future. You have transcended all three; then there is no season for you. Then you are sad in your happiness and you are happy in your sadness. Then you are old in your youngness and you are young in your oldness. Then you are a child at the time of death and you are an old man at the time of birth.

It is said of Lao Tzu, the master of Chuang Tzu, that he was born old, eighty years old, that he remained in his mother's womb for eighty years. It is a beautiful story. And it is said that he was born old with a white beard and white hair – snow-white. This is just the other side of the coin. Jesus says: If you are a child again you will enter into the kingdom of God. This is one aspect. Lao Tzu has another aspect. He says: If you are born old you have already entered. But both are the same, and this is the problem for the mind to understand: one who is born old will be a child when he dies. If you are a child when born, you will be old when you die. So either become old when you are born, which is difficult – very, very difficult, but there are methods – or die and then become a child. But both are related, because life and death are a circle.

When you die here, you are born somewhere else. If you can die here as a child – fresh, unburdened, innocent – you will be born old. Because you will be so experienced, you will be so wise, you will be old. That is what it means: to be wise from the very first moment. If you die fresh and young you will be born wise, because wisdom happens in an empty and innocent mind. And if you are born wise, old, you will not move in the ordinary foolishness that everybody is prone to, and you will remain fresh, wise. Then there is no death.

So a wise man is born only once; all other lives are just preparations. Only once can he come back before his final merging into the universe; before his *mahanirvana,* he can come once. If you die almost a child you will be born once more, but you will be born as an old man. You will be wise from the first day and then there will be no more birth; then you attain to the birthless and deathless.

> *Gazing out at the far horizon he came to his senses and murmured to the Ocean God, 'Well, the proverb is right. "He who has got himself a hundred ideas thinks he knows more than anybody else." Such a one am I. Only now do I see what they mean by expanse!'*

When you come to the superior, when you come to a man of Tao, only then do you realize what it means to be wise, what it means to be intelligent, what it means to be mature, what it means to be expanding, what it means to be really conscious, total, integrated. When you come to an enlightened person, only then do you feel what it means to be here at all. Before, you moved in a dream, in shadows; you never came into the sunlight, you were never under the sky. You lived in dark caves, caves of the ego.

> *The Ocean God replied, 'Can you talk about the sea to a frog in a well?'*

It is impossible, because the language differs. The frog in the well speaks the language of the well.

You must have heard this story:

Once a frog from the ocean came and jumped into a well. He got acquainted with the frog in the well and the well frog asked, 'From where do you come?'

He said, 'I have come from the ocean.'

The well frog asked, 'Is it bigger than this well?' Of course suspicion was in his eyes, doubt in his mind, 'How can anything be bigger than this well where I live?'

The ocean frog laughed and said, 'It is very difficult to say anything because there is no measure.'

The well frog said, 'Then I will give you some measure so that you can.'

He jumped one quarter of the well, one fourth of the way across, and said, 'Is it that big?'

The ocean frog laughed and said, 'No.'

So he jumped half of the well, and said, 'Is it that big?'

Again the ocean frog laughed and said, 'No.'

Then he jumped three quarters and said, 'Is it that big?'

Again the ocean frog said, 'No.'

Then he jumped the whole well, the whole length, and said, 'Now – now you cannot say no.'

The ocean frog said, 'You may feel hurt, and I don't want to be offensive, but still the answer is no.'

Then the well frog said, 'Get out from here, you liar. Nothing can be bigger than this well!'

Whenever you doubt, it is always the well frog in you. Nothing can be bigger than you, nothing can be higher than you, nothing can be more divine than you, nothing can be holier than you. No! That is why you go on rejecting Buddhas, Christs; you have to, because they come from the ocean. They bring a message of the immeasurable, and you have your measuring sticks. You should not be too hard on the well frog because what can he do? You can only have compassion; you cannot be too hard because that is all he has known. He has never been to the ocean so how can he conceive of it?

Hence the compassion of the buddhas. You go on disbelieving them and they go on giving their compassion, because they know – what can you do? You have lived in a well for so long. A well frog even looks at the sky, but the sky is also surrounded by his well, it is just a hole. Even the sky is not bigger than his well, because he cannot know that his well is just a window and that the sky is not fixed in the window. But you are standing behind the window. Then the same structure of the window becomes the structure of your sky and you think, 'The sky is the same as my window.' This is how everybody thinks.

And buddhas cannot do anything else but be compassionate. Jesus died on the cross and still he said, 'God, forgive these people because they don't know what they are doing.'

This is what that well frog was doing. And the ocean frog must have prayed in the depth of his heart, 'God, forgive this frog because he does not know what he is doing and what he is saying.' He said, 'Get out from here, you liar. You cannot deceive me, you must have some plans to deceive me. I cannot believe in such an absurdity, that anything can be bigger than this well.'

The Ocean God replied, 'Can you talk about the sea to a frog in a well?

That is why buddhas cannot talk about what they know; it is impossible to communicate. It is incommunicable because languages differ; you have a different pattern of language. If it is put in that pattern of language then the ocean will have to be put in a well, but the ocean will not go, so everything will become false. That is why buddhas go on saying, 'Whatsoever we say, just by saying it, it becomes untrue.'

Says Lao Tzu: The truth cannot be said, and that which can be said is no longer true. This is the problem – not the truth. You are the problem, and your language of the well is the problem, not truth. Truth can be said, but then two buddhas are needed to talk about it. And they don't need to talk about it because when two buddhas are there, there is no need to say anything – they show it. They *are* the truth; there is no need to talk. And whenever there is any need to talk, the problem arises.

> *'Can you talk about the sea to a frog in a well? Can you talk about ice to a dragonfly?'*

The dragonfly lives in fire; how can you talk about ice to a dragonfly? She has never known it, ice never existed for her; fire is her world. You can talk about fire, you cannot talk about ice. You cannot say that there are things as cold as ice. She will not believe you because to her everything is fire.

Can bliss be taught to you – to you who live in the fire of misery and *dukkha*? Can bliss be taught to you who live in anguish, who are dragonflies? How can you understand the coolness of a buddha? You cannot understand. How can you understand that in the head of a buddha there are no thoughts moving, no clouds? You don't know, you have not even had a glimpse; not even for a single moment has the process of thought stopped. You know your head as a mad crowd: how can you believe that a buddha simply sits and there is not a thought in his head? That is inconceivable! You live in fire; Buddha lives in a cool, very cool world. And there is no bridge between fire and ice. Unless you become cooler and cooler and cooler you will not be able to understand. Buddha becomes communicable only when you become more silent and cool; otherwise everything is missed.

> *'And can you talk about the way of life to a doctor of philosophy?'*

Impossible! And I will tell you that it is even possible sometimes to talk about the sea to a well frog, it is possible to talk about ice to a dragonfly, but it is not possible to talk about truth to a philosopher, to a doctor of philosophy. Why? Because howsoever small the well may be it is still part of the ocean – at least the water is part of the ocean. And howsoever opposite the fire may be to the ice, they are degrees of the same phenomenon.

Heat and cold are not two things, but the same energy. Energy becomes heat, the same energy becomes cold; the energy is the same, degrees differ. That's why with one thermometer you can measure both heat and cold – because the energy is the same. Where does cold become heat, can you say exactly where? At which degree does the cold cease to be cold and become heat? You cannot say, it depends.

Try a simple experiment. Put one hand, your left hand, on an ice cube and your right hand near a fire. Let the right hand become hot, let the left hand become cool. Then put both the hands together in a bucket of water and tell me whether it is cool or hot. You will be in difficulty, because one hand will say it is hot, and one hand will say it is cool, it is cold. What is it – cold or hot? They are degrees of the same energy.

So I say to you, even to a well frog it is possible to communicate something about the sea. And if the messenger is really inventive, he can create devices to communicate. That is what a Buddha is doing, a Jesus is doing – creating devices to communicate something of the sea to well frogs. Because there is one thing in common, the water. If there is one thing in common, then communication is possible, a bridge exists.

Even to a dragonfly something can be communicated about ice. Even if we say it is not hot like the fire, something has been said about the ice – negative, of course. That is why all great scriptures are negative. They don't say what truth is; they always say what truth is not, just to make the message meaningful to dragonflies. So we cannot say what the ice is, but we can say that the ice is not fire – this much can be communicated.

But even by that method it is impossible to talk to a philosopher about the way of life, or to talk to a philosopher about existence.

Even if the philosopher is an existentialist, then too it is impossible to talk about existence, because between a word and the corresponding reality there is no bridge. A rose and the word 'rose' are not related in any way; all relationship is arbitrary. What is the relationship between the word rose – r-o-s-e – and the rose? If there is some relationship then you cannot call it a *gulab*.

There are three hundred languages in the world and three hundred words for rose; there is no relationship, all relationship is arbitrary. Cold is related to hot, well is related to the ocean. Their relationship, howsoever indistinct, is there – real, not arbitrary. But between a word and reality there is no relationship, they are not related at all. So you can have your own words, a private language, you can call anything by any name. If you like to call it something else the rose will not fight in a court. And nobody can prove that their word is more correct than yours, nobody can prove it because no word is more correct or less correct. Words are irrelevant, they are not related. And a philosopher lives in words.

A philosopher is the falsest thing in existence, and the more you become philosophic, the less you live. Then you think about love, you never love; then you think about God, you never become divine. Then you go on talking and talking and talking and your whole energy is wasted in words; there is not a single moment to enter into existence.

Chuang Tzu says: Be aware of all philosophies, because their base is the same – they depend on words. And reality is not a word. Move into the real: you are real, existence is real. Move into the real. Don't create a wall of words between you and reality, otherwise it is impenetrable; you will be enclosed within your wall. And then it will become almost impossible to come out of it.

Don't be a philosopher. And everybody is a philosopher! It is difficult to find a man who is not a philosopher. Some philosophers are good, some bad, but everyone is a philosopher. Some are more logical, some are less, but everybody is a philosopher. Drop out of the trip – the trip of philosophy. Only then you enter the real, the existential.

CHAPTER 8

THE TURTLE

Chuang Tzu with his bamboo pole was fishing in the Pu river.

The Prince of Chu sent two vice-chancellors with a formal document: We hereby appoint you Prime Minister.

Chuang Tzu held his bamboo pole. Still watching the Pu river, he said, 'I am told there is a sacred tortoise offered and canonized three thousand years ago, venerated by the prince, wrapped in silk, in a precious shrine on an altar in the temple.

'What do you think? Is it better to give up one's life and leave a sacred shell as an object of cult in a cloud of incense for three thousand years, or to live as a plain turtle dragging its tail in the mud?'

'For the turtle' said the vice-chancellor, 'better to live and drag its tail in the mud!'

'Go home!' said Chuang Tzu. 'Leave me here to drag my tail in the mud.'

Every child is born sane, but every man becomes insane. The whole of humanity is neurotic. Neurosis is not a problem for only a few people, the human being as such is neurotic. And this neurosis is created through such a subtle mechanism that you cannot even become aware of it. It has become an unconscious thing, it goes on influencing you: your behavior, your relationships, your whole life is colored by it. But it has gone so deep into your roots that you cannot find from where your misery, conflict, anxiety and neurosis have arisen.

A few things have to be understood; then this story will become clear, and very helpful. First, if you condemn yourself you are creating a division, and that division will be your misery and your hell. If you condemn yourself, it means you condemn nature, and there is no victory against nature; there cannot be. You are just a tiny part in a vast ocean of nature, you cannot fight it.

And all so-called religions teach you to fight it. They condemn nature and they acclaim culture. They condemn nature, and they say: 'This is behaving just like animals, don't be like animals!' Every parent is saying: 'Don't be like animals.' What is wrong with animals? Animals are beautiful! But in your mind animals are something to be condemned, something bad, something evil, something not worthy of you. You are superior, you are not an animal, you are born of angels. And animals – they are just to be used, exploited; you don't belong to them.

That is why when Darwin first declared that man has come out of the same heritage as animals, that he belongs to the animal world, the whole of humanity was against him. From every church pulpit, from every temple, from every mosque, he was condemned as a heretic. They said that he was teaching something absolutely wrong, and if he were believed then the whole culture would be lost.

But he was right! Man is as natural as other animals, trees and birds. And trees and birds and animals are not neurotic, they never go mad – unless you put them in a zoo. In a zoo it happens: animals do go neurotic. Even to be in contact with man is dangerous. Man is infectious. Sometimes dogs go mad, but never when they are wild, only when they are domesticated.

Domestic animals go mad; living with man is living with something unnatural. In the wild no animal commits suicide, no animal goes mad, no animal murders. But with man even animals turn unnatural, they start doing things they have never done in the wild: they become homosexual, they become neurotic, they murder, and sometimes they have even tried to commit suicide.

What happens when you bring a dog to your home? You immediately start teaching him, as if he lacks something. He is perfect! Every dog is born perfect. Nature has given him everything that is needed; he is already equipped, you need not teach him.

What are you doing? You are trying to make him a part of human society. And now the trouble starts: now even the dog will learn to condemn himself. If he does something wrong, inside he feels guilty; condemnation has entered.

I have heard:

It happened once that a bum, a beggar, caught hold of a rich man and asked for a dime, just for a cup of coffee. The rich man said, 'You seem to be healthy enough, why are you wasting your life? Why don't you go to work and help yourself?'

The bum said, with very deep condemnation in his eyes, 'What! To help a bum like me?'

You are continually not accepting yourself. From the very beginning you have been taught that nature is not enough, you have to be more than nature. And you have tried, and that effort has failed – it is impossible, you can never be more than nature. And if you try too much you will be less than nature. You can never be more than nature because nature is perfect: nothing more is needed, no polishing is needed, no effort is needed to make it better – it cannot be made better. But if you try too much you will fall from the perfection of nature and you will become a neurotic animal. Man comes from animals, but he is not a higher animal. He has become a neurotic animal.

And the problem is that nobody teaches you to accept yourself and to accept your nature. Worship it, be thankful to the divine for it, be grateful to the whole! Whatsoever has been given to you has a meaning, it is significant; you cannot cut it down and change. If you try, you will be in trouble. And you *are* in trouble – everybody on this earth is in trouble.

Why does man condemn himself? Why can't he accept nature? Because through condemnation the ego is created. There is no other way to create the ego. To create the ego you have to fight. To create the ego you have to condemn something as bad, and applaud something as good. To create the ego, first you have to create a God and a Devil, and then you have to fight with the Devil and try to reach the God. A conflict is needed for the ego. If there is no conflict, there cannot be any ego. Just think … if there is no fight within you, if you accept yourself totally – you are happy as you are, deeply content, deeply satisfied, not even a single note of complaint, thankful – how can the ego exist? How can you say 'I am'? The more you fight, the more 'I' is created.

That is why if you go to your so-called saints you will find more neurotic people there than anywhere. And this is something to be observed, that wherever there are many saints there are many more madmen. Madness exists less in the East, it exists more in the West. But if you simply do ordinary arithmetic you will be surprised: in the East many mad people are worshipped as saints, so they are not in madhouses. In the West, the same people who should be in the madhouses are on the couch of the psychiatrist; they are not thought to be mad, but they are, because ego *is* mad.

Look at your saints. They have such subtle egos – refined of course, polished, very cultivated, decorated, but they are there. If you fight with somebody else you cannot have a very subtle ego, because with the other the possibility of being defeated always exists. Even if you have won, the other is there; any day there is every chance that he will gather strength and you may be defeated. The victory cannot be absolute and you can never be certain; the enemy is there. And there is not only one enemy outside, there are millions of enemies, because with whomsoever you compete, he is your enemy. You will always be shaking and wavering, your ego cannot be on solid ground; you have made your house on sand. But if you are fighting with yourself, then you are working on solid ground, you can be certain; you can be a more subtle egoist.

To have the 'I' you have to kill nature, because in nature no ego exists. Trees are there, but they don't know the 'I'; animals are there, but they don't know the ego – they live unconsciously. They simply live without any fight or struggle. When they are hungry they search for food; when they are satisfied they go to sleep. They make love, they eat, they sleep – they just exist; they don't say, 'We are.' They are just waves in the vast ocean of life, they come and go without leaving any trace. They have no history, no autobiography; they come and go as if they had never been there.

Lions have existed, elephants have existed, but they don't have any history, they don't have any autobiography. A lion comes like a vast big wave and then disappears; no trace is left behind. Ego leaves traces, footprints. If the ego wants not to die, autobiographies are written, history is created. And then comes the whole foolishness – neurosis. To create the ego, man has created a conflict, and this conflict has two aspects. One aspect is with outer nature – that is how science is created. Science is a fight with nature outside, nature without. That is why even a person like Bertrand Russell goes on talking in terms of conquering nature. How can you conquer nature? How can a wave conquer the ocean?

It is patent foolishness! A part cannot conquer the whole; and if the part tries, the part will go mad. The whole will not lose anything, the part will lose everything, because the part exists with the whole, never against it. Science has become destructive because of this conquering attitude.

And there is another aspect of conflict: that aspect you call religion. One aspect is to fight nature outside; science is created, it is destructive. The ultimate goal can never be anything other than Hiroshima, and it will be reached – the whole earth will become a Hiroshima. Fighting leads to death, conflict ultimately leads to ultimate death; science is leading towards that.

Then there is the other conflict, the inner conflict; to fight with oneself. That is what you call religion – to conquer oneself. Again the fight, and it too is destructive. Science destroys nature from the outside, and so-called religion destroys nature from the inside.

Chuang Tzu is against both types of conflict. So-called science and so-called religion are not enemies: they are partners, they have a deep affinity.

To understand Chuang Tzu and Lao Tzu, to understand Tao, you will have to understand that they don't believe in fighting of any sort. They say: Don't fight, live! Just be in a let-go, so nature can penetrate you and you can penetrate nature. They say: Just be ordinary, don't try to be extraordinary. Don't try to be somebody – just be nobodies. You will enjoy more because you will have more energy left, you will be full of energy.

There is tremendous energy, but it is dissipated in fighting; you divide yourself and you fight from both sides and the energy is dissipated. The same energy can become ecstatic if allowed to move in an inner harmony, not fighting.

Acceptance, accepting whatsoever is, is the basis of Tao. Tao does not create any 'ought'. Chuang Tzu says: Don't say to anybody that you ought to do this, you should do this, you ought not to be like this. Chuang Tzu says these things are dangerous, they are poisonous. There is only one thing to be followed and that is your nature: wherever it leads, trust it.

But we are afraid to follow nature, not because nature is bad but because of the moral teachers, because of the poisoners of the very source of life. They have taught you so many things, so many 'oughts', that you cannot look directly at the *is* – that which is. You always look for the 'ought'. Even if you look at a rose you immediately start to think how this rose ought to be: it could be a little more red, it could be a little bigger, you could inject chemicals into it and it will become bigger; you could paint it, it will become more red ... but you cannot accept it as it is. Small or big, red or not so red, it is there. Why not enjoy it at this very moment? ... First make it more red, make it bigger, and then you will enjoy it.

You don't know that you are postponing – and the postponing becomes a habit. When it has become bigger the same mind will say, 'Still more is possible.' And the same mind will go on postponing until death knocks at your door. Then you will be surprised: 'I have been wasting my whole life with "oughts", and the "is" was there.' And the 'is' is beautiful. The 'is' is the only religion for Chuang Tzu.

The conflict between 'is' and 'ought' is very foundational. If you can drop your 'ought' you may not be as respectable as you are right now. Because of your 'ought', people respect you. They say, 'This man is beautiful, he is never angry, he always smiles,' and they don't know that those smiles are false – because a man who can never be angry cannot be truly smiling. This is the problem – if he is not authentic in his anger, he cannot be authentic in his smile.

Children are authentic; when they are angry they are really angry. You look at them – their anger is beautiful. They become just like wild animals, jumping and screaming, their faces completely red. They are like lions, they would destroy the whole world at that moment. Their anger is true, and whatsoever is true is beautiful.

Look at a child when he is angry. Just watch him and you will see a beautiful flowering, a flowering of strength, power, energy – energy moving. And the next moment the child is happy, smiling. Now the smile is also true, now his smile is also beautiful. Whatsoever is natural is beautiful. But you say to the child, 'Don't be angry, suppress your anger. This is not good, you are not supposed to be angry!' But who is this who is supposing these things? Is there any possibility to go beyond nature? Who are you?

At the most, you can do this one thing – you can force him. A child is helpless; if you force him he will have to follow you. He is weak, he depends on you because you can withdraw your love. He needs your love, he will have to follow you. When he feels angry he will not express it. Now the anger will move into the blood, and because anger is chemical his whole body will be poisoned. Expressed, it is a beautiful phenomenon; suppressed, it is disease. Now when he smiles, this smile will carry that anger, that poison; now it is in the blood.

And you have suppressed so much that whenever you want to smile something holds you back; something is afraid in any sort of let-go, because a smile is a let-go. If you smile – just stand before a mirror and smile – you will see that behind your smile there is anger, there is sadness, there is lust; it is not pure. It cannot be, because the very source is poisoned. Nothing is pure – not only are things in the market adulterated, *you* are adulterated. Then you cannot smile, and if you cannot smile, how can you kiss? Your kiss will be just poison, it will be poisonous. How can you love? How can you enjoy sheer being? No, you cannot do anything. Now you can only follow 'oughts', 'shoulds', and 'should nots'.

You are afraid to live. You go on postponing – somewhere in the future you will live – and because of this postponing you have created heaven and hell. Heaven is your final postponement of everything that is worth living for. You say that in heaven there is eternal beauty. The eternal beauty is here and now, not in heaven.

You say that in heaven love is pure and eternal! Love can be pure and eternal here and now, there is no need to wait for heaven. Wherever love is, it is eternal and pure, because for love time does not exist.

Eternal does not mean permanent; eternal means nontemporal, eternal means there is no time. Even if a single moment of love is there, it is eternal. In that moment is such depth that in that moment time ceases; in that moment there is no future, no past; in that moment you are simply so much that you spread all over existence – the whole existence belongs to you and the whole of you belongs to existence. That moment is eternity unto itself. Wherever love is, there is eternity, and then there is the possibility of prayer. If your smile is false, your kiss will be false, your love cannot be true; and all your prayers will be just words and nothing else.

How can you find a god, how can you become god-like if you are not true? You seek truth but in your life you are always untrue. How can an untrue person meet the truth? This seems an almost impossible thing. The truth will knock at your door, you need not go anywhere; just be true. And when I say just be true, I am saying just be natural.

Nature is truth, and there is no other truth than nature. This is the message of Chuang Tzu, one of the greatest messages in the world.

Now we will try to enter this beautiful story.

Chuang Tzu with his bamboo pole was fishing in the Pu River.

Can you conceive of Buddha fishing in the Pu River? Can you conceive of Mahavira fishing? Impossible!

Chuang Tzu with his bamboo pole was fishing in the Pu River.

What does this mean? It means Chuang Tzu is an ordinary man.

He does not claim anything whatsoever, he just enjoys being ordinary. He does not live by principles, he lives by instinct. He does not superimpose his ego on his nature, he simply flows with it – he is just an ordinary man.

This is the meaning of his fishing in the Pu River; only an ordinary man can do that. Extraordinary people – how can they do it? They have much 'ought' in them: this should be done, that should not be done. They live by morality, they live by principles. What are you doing? A man of knowledge, fishing? Impossible to conceive you are killing fish!

Chuang Tzu believes in nature. He says whatsoever is natural is good. He is just an animal and he will not create any morality just to feel superior. The story says just be ordinary and enjoy being ordinary, only then can you fall by and by into the natural; otherwise you will become unnatural. This fishing is just symbolic. Whether Chuang Tzu fished or not is not the point, but he is the sort of man who can fish, who can sit with his bamboo pole.

That is why you cannot make a statue of Chuang Tzu – it is difficult. A Buddha is perfect, you can make a statue of him; it is as if he were born just to have statues made of him. You cannot find a better man, so statue-like. That is why, naturally, millions of statues exist of Buddha, more than of anybody else. He looks perfect, the perfect model for a statue, sitting under the bodhi tree with closed eyes, not doing anything. He looks the perfect ideal, the perfect 'ought', as man should be – absolutely nonviolent, absolutely truthful, absolutely meditative. He is just like marble, not a man at all.

You cannot make a statue of Chuang Tzu. You will find him in such wrong places! He is just an ordinary man – and this is the beauty of it, this is the whole message of it. Just be ordinary, with a bamboo pole, fishing, and Chuang Tzu says that this is enlightenment.

I also say to you that Buddha may have attained enlightenment

– it may have been easy for his nature to sit under a tree – but if you follow Buddha you will become just stones. Chuang Tzu will be better for you.

Just be ordinary. For Buddha that may have been ordinariness … to sit. Hence he attained. But as I know you, and the common human man, the common humanity, the vast humanity, Chuang Tzu is better. And when I say better, I am not making any comparison, I am simply saying that he is so ordinary that you can easily be with him without becoming neurotic. If you follow Buddha you may become neurotic. If you follow Chuang Tzu you will become more and more natural.

Chuang Tzu with his bamboo pole was fishing in the Pu River.

The Prince of Chu sent two vice-chancellors with a formal document: We hereby appoint you Prime Minister.

Politics is of the ego, it is the ego trip, the ego game. But Chuang Tzu was known far and wide as a wise man, there was no need to advertise it. When wisdom exists it is such an illumination that you cannot hide it, even a Chuang Tzu cannot hide it. You cannot hide ordinary love. If a young man falls in love, or a young woman falls in love, you can tell just by their very walk that love has happened. You cannot hide it because every gesture changes, becomes illuminated; a new quality enters. You cannot hide it.

How can you hide being in love with the whole existence? When prayer exists, how can you hide it? Even a Chuang Tzu – who says hide it – cannot hide it. It is impossible, people will suspect.

How can you hide light? If your house is lit up, the neighbors will come to know because the light will show from your windows. No, you cannot hide it, but the effort to hide it is good.

Why does Chuang Tzu say hide it when the inner lamp is burning? He says it just to bring you from exactly the opposite pole, because you would like to advertise it. There are people whose light does not yet exist, whose flame is not yet there, whose house is dark, empty, but they would like to advertise that they have become wise. Ego would like to pretend even about wisdom. Hence, Chuang Tzu says: Don't say anything about what you are, who you are; just hide yourself. Those who have eyes, they will seek and follow you themselves; they will come to you. You need not go and knock at their doors; the very phenomenon will attract them, and seekers will follow you and seek you wherever you are. And those who are not seekers, don't bother about them, because their coming is of no use. They will just be a disturbance, and they will create hindrances for those who are seeking. Hide the fact.

But still people will come to know. The prince must have come to know that Chuang Tzu had become enlightened.

The Prince of Chu sent two vice-chancellors with a formal document: We hereby appoint you Prime Minister.

In the old days prime ministers were not chosen by the vote of the people, because how can you choose by the vote of the people? How can people choose their leaders? They would like to, but they are not capable. Democracy is just a dream, it has not happened anywhere – it cannot happen. And wherever it happens it creates trouble; the medicine proves more dangerous than the disease itself.

In the old days a prime minister was not chosen by the people. A prime minister was appointed by the king, and the king had to seek out a wise man. A *brahmin* had to be sought, searched for, because a wise man would not stand in an election, he would not go knocking at doors to ask for votes – rather he would hide himself. Kings would go and seek, and wherever there was a wise man he had to be brought to the world so the world could have the benefits.

The prince must have come to know that Chuang Tzu had become enlightened. He sent two messengers and appointed him as the prime minister.

Chuang Tzu held his bamboo pole.

Nothing changed. The vice-chancellor was standing there with a formal document saying: You are appointed prime minister. It was the greatest post, but Chuang Tzu remained as he was. Chuang Tzu held his bamboo pole still watching the Pu River. He didn't even look at those vice-chancellors. He didn't look at the document, as if it was not worth it.

> *Still watching the Pu River, he said, 'I am told there is*
> *a sacred tortoise offered and canonized three*
> *thousand years ago, venerated by the prince, wrapped*
> *in silk, in a precious shrine on an altar in the temple.'*

That turtle is still there; the turtle is covered with gold and precious stones. In the forbidden city of Peking, the imperial city, which is not open to everybody, it is still there. Now it is almost six thousand years old – a dead turtle, covered with gold and very precious stones, enshrined. It was worshipped by the prince himself.

Asked Chuang Tzu:

> *'What do you think? Is it better to give up one's life*
> *and leave a sacred shell as an object of cult in a cloud*
> *of incense for three thousand years, or to live as a*
> *plain turtle dragging its tail in the mud?'*

Chuang Tzu asked: What is better – just to be a plain turtle and live, or to be dead, covered with gold, and to be worshipped? This is the problem with everybody, before everybody, and these are the two alternatives. People can worship you, but they cannot worship you if you are alive, because life is amoral – it is neither moral nor immoral. Life does not know any morality, it is amoral; life knows no 'oughts', it simply lives from the unconscious.

If you are simply alive it is very difficult for anybody to worship you. If you simply live plainly, enjoying, you cannot expect incense to be burned around you and a temple to arise, and a cult, and a sect, and people to worship you for thousands of years. No!

They worship a Jesus not because he was enlightened, they worship a Jesus because he was crucified. Just think about the story of Jesus: if the crucifixion had never happened there would have been no Christianity. It is not because of Jesus that there is Christianity, it is because of the cross; that is why the cross has become the symbol of a Christian. Why the cross? The human mind, the neurotic mind, worships death, not life: the more dead you are, the more you can be worshipped. If you are alive then you are not worth worshipping because you are not sacrificing anything! Sacrifice can be worshipped because sacrifice means sacrificing life, a gradual crucifixion. If others crucify you, people will worship you, and if you crucify yourself, people will worship you more. People worship death; Jesus is worshipped because he was crucified.

If you just drop that part of the story, then who is Jesus? Then it will be difficult for you to even remember, because Jesus was a vagabond just like Chuang Tzu. The only difference in the story is that Chuang Tzu was never crucified and Jesus was crucified – otherwise he is the same man. You could have found him on the riverbank with a bamboo pole, fishing – he was very friendly with fishermen. He must have fished around the Sea of Galilee – fishermen were his followers. You would have been able to find him staying with a prostitute, because the prostitute loved him, worshipped him, and he knew no distinctions. He moved with gamblers, drunkards, people rejected by society – and that was his crime! He was crucified because this was his crime: he was moving with ordinary people living an ordinary life. That cannot be tolerated by the respectable world – that cannot be tolerated. This man who moves with prostitutes, gamblers, drunkards, who is found in wrong company, this man says that he is the son of God! This is heresy! This man is claiming too much, he has to be punished, because if such things are left unpunished then the whole morality will be destroyed. And this man lives against all rules, he has no rules except life.

Jesus and Chuang Tzu are similar. Just one thing differs: Jesus was crucified. Jews are very much rule-oriented, they live by rules; they are Confucians, and it is difficult for them to concede that somebody who lives without rules can be good. Jews are very moralistic and their conception of God is very revengeful.

The Jewish God is very revengeful, he will throw you in fire if you don't obey him. Obedience seems to be the greatest rule. And this Jesus, the son of a carpenter, an ordinary man, is moving with suspicious people and claiming that he is a prophet, the prophet for whom the whole Jewish world has been waiting. No, he has to be punished!

China was more tolerant. Chuang Tzu was not punished because China had no conception of a ferocious God; in fact there was no conception of God. Confucius never believed in God, he believed in rules; and he was the basis for China. But he said that rules are human, there is no divineness about them; they are arbitrary, relative – you can change them. One has to follow them but there is nothing divine about them, no absoluteness about them. That is why Lao Tzu and Chuang Tzu could live without being crucified.

But one thing you have to remember: if Chuang Tzu had also been crucified, there would have been a great following. There is none. Chuang Tzu has no followers, he cannot have, because people worship death. And he refused to be a turtle, canonized, because the condition is: Be dead! Don't do this, don't to that; just go on cutting and sacrificing yourself; just sit, not even breathing is allowed. Then people will worship you, then you will have become a dead turtle.

Asked Chuang Tzu:

> *'What do you think? Is it better to give up one's life and leave a sacred shell as an object of cult in a cloud of incense for three thousand years, or to live as a plain turtle dragging its tail in the mud?'*
> *'For the turtle,' said the vice-chancellor, 'better to live and drag its tail in the mud.'*

Of course, it is logical for the turtle: *'Better to live and drag its tail in the mud!'* Chuang Tzu said: Go home, leave me here to drag my tail in the mud! Let me be just a plain turtle. Please, don't you try to canonize me, because I know your condition – first I have to die and leave a shell, a dead shell, then you can canonize me, then you can make a cult of me, then you can have a temple around me, and incense, and clouds of incense, and then you can worship me for three thousand years. But what will I gain out of it? I am the turtle, what will I gain out of it? What does a turtle know about gold and precious stones? They are human foolishnesses, a turtle never believes in them. The turtle believes in the mud, the turtle drags its tail in the mud and enjoys it.

The symbol is very meaningful, because mud for us is something dirty. But mud is nature; dirty or not dirty – those are your interpretations. Mud is nature, and a turtle dragging its tail in the mud and playing the game for the time it lasts – enjoying the mud – is a good symbol. This is how a natural man should be: not condemning the mud, not saying this body is nothing – dirt unto dirt, dust unto dust. This body will fall back into the mud, this is just mud.

> *' … dragging its tail in the mud.'*

Nature is muddy, it is there. You are made of it and you will dissolve into it. But if you want to be worshipped for thousands of years then there is no problem. If you want a cult around you, if you want to become a deity, placed in a temple shrine, enshrined, canonized, then it is okay, but then you have to give your life. Is it worth it? Is it worth it to give your life and gain respect? Is it worth it to lose a single moment of life and gain the respect of the whole world? Not even then is it worth it, no. If the whole world worships you, that too is not enough to lose a single moment of being alive. Only life is precious; there are no precious stones. Only life is gold, there is no other gold. Only life is the temple, there is no other temple. Only life is the incense, the fragrance, there is no other fragrance. This is what Chuang Tzu says: Let me be alive. You may condemn me, because I am just a turtle dragging his tail in the mud, but for the turtle this is the best. Even you agree with me. So go home. I am not coming to the palace, I am not going to become a prime minister; that is not for me, because you will kill me.

There are many ways to crucify a man, crucifixion is only one. You can also put him on the throne; then too he is crucified, and in a subtler way – very nonviolently you kill him. Whenever you start respecting a person you have started killing him, because now he has to pay; he has to look at you – what to do, what not to do.

I once stayed in a home with a *Jaina* family. They had never met me but they had read my books and through books they had much respect for me. Then they invited me to stay with them as I was in their town – a very rich family. So I stayed.

At evening time a few people had come to see me. And *Jainas* take their food before sunset: they are very traditional. The woman came and she said, 'It is getting dark, you must finish with these people, otherwise you will be late for your food.'

I said, 'I can take my food a little later, there is no hurry. But these people have come from very far, from a far-off village, and they are really seekers, so I must tell them something; before they go I must give them something.'

She wouldn't believe me, and by the time those people left it was already late, the sun had set, it was dark. So again the woman came and said, 'Now you cannot eat, or are you ready to eat even at night?'

So I said, 'For me there is no difference, because hunger knows no day, no night. I am hungry and I will eat.'

As if her whole image of me was shattered, she said, 'We thought that you were an enlightened man, but now you have shattered the whole image. How can an enlightened man eat at night?'

This is impossible for a *Jaina* to conceive, because they live by rules and they go on living by dead rules. If you want their respect you have to follow their rules. If you follow their rules, you are imprisoned. So I said, 'It is better not to be enlightened, because I would not like to go to sleep hungry, that is too much. I can leave enlightenment.'

And that day I told them this story: 'Let me drag my tail in the mud, it is not worth it.' Somebody thinks that I am enlightened, and just to keep his image, am I to kill myself?

But this is how things go.

Never ask for respect, because respect is asked for by the ego. Never seek respect from others, because that is a subtle bondage and you will soon be imprisoned and enclosed in it. Just live plainly, just live as you feel, natural, and don't bother about anybody else.

Nobody else is responsible for your life except you. Be responsible only to yourself and nobody else, then it will be difficult for you to create a cult around yourself. But if people come, they will be the right seekers. If you seek respect, wrong people will come around you; if you don't seek their respect, if you don't bother about them, if you simply follow your natural course, then only the right seekers will come and they will not be an imprisonment to you. And only those people who are not an imprisonment to you can be helped; otherwise followers lead their leaders, disciples impose rules on their masters. What nonsense! They both remain in darkness.

Remember one basic thing always: there cannot be anything more than nature. Nature is the whole. So you have to find a way to fall back from the cultured pattern of your life into the natural flow.

You are as frozen as you are cultured. How to melt again and become a river? It is arduous, because frozen ice is worshipped and the ego will say, 'What are you doing? Now nobody will respect you, now you will not be a respectable person! What are you doing?' The ego will say, 'Just follow the rules, what is the harm?' There is so much investment in the rules. If you follow ordinary rules, everybody will worship you. But what is gained by worship? It is not a substitute for life. What is gained by respect? It is not a substitute for existence.

Be existential, let things happen.

If somebody respects you, even then it is for him to decide, it should not be your concern. If it is your concern then you will become neurotic; that is how everybody has become neurotic. And there are so many people around and they are all expecting you to do this and to do that. So many people, so many expectations, and you are trying to satisfy all of them! You cannot satisfy all of them. The whole effort will end in your deep dissatisfaction, and nobody will be satisfied. You cannot satisfy anybody; the only satisfaction that is possible is your own. And if you are satisfied then a few will be satisfied with you – but that is not your concern.

You are not here to fulfill anybody else's expectations, their rules, their maps. You are here to fulfill your own being. That is the whole of religion, the all of religion; you are here to fulfill your own being. That is your destiny. Don't waver from it, nothing is worth it.

But there are many allurements all around and they seem so

innocent; the allurements seem very innocent. They are not so innocent, they are very cunning. Somebody says, 'What is wrong if you don't eat at night? People will give you respect.' Eating or not eating is not the point. If you don't feel like eating, it is good, don't eat. People say that if you get up early in the morning at five o'clock, then Hindus will respect you. Nothing is wrong; if you feel good, get up, but don't think of the Hindus. If you get up because of them then you are missing yourself, and by and by you will get more and more entangled. Because there are some people who will be unhappy the whole day if they get up at *brahmamuhurt*, at five o'clock.

There is a particular time which has to be passed in sleep, two hours every night. Now scientists have discovered that out of twenty-four hours there are two hours every day when the temperature of the body falls; those two hours are the deepest for sleeping. If you miss them, then for the whole day you will feel that something is missing. If you can sleep during those two hours then there is no need to sleep for five or seven hours, they will be enough. But those two hours are different for everybody, and rules are not different for everybody – this is the problem! If somebody has those two hours when his temperature drops between three and five, then at five he can get up absolutely fresh – that is his *brahmamuhurt*. But somebody else who really falls asleep at five, whose temperature falls between five and seven, if this man follows Hindus, his whole life will be lost.

You have to seek your own, and it differs from individual to individual. Everything differs from individual to individual. There is no rule that you have to fix and fit into, you have to find your own rules.

Just try to understand: whatsoever gives you happiness and blessings and peace and silence, seek in that way. More will be coming soon. And that is the criterion: if you are happy, I say you are a religious man although you may not be going to the temple.

If you are unhappy and you go continuously to the temple, I don't call you a religious man. If you are happy, blissful, if your whole being exudes ecstasy and peace, 'at homeness' in existence, you are a religious man – whether you believe in God or not. Those are just words, don't bother about them.

Find your peace, find your mud where you can drag your tail and be alive; that is your temple. Nobody else's temple will suit you – cannot suit you, because every temple was made by somebody for somebody.

Buddha lived in his own way, then a temple was born; then thousands followed and they started living like Buddha. They missed their goal. Buddha never followed anybody, his way was his own, he was happy – then it is okay. But you will be unhappy following him. Don't follow anybody, otherwise you will be unhappy. And you are unhappy enough because you have been following your father and mother, teachers, religion. You have been following so many, and all those voices are different, contradictory, inconsistent. You are being pulled in all directions; how can you be together? You are a disintegrated phenomenon, a crowd, one part going to the east, another part going to the west; the lower body has gone to the south, the upper body has gone to the Himalayas, north. You are a disintegrated phenomenon, not together. Be together!

And I tell you, if you remain together, if you don't listen to anybody, if you only listen to your own voice – even if you have to err sometimes, even if you go wrong sometimes; don't bother. You will go wrong, because you have become accustomed to following others so much that you have lost your inner voice. You don't know what the inner voice is. Many voices are there and they are all from others. Sometimes the mother speaks – do this! Sometimes the father speaks – don't do this! Sometimes somebody else, a Buddha, a Jesus, a Christ, a Chuang Tzu … drop all those voices. Listen!

Meditation is a deep listening, listening to the inner voice. As you become silent, voices cease. Chuang Tzu goes to his home,

Buddha goes to his home, Jesus is no longer there, your father and your mother are really gone; everybody goes, only you are left, alone in your emptiness. Then your nature asserts itself – and that is a flowering. As a seed breaks and comes out, sprouting, so your inner voice comes out, sprouting. And then follow it: wherever it leads, follow it. Don't listen to anybody; that is your way to God. And all that a master can do is to bring you to your inner voice. The master should not become the substitute; otherwise you will become even more crowded than you were before.

Don't make me your voice, I am not your enemy. Don't listen to me! Only this much is enough: that you go deep within yourself and listen to your own voice. If I can help you towards that, then I am a master to you, otherwise I am an enemy. And once you have started listening to your own voice I am not needed, you can discard me.

Listen. Just as there is a third eye, there is a third ear – it is not talked about in the scriptures. There is a third ear, and as the third eye will give you glimpses of your being, so the third ear gives you glimpses of your inner voice. When these two outer ears stop functioning – when you are not listening to anybody, you have become completely deaf, no voice penetrates and you have thrown all the voices from the inside outside, when you have thrown all the rubbish out, you are just empty, settling within – you will feel the voice. It is always there.

Every child is born with it, every tree is born with it, every bird lives with it – even a turtle is born with it. And you cannot confuse a turtle, you cannot convince him by saying, 'Come and be dead and we will enshrine you.' The turtle will also say, 'Go home, leave me here to drag my tail in the mud.'

Once you can feel your voice then no rules are needed, you have become a rule unto yourself. And the clearer the voice, the more your steps fall in the right direction. It becomes a progressively stronger and stronger force; every step leads nearer to your destiny and you feel more at ease. You will feel a deep contentment that nothing is wrong and you can bless and you can be blessed by all.

Religion is rebellion, rebellion against the others, rebellion against the well-wishers, rebellion against the do-gooders. It is the greatest rebellion, because you are alone, nobody else is there, and you have to travel the path alone. It is the rebellion of the individual against the crowd.

The crowd is very, very powerful. It can crush you, it has already crushed you. You are crippled and crushed, you are almost dead. To leave you alive is dangerous for the crowd because then you will follow your own path, and the crowd has its own path – it wants you to follow it. The crowd wants you to become a clerk in a post office, a teacher in a primary school, a nurse in a hospital, and your inner voice may not be ready for it. Your inner voice may be moving you to become a poet, or a dancer, or a singer. Your inner voice may be moving you to become a Buddha or a Chuang Tzu. But the society does not need a Buddha – it needs a perfect executive. What is a Buddha needed for? He is useless economically, a burden.

Once it happened that Mulla Nasruddin went to a psychiatrist wearing a beret, a smock, a flowing beard. The psychiatrist asked, 'Are you an artist?' Nasruddin said, 'No, not at all!'

The psychiatrist said, 'Then why this beret, smock and beard?'

Nasruddin said, 'That's what I am here to inquire: Why? I never wanted it. This is my father, he wanted me to be a painter, a great artist. That is why I am here: to inquire.'

You are in such bad shape because so many people have wanted so many things of you. If you fulfill them you will remain unfulfilled, because nobody can expect the thing that you are here for – for that you have to search, it is an inner inquiry. That is the soul. You may call it God, you may call it truth. Names differ, but the real thing is to find the authentic destiny that you are here for; otherwise one day or other you will have to go to the psychiatrist and ask. And everybody is getting nearer the door of the psychiatrist! Even the psychiatrist himself is in bad shape, because he goes to some other psychiatrist for his own analysis – they do each other's psychoanalysis. And this is really something: more psychiatrists commit suicide than anybody else, twice as many as any other profession. Twice as many as in any other profession go mad, and they are here meaning to help others! Everybody is in bad shape because nobody has listened to his authentic being. Listen to it, and don't listen to anybody else.

It is going to be arduous, you will have to lose much, many investments will be lost. This is what I mean by *sannyas:* it is a renunciation of false investments, it is a renunciation of others and their wishes and their expectations, and it is a decision to be authentically oneself.

CHAPTER 9

DUKE HWAN AND THE WHEELWRIGHT

Duke Hwan of Khi, first in his dynasty, sat under his canopy reading his philosophy. And Phien the wheelwright was out in the yard making a wheel.

Phien laid aside hammer and chisel, climbed the steps, and said to Duke Hwan, 'May I ask you, Lord, what is this you are reading?'

Said the duke: 'The experts, the authorities.'

Phien asked, 'Alive or dead?'

The duke said, 'Dead a long time.'

'Then,' said the wheelwright, 'you are reading only the dirt they left behind.'

The duke replied, 'What do you know about it? You are only a wheelwright. You had better give me a good explanation or else you must die.'

The wheelwright said, 'Let us look at the affair from my point of view. When I make wheels, if I go easy they fall apart, and if I am too rough they do not fit. But if I am neither too easy nor too violent they come out right, and the work is what I want it to be.

'You cannot put this into words, you just have to know how it is. I cannot even tell my own son exactly how it is

done, and my own son cannot learn it from me. So here
I am, seventy years old, still making wheels!
'The men of old took all they really knew with them to
the grave. And so, Lord, what you are reading there is
only the dirt they left behind them.'

I t happened that on a back-country road a motorist found that
something was wrong with his engine. He stopped the car,
opened the hood and looked inside.

Suddenly he heard a voice, 'If you ask me I can tell you what the
trouble is.'

Surprised, he looked around because he thought that there was
nobody else there. Yes, there was nobody but a horse, standing in
a farm just nearby. The man became afraid and scared; down the
road he sped! After twenty minutes, he reached a filling-station.
When he caught his breath, he told the man, the owner, what had
happened: 'There was nobody else but a horse, and I heard
a human voice say that if I asked him, he could tell me what the
trouble was.'

The owner said, 'By any chance was the horse black, sway-
backed, bow-legged?'

The man said, 'Yes, that is right.'

Said the owner, 'Don't mind him, he is just an old philosopher,
dead long ago, still haunting the place. Just because of his old habit
he goes on seeking people to ask him questions. He does not know
a thing about engine trouble. And he is not a horse, he is just using
that poor old horse as a medium. So don't mind him.'

But this is how it happens on all the roads of life. The old ghosts
go on haunting, and they know all the answers – you have only to

ask. Just for the asking they are ready to give you all the answers. And life goes on changing and they don't know a thing about engine trouble. Life goes on changing moment to moment. You cannot find the answer in the past because nothing is the same today. You cannot find the answer in the past because the answer is not the thing, it always dies with the man who has discovered it. But ghosts go on haunting. Your Vedas, Korans, Bibles, Gitas, they are ghosts. They are not realities now, they are long dead, but they have an appeal.

So first try to understand why the dead have so much appeal, why the dead past has so much appeal over the living, why the dead go on pulling your legs. Why do you carry them? Why do you listen to them? You are living, you are fresh. Why do you look to the past, to the authorities and to the experts?

The first thing: the longer a person has been dead, the greater is the tradition. Time ... time hallows everything. If Buddha is alive you can barely tolerate him. At the most, if you are very kind to him, you may go and listen. But you cannot believe that he is a *Bhagwan*. You cannot believe that this man has known the ultimate because he will look just like you: a man of blood and bones, young or old, ill or healthy, as prone as you are to death – just like you. Hungry, he needs food; sleepy, he wants a bed; ill, he has to rest – just like you. Thirsty, he drinks the same water; hungry, he eats the same bread – just like you! How can you believe that he has known the ultimate, the deathless? Difficult, almost impossible.

Even if you try, it never happens; even if you force yourself, deep down the doubt remains. But now, twenty-five centuries later, Buddha is no longer a man of bones and blood. He never falls ill, he is never hungry, never needs food, never needs any medicine. He will never die now, he is immortal. Time hallows everything and by and by you forget that he belonged to you. By and by the dead image becomes golden. It reaches higher and higher, it is completely lost somewhere in paradise, you can have only a glimpse. Then you can believe.

Hence the past goes on haunting you. If Buddha comes again, you will reject him. That is why Jesus is worshipped now and yet he was crucified when he was alive. Alive, you crucify him; dead, you worship him. Why does death make him so meaningful, so significant? Death destroys the body, and then the link with you is broken. Then you have a spiritual image: bloodless, boneless, superphysical. Now you can imagine, and it is up to you to give all the qualities to him – you project.

It is difficult to project onto a living man because the reality is there, and he will destroy all your projections. He will not be ready to become a prisoner of your projections. But dead, what can he do? What can Jesus do? What can Buddha do? Helpless whatsoever you do, they have to suffer.

That is why more imagination is possible with a dead master – now *you* can give the significance, the superiority, the other-worldliness.

But with a living person it is impossible unless you have a heart of faith, total faith; and for those who have a heart of total faith Buddha is never the body, alive or dead. He is never the body. Because they penetrate deeply, the Buddha is transparent. He may be in the body but he is not the body; he may be living amongst you but he does not belong to you – he is from somewhere on high. That is the meaning of a Christ, the son of God; that is the meaning of an *avatar,* a descendance of the divine; that is the meaning of a *tirth-ankara* – a buddha. He comes from the invisible, but that can be seen only through the eye of faith. The mind cannot look at it. But when he is dead the mind can project.

So the first thing is that the longer the period, the gap – the more the time between you and Buddha, Jesus, Mahavira – the more your imagination has freedom. You can project, you can create a dream around them. Then they become more a myth and less a reality, then a whole myth is created around them. Then you can worship, then you can listen to them.

But the trouble is that when a buddha is alive he can help you. When a buddha is alive you can imbibe his spirit. When a buddha is alive it is possible for something to be communicated, transferred. But when he is dead, it becomes more and more impossible. Why? Because that which is to be given cannot be given through language. If it can be given through language, then there are scriptures, then there is the word of the Buddha. But it cannot be given through the word. The word is just an excuse. Buddha speaks to *you*: it is just an excuse to create a contact on the plane of the mind. And if you are receptive, something is constantly happening on the side; just between the words, or between the lines, Buddha is reaching to you – that is a living experience.

He has to transfer not a theory, but himself. He has not to communicate a hypothesis, a philosophy, but a living experience, and that is more like a skill and less like a philosophy. Even if you know how to swim you cannot teach somebody just through words. What will you say? Whatsoever you say, you will feel it is not adequate. The only way is to take the disciple with you to the river. First show him how you swim – give him confidence, give him courage – then tell him, come. And if he trusts you, he will come with you. Then by and by let him pass through the experience.

Only experience can teach. And spirituality is just like swimming: you cannot say anything about it. You can describe it, but the description is dead. It is an alive experience. Something happens when somebody is there who knows the skill. He cannot tell it to you, but you can learn. And this is the mystery: he cannot teach it to you, but you can learn if you are receptive.

So remember, more depends on the disciple and his receptivity, and less on the master. He is there, he is present. Now you have to be receptive and imbibe; you have to be receptive and allow; you have to be receptive and let him penetrate into you. If you are afraid the whole being shrinks; you are closed. When you are closed, the master can go on knocking at your door but there will be no response. The more he knocks the more you will shrink and become scared. So he will not even knock because that too is aggression. He will simply wait at the door. Whenever you are ready and open, he can give it to you, he can deliver it instantly. But the disciple has to be ready.

This possibility is there only with a living master. With a dead master, you cannot learn anything. The word is with you, the Bible is with you; you can become a great scholar, a philosopher, you can think and spin many theories around it, you can create a theology of your own – but Jesus will not be there. You have to live with Jesus. His presence is the most significant thing.

The second thing to be remembered is that mind always likes theories, words, philosophies. It can tackle them, it is a game the mind likes very much because nothing is lost. On the contrary, mind is more strengthened through them. The more you know, the more information you gather, the more your mind feels, 'I am somebody.'

With a living master the problem is this: you have to surrender, your ego has to be dissolved. It is really a death experience to live with a master, you have to die. And unless you die nothing is going to happen. Only through your death will rebirth happen. When you are no longer there, suddenly the divine is. So a living master is a death experience for the mind – a rebirth of the soul, but a death of the ego. With dead masters you are not scared. The mind can go on playing the game with the experts and the authorities, and the interpretation depends on you. In any theory the meaning is not there in it; you have to put the meaning in, it is a game. You think you are reading the Gita, the word of Krishna: you are wrong. The word is there, but who will give the meaning? You will give the meaning.

So every scripture is nothing but a mirror: you will see your own face in it. You can read anything that you like, but because the mind is very cunning it will simply not listen to anything that goes against it. It can interpret in its own ways, and Krishna is not there to say, 'No, this is not my meaning.'

It happened that when Sigmund Freud was alive but very old, just in his last year of life, he gathered all his disciples – and he had a big following all over the world. He had created a very significant school of psychoanalysis, and he was revered.

Twenty of his closest disciples were taking lunch with him. They started discussing what Freud meant about something and they completely forgot that Freud was there. They became so much absorbed in the discussion, contradicting each other, arguing with each other. One theory – twenty interpretations. And the master was alive, he was sitting there, but they had forgotten him completely! Then he hammered on the table and said, 'One thing please! I am still alive, you can ask me what I mean. Listening to you, I have become aware of what you are going to do when I am dead. I am alive, yet nobody asks me what my meaning is. And you have twenty meanings already! When I am dead, you will have two hundred, two thousand, two million meanings, and then there will be no possibility to ask me what I mean.'

That is how sects and creeds are born.

Jesus was a simple man, but look at the Catholics, the Protestants, the hundreds of sects of Christianity and their interpretations. Jesus was a simple man, the son of a carpenter; he never used the jargon of theology. He was not a man of words, he was a man of experience. He talked simply in small stories, anecdotes, and parables. And he was talking to illiterate people, his meaning was simple. But look ... the Protestants, the Catholics, their theologians, they have made so much out of him – a mountain! On simple things they go on discussing and arguing, and they get so lost in it that Jesus is completely forgotten.

When a living Freud is forgotten how can you remember a dead Jesus? Ask Hindus; they have one thousand interpretations of the

Gita already, and every year interpretations go on being added, new interpretations, and nobody agrees with anybody else. Shankara says that the message is of renunciation, that the Gita's message is of renunciation, inaction. Lokmanya Tilak says that the message is of action – just the opposite. And Ramanuja says that the message is of devotion, not action, not renunciation. And so you go on: one thousand interpretations, nobody agreeing with anybody else. And when you read the Gita that will be one thousand and one interpretations, because that will be yours. You will bring your mind into it and mind feels strengthened by knowledge, information.

Mind is never in any danger except in the presence of a living master. Then it is just on the verge of death. You escape Krishnas, and you carry Gitas in your head. You escape Jesus and you always keep the Bible in your pocket. The Bible can be kept in your pocket, not Jesus. The Bible will belong to you, but with Jesus you will have to belong to Jesus. That is the difference: you can own a Bible, you cannot own Jesus. You will have to be owned by him.

And thirdly, science can be written, there is no problem, because it is not a skill, it is theorizing, it is *theoria*. It can be written, it is description, it is not a mystery. The whole basis of science is to demystify everything. It has principles, laws, they can be written; and if you decipher the law, everything is known.

Religion is not like science, it is more like art – it is symbolic. The first thing is that it is not realistic, it is symbolic.

Once it happened that a friend came to see Picasso. The friend was in the military, in the army. He looked into Picasso's studio, and he said, 'What nonsense! Everything is unreal, not even a single painting represents reality.'

You cannot find anything like Picasso's painting in reality; it is not there, it is only Picasso's feeling of reality.

Science tries to discover the objective, art goes on trying to find the subjective in the objective. You look at a flower; if you ask a scientist about it he will talk of the chemical compounds of the flower. Of course they are there, but they are not the flower, because they don't carry the beauty, they don't carry the meaning. For the beauty you have to ask the artist, but then he will not talk about chemical compounds or anything else. He will give you a poem, and it will be nearer the truth than anything a scientist can give, but it will not be objective.

Picasso listened quietly. He was a soldier, this friend, and you cannot expect a soldier to understand too much subjectivity – he lives in the world of objects. Later on they talked of other things, and then the soldier showed a picture of his girlfriend to Picasso, a small picture. Picasso started laughing and he said, 'Is that girl so small? It will be very difficult to make love to such a small girl.'

The soldier said, 'What are you saying? This is just a picture.'

So Picasso said, 'A picture is not objective, it is symbolic; it simply represents, indicates, shows. It is not a description, it is not exact in proportion; it is just an indication, a hint.'

Remember, religion is more like art than like science. And it is even more subtle than art, because art represents the objective and religion represents the subjective. Art has symbols to show the objective world. The artist paints a picture of a rose, but the rose is there. Van Gogh's rose or Picasso's rose may not be exactly as it is in the garden, but still it is a rose. You can find some similarity, you can find something which corresponds.

But when a Buddha talks about *nirvana*, it is not in the outside world; you don't have anything to correspond to it. When Jesus talks about the kingdom of God, it is not there in the objective world. Art represents the objective: the symbol is difficult, but you can still find something corresponding to it in the world. Religion symbolizes the subjective, you cannot find anything like it in the world. Unless you go within yourself you will not be able to find the meaning, the significance. Then you will carry the word, and the word is not the reality. Then you may repeat the word 'god' and you don't know anything about God. It is more like an art, and even more like a craft.

What is a buddha doing? He is a craftsman, he makes gods out of you. Just like a sculptor he goes on hammering on the stone, cutting this and that piece, throwing away all that is inessential – then by and by an image is discovered. It was there. Before the artist started with his chisel and hammer it was there, but the inessential was there also. The inessential has to be broken and thrown away so that the essential comes up and is discovered. So what is a buddha doing? You are like a stone; he will go on working with his chisel and hammer, he will cut away the inessential, and then the essential comes in its total glory. Then the magnificent is born, then the other world penetrates into this world. He is not bringing anything new into the world, he is simply changing you, transforming you.

You are already carrying the other world within you, but it is mixed too much with this world. A separation is needed: a separation of that which is essential from that which is non-essential; a separation of that which is you from that which you possess; a separation of the possessor from the possession, of the spirit from the body, of the center from the circumference. It is like a skill.

No painter can tell you how to paint, you have to live with the master. If you go to Picasso and say, 'How do you paint? Tell me something, give me some guidelines,' he cannot give you any guidelines because he himself is not aware. It is such a tremendous phenomenon, it is so unconscious, that when Picasso is painting he is not aware of any rules, regulations, any laws, any guidelines. He becomes his painting; he is no longer there, he is completely absorbed in it. You have to be with him when he moves into his painting, when the painter is lost and only the painting remains, when the painting is no longer a conscious effort, when the unconscious takes over – you have to see that phenomenon to feel it, what it is. Then those are not the hands of Picasso, then the unconscious Tao, nature, has taken over. Those hands are instrumental, they work as vehicles: some other energy is there. Watch Picasso painting – he is no longer a man. He is not at all a part of you; he has become a creator, he is not a creature. That is why when the painting is born it brings something of the other world.

But this is nothing. When a buddha speaks he is not the speaker. When a buddha moves he is not the walker. When a buddha puts his hand on your head he is not the hand. Tao – you may call it God, or whatsoever name you choose – has taken over. Now the hand is not of Buddha, it is instrumental. God is touching you through him and Buddha is not there at all, not standing between you and God. But this has to be experienced. It is impossible to learn anything from a dead buddha. And if you cannot learn from a living one, how can you expect to learn from a dead one?

It is a skill, the greatest skill, and it is so delicate and subtle that nothing can be done consciously, you have simply to be near and imbibe. This word has to be remembered – imbibe. A buddha has to be imbibed, eaten. He becomes your blood and bone, he flows within you. His presence has to be absorbed and you have to carry it within you.

This is the greatest skill in the world – to make a god out of a man. A man who is always prone to become an animal – to make a god out of him, to change the mind, to drop the ego, to allow the ultimate to happen in him. It is bringing the ocean to the drop, it is dropping the ocean into the drop. It is the highest, most supreme skill. No scriptures can carry it, they can only indicate. You have to be near a living buddha to know what it means. And it happens only once in a thousand years, in two thousand years, that a person like Buddha is there. And then dead cults are born, and people go on worshipping without knowing what they are doing.

Now try to understand these words of Chuang Tzu. It is a beautiful parable: Duke Hwan and the Wheelwright.

Duke Hwan of Khi, first in his dynasty, sat under his canopy reading his philosophy. And Phien the wheelwright was out in the yard making a wheel.

He is a craftsman.

Phien laid aside his hammer and chisel, climbed the steps, and said to Duke Hwan: 'May I ask you, Lord, what is this you are reading?'
The duke said: 'The experts, the authorities.'

Remember well that all your experts and authorities are always dead, because by the time the news reaches you, the person has disappeared. By the time you come to know that there is a buddha, the buddha is dead. Your consciousness is such a lazy and lousy affair, you are so unaware of what is happening that by the time you come to know that the flower has flowered and you rush to the garden, the flower has disappeared.

It takes time for you to realize somebody is there – and it takes so much time! Sometimes centuries afterwards you come to feel that Buddha was there, but then nothing can be done. Be more alert, be more conscious, so that you catch the train in time. You have always been missing the train. You are not here for the first time, you were there when Gautama became Buddha. Somewhere on this earth you were there; it cannot be otherwise, because nothing dies. You missed him. Somebody must have told you, you must have argued. You must have said: 'We have heard many stories, these are just stories.' You must have thought: 'How can somebody else become enlightened when I have not become enlightened? How can somebody else be superior to me?' And faith? You must have said: 'I am a rational man and I cannot believe so easily. There is doubt, and first I have to satisfy my doubt…'

It takes time, sometimes centuries, and even then the doubt is not satisfied. Remember, one has to take the jump, even with the doubt. If you wait to let the doubt subside first, then the time will never come for you to take the jump, because doubt is a self-creating process. One doubt creates another; another doubt creates another. And the same happens with faith – one faith creates another, another faith … then a chain is created. When you start there is always a wavering. Nobody can start with a total heart because then there would be no need. One has to start with doubt. But don't pay much attention to the doubt, pay much attention to trust. Then the energy moves to trust, and the trust becomes a chain. By and by the energy from doubt is absorbed by the energy in trust.

Remember, one has to sow the seeds. If you wait, and say, 'When doubt is no more then I will sow the seeds of trust,' then you will never sow the seeds.

You must have heard, somebody must have told you that this Gautama had become enlightened. You must have laughed, you must have said: 'Nobody becomes enlightened, these are just stories that people go on creating. And I know this Gautama, I even know his father. I know his family and I cannot believe because I am a skeptic, I am a rational man. Without reasoning I cannot move a single step.'

And not only with Buddha – you were there when Jesus was there, you were there when Chuang Tzu was there. You have always been here, but you have missed many times. Why? The reason is always the same – you cannot trust. You go on finding arguments against taking the jump; and there are infinite possibilities to go on finding arguments again and again and again. Because once you feed doubt it becomes a cancerous growth – then it perpetuates itself, there is no need to help it. It is a cancerous growth, it goes on and on, and it grows. The same thing happens with trust.

So remember that it is not a question of 'When there is no

doubt then I will trust.' It is impossible, that time will never come. You have to trust while doubt is there. And look at the beauty of it, if you can trust while doubt is there! And this is how human mind is: frail, weak, divided – you have to trust while doubt is there. And I tell you, if you can trust while doubt is there, it means that you pay more attention to trust and less attention to doubt; you are indifferent to doubt, your whole attention is toward trust. Then a day comes when the doubt has disappeared, because if you don't give attention, you don't give food – attention is food. If you don't give attention the doubt cannot persist in its chain. But you always find reasons. The ego always says, 'Don't surrender, don't let go. What are you doing? You will be lost.' And you never think that you are already lost. Where are you?

You must have met a person who is known as an auto-nut. There are persons who simply enjoy driving, they are auto-nuts. They will go from Bombay to Delhi, nonstop, and the first thing they will say on reaching Delhi is, 'We made it in twenty-four hours.' This is an auto-nut!

Once it happened that an auto-nut was driving me somewhere. He was going fast, at a mad speed along the highway. And we were supposed to reach a village by the afternoon. But we had not reached it and it was already evening. So I looked at the map and told him that it seemed that he had taken a wrong route. He said, 'Don't bother about the map, it does not matter. We are enjoying the ride.' And on he sped, without even stopping to look at the map. There are people who simply go on moving fast, thinking that just by moving fast they will reach somewhere.

It is not movement that leads you somewhere, it is direction. It is not just by running that you will reach your destiny; you may be running in a circle. Where have you reached? What have you got to lose? Nothing whatsoever! Then why are you afraid? Afraid to lose nothing?

People come to me and they say it is difficult to surrender. I always look at them and simply cannot understand what they are talking about, because they have nothing to surrender, nothing to lose, nothing to renounce. If you have attained something then renunciation means something. You have not attained anything: you have gathered worthless rubbish. And you think this is something?

But you don't want to look at it because if you look, you become afraid; then the ground underneath becomes shaky. You don't look at it. You simply go on believing that you have much and I have nothing, because with the exception of enlightenment there is nothing that I have got that is worth mentioning. Except a fully aware consciousness, a flame within of the deathless, there are no other riches. There cannot be.

> *Phien laid aside his hammer and chisel, climbed the*
> *steps, and said to Duke Hwan: 'May I ask you, Lord,*
> *what is this you are reading?'*
>
> *The duke said: 'The experts, the authorities.'*

A person becomes an expert only when he has a long tradition. He becomes an authority only when much time has passed and many people have worshipped him. If nobody worshipped Jesus, would he be an expert or an authority? You count the followers: the more followers, the greater the expert and the authority.

In New Delhi on a confectioner's shop there is a sign. If you go, you must visit this shop. On the sign it is written: 'Eat here, a million flies cannot be wrong!'

This is how you feel: if a million people follow, a million people cannot be wrong. When ten million people follow, then you feel that this is the authority. But these are flies!

How many people are following Buddha? How many are following Jesus? You count the followers as if the master depends on the quantity of the followers. Religion is not politics, following is not the question. Even if nobody follows a buddha, a buddha is a buddha. And if the whole world follows, it makes no difference, because people always follow for the wrong reasons. Don't look for followers. But that is how you feel who is the authority: how many people follow. You always move through wrong arguments.

Said the duke: 'The experts, the authorities.'

Phien asked: 'Alive or dead?'

That old Phien must have been a man of knowledge, a really wise man, because it is difficult to find a person who believes in an alive authority. How can a person who is alive be your authority? It takes time, a long time – only then somebody becomes the authority.

It happened that I was visiting a Buddhist *vihar* – a monastery – and the inmates gathered and asked me to say something about Buddha and so I said something. The head priest was a little uncomfortable. At the end, he asked me, 'I have never found the story that you told in any scripture and I have read all that Buddha has said. No authority quotes it, I have heard it for the first time. Where did you get it from?'

So I told him, 'I create stories, and if it is not written in your scriptures, you can add it. I am my own authority.'

How are scriptures created? If somebody wrote it one thousand years ago, then he is an authority. But if I add a story, then no! But why? It is just time. Buddha died and after five hundred years stories were written – but not at the time. So if after five hundred years stories could be written, then why not after two thousand five hundred years? The head priest couldn't believe that I could say this.

This Phien must have been a very wise man. He said, *'Alive or dead?'* Authorities are almost always dead, and I tell you, that if you can believe in a living authority you will be transformed. Carry the dead and they will make you dead – that is how you have become dull and insensitive. Be with the living and you will become more alive, because whatsoever you do changes you. If you believe in the dead, you believe in death not life. If you believe in the living, you believe in life not death.

The duke said: 'Dead a long time.'

And really, every religion tries to prove that their authorities are very, very old, extremely ancient. Ask Hindus – they say their *dharma sanatan* has no beginning. They are the most cunning: they say it has no beginning so you cannot prove your religion is more ancient than theirs. They have finished it; it has no beginning. They say that the Vedas are the most ancient, and they think that if you can prove that Vedas are the most ancient then they are more authoritative.

Somehow the mind thinks that the older a thing is the better; as if truth is a wine – the older the better. And all interpretations are nothing but putting old wine in new bottles. Truth is not a wine, truth is not at all like wine, it is just the opposite: the newer it is, the fresher, younger it is, the deeper. The more alive it is, the more profound. The dead is flat – dust left by the past, nothing else.

But Hindus prove their Vedas are very, very old and they go on pushing the date of the Vedas backwards. And they become very angry if somebody proves that they are not so old; they think you are irreligious, you have gone mad. Ask the *Jainas*: they prove that their *tirthankaras* are older than the Vedas. And they have a point, because their first *tirthankara* is mentioned in Rig Veda, so that is a clear proof. If the first *tirthankara* is mentioned with respect in the Rig Veda it shows that he must have already been dead long before; otherwise how can you show such respect to a living person? And not just mentioned, but mentioned with respect, as a god, in Rig Veda, that means he must have been dead for at least five thousand years. Only then a man becomes a god! So *Jainas* say their religion is the most ancient – and this is how all religions try.

Why this effort to prove that you are the most ancient? Because the mind believes in death, the mind believes in past. Mind is nothing but past. So you think that your mind will be greater if your authority is ancient, because the greater the gap of time, the accumulation of tradition, the longer the stretch for the mind to move. Mind needs time to move and mind is nothing but accumulated past, so you will have a bigger mind if your past is bigger and you will have a smaller mind if your past is not so big. That is why all the old traditions, countries and races, always look at Americans as childish because they have no past – just three hundred years! Is it a past, three hundred years? It is nothing. Not only that but if you follow a master and he says that his age is five hundred years then he will collect more followers.

I have heard that it was rumored about a lama in Tibet that he was one thousand years old. An Englishman visited him, he traveled from London just for this purpose – because the lama was one thousand years old. This was rare. He visited the lama and he couldn't believe it, the man looked not more than fifty. So he inquired. He asked the lama's chief disciple, 'Is it true that your master is one thousand years old?'

The disciple said, 'I cannot say because I have only been with him for three hundred years.'

But this is how it is: the older a thing the more authority it has. Even if somebody says that his guru is one hundred and fifty, suddenly you feel that here is something very valuable. Just by becoming old, you think something valuable happens. You can be one hundred and fifty years old and be just a one-hundred-and-fifty-year-old fool – because age cannot bring wisdom, it is not concerned with it. On the contrary, children are more wise; they have to be. God cannot be wrong, because he always kills the old men and replaces them with children; that means he believes in children more than in old men. Old men means: discard, throw them out, they are of no use now. God believes in the new and man believes in the old; God always believes in the new leaf, that is why the old leaf is shed. And he replaces it by the new, by the fresh, by the young.

God is eternally young and new, and so is religion. But authorities ... So you cannot believe in God's authority. If you look at the divine creativity all around, you will always see that he looks a little crazy, because by the time a man has become wise, he withdraws him. You have become ninety years old, lived your life past all seasons, known much, gathered experience, and by the time you have become wise, he calls you, 'Come on, go from life.' And he replaces you with a small child; you are replaced by a small child who does not know anything. It seems that he loves innocence more than knowledge and he loves fresh leaves more than old, pale leaves. And it should be so, because life has to be young, and if he is eternal life, he has to be eternally young.

That is why Hindus never depict Krishna or Rama as old. That is symbolic – they are always young. Have you seen any picture of Rama looking very old, or of Krishna with a staff in his hand, bent over it? He lived eighty years, he was old, but Hindus have simply dropped the idea of depicting him as old, because if you look at God he is always young. So it is just to show that God is always young and religion is always fresh, just like an innocent babe, just like the morning dew, just like the first star in the night. But then God cannot be an authority, because authority means the weight of the past; without the weight of the past authority is not created.

> Phien asked: 'Alive or dead?'
> The duke said: 'Dead a long time.'
> 'Then,' said the wheelwright, 'you are reading only the
> dirt they left behind.'

Whenever you are too engaged with the past you are engaged with dirt, with graves; you are a grave digger. You live in a cemetery, you are no longer a part of the living phenomenon that is life.

> *The duke replied: 'What do you know about it? You are only a wheelwright. You had better give me a good explanation or else you must die.'*

The duke could not believe his own ears that just an ordinary wheelwright would like to teach him wise things. People who are ready to learn are ready to learn from everywhere. This man is ready to learn from dead authorities but not from a living wheelwright. And I tell you, a living wheelwright is better than a dead king because he is alive. Nobody is going to worship him but God still trusts him; that is why he is alive.

The duke was very angry, he said:

> *'You had better give me a good explanation or else you must die.' The wheelwright said: 'Let us look at the affair from my point of view. When I make wheels, if I go easy they fall apart, and if I am too rough they do not fit. But if I am neither too easy nor too violent they come out right, and the work is what I want it to be.*

> *'You cannot put this into words, you just have to know how it is.'*

The wheelwright was saying, 'I don't know about authorities and experts. Let us look from my view point. Yes, I am just a wheel-wright, but I know my craft, and I have learned something from it. And that is this: it is a skill, and so subtle and delicate that it cannot be put into words.'

If you move to the extremes the wheel never comes out as it should. You have to remain just in the middle. And how can you put it into words? Ask a tightrope walker, how can he put it into words? How does he walk on the rope stretched between two hills over a valley, where if he falls he falls forever, he will be dead – how does he walk on such a rope? Can he put it into words? He will say, 'If I lean too much towards the right immediately I have to balance and lean towards the left. If I lean too much to the left again I have to lean towards the right, towards the opposite direction, to balance.'

This can be written, but just by reading it, don't stretch a rope and go for a walk; you will never come back! Because it is not a question of knowing intellectually, it is a question of feeling through your whole being – how much to lean? And there cannot be any fixed formula, each person is different. It will depend on the person, on the weight, the height, and the situation, the wind blowing. And it will depend on the inner mind. You will have to feel it, you cannot have a fixed formula and follow it. You will have to learn through a master; you cannot go to a college and learn it.

In college you can learn philosophy, you can learn mathematics, you can learn science – everything, but you cannot learn a skill. A skill is learned only through a master who knows, and simply by watching him you start feeling him. And you have so much trust in him that if he moves to the right, your inner being also moves to the right. If he moves to the left, your inner being feels it and you move to the left. You become his shadow, and by and by you start.

The wheelwright said: 'Let us look at the affair from my point of view. When I make wheels, if I go easy they fall apart, and if I am too rough they do not fit. But if I am neither too easy nor too violent they come out right, and the work is what I want it to be.

'You cannot put this into words, you just have to know how it is.'

I cannot even tell my son exactly how it is done, and my own son cannot learn it from me. So here I am, seventy years old, still making wheels!'

What is he saying? He is saying one of the most profound truths: that there are things which can be learned only through your totality; intellect alone will not help. You can make a formula but then you will miss, because in every changed situation you will be carrying a dead formula, and it will not help. In every changed situation a changed response is needed. That means only consciousness will help, not knowledge. You have to carry a light within you so that in every situation you can feel the situation that is here and now. And you need not fix the situation in a formula; rather, on the contrary, you have to discover the formula every time there is a new situation.

Life goes on moving, it never repeats itself; even if it appears to be repeating, it never repeats itself. It cannot. If you feel that life repeats, it is only because you cannot feel the new, you are so dead. Otherwise it never repeats. A cloud that you have seen this morning will never again be in the sky – it cannot be. The sun that has risen this morning will not rise again, because the whole universe will be different tomorrow morning. It is such a vast thing and everything is changing.

Everything goes on changing. Nothing is old ever, except the human mind. That is the only old thing – the only museum in the world, a collection of fossils, the only graveyard. Otherwise everything is new. Just look! Drop the human mind! Can you find anything old in this world? Everything is changing, even the Himalayas. They go on changing; they say that they are rising one foot every year. Everything goes on changing: the oceans change, the Earth changes, even the continents go on moving.

Now scientists have discovered the fact that the continents have moved much. Once Africa was joined to India. Once Ceylon, Sri Lanka, must have been very near to India, otherwise the monkey Hanuman could not have jumped across. There must have been just a small river, a stream between the two. Now scientists have proved that continents move, they go on changing. Everything is changing, nothing is static.

Eddington is reported to have said that in his life he had come to understand that there was one human word that was absolutely wrong and that was 'rest', because there is no rest. Everything goes on moving, nothing is in a state of rest, nothing can be – life is a flux. If life is a flux, then this wheelwright is right, because he says that nothing can be said, with every wheel it is different: the wood is different, the cart is different, the situation is different, the road is different – and one has to be conscious about it. 'I cannot put it into words, I cannot even teach my own son.' And it is really difficult to teach your own son.

Have you ever heard that Buddha could teach his own son? Have you ever heard what happened to Chuang Tzu's own son, what happened to Lao Tzu's son?

It is very difficult for a father to teach his own son, because their egos are always antagonistic. It is very difficult, because a son is always fighting with the father. He wants to prove something, that he is better than the father. He thinks that his father is just an old fool. And the father cannot believe that his son can learn anything. He is just a son and he remains a son. Even if the son is seventy and the father is ninety he thinks that he is just a baby. It is very difficult to find a meeting point between a father and son; the bridge is impossible, almost impossible.

This wheelwright says that he cannot teach even his son, who is so near to him. He cannot say what he means and so here he is, seventy years old, and still making wheels. He is saying, 'It is time for me to retire. I am old enough now. The body is in tatters and I cannot work anymore. But what to do? Nobody has been able to learn the art, and I am still here making wheels.'

Remember that the Sufis are the only ones who have used this story very beautifully, because they always teach through a craft –

only Sufis. They teach through a craft. The craft may be anything: the craft of a carpenter or a wheelwright, the craft of a painter, shoemaker, or anything whatsoever. Sufis teach through crafts; first you have to learn the craft from the master and then he will teach you the innermost thing. Why? This seems absurd!

For ten years the disciple learns how to make shoes, and then after ten years or twelve years or even twenty years, when he has become a perfect master in making shoes, the master starts teaching him about the inner world. This seems to be a sheer waste of time. It is not, because Sufis say that the question is not what you learn – the subject matter is not the question – but how you learn.

Once you have learned how to learn then the innermost keys can be given to you immediately. In ten or twenty years of living with a master and learning how to make shoes, the disciple imbibes the spirit. The more he imbibes the spirit of the master, the more he becomes a perfect shoemaker. Spirituality is not touched at all, not talked about – just the learning to imbibe. And anything will do – whatsoever the master feels fits, or whatsoever he is skilled in. And by the time he feels that you can now imbibe, you have imbibed the art, then he will teach you the inner world. Then he will bring you to the door of the temple. Then he will say that now I can hand over the key. And if you cannot even learn shoemaking, how can you learn the divine?

Sufis use it, and this wheelwright's standpoint is absolutely right: '*So here I am, seventy years old, still making wheels!*' Nobody has been able to learn from me while I am alive, so how can you learn from the authorities which are dead? And if not even wheel-making can be learned, how can you learn the most supreme art of life – the most supreme craft of bringing the divine to man or bringing man to the divine?'

'The men of old took all they really knew with them to

*the grave. And so, Lord, what you are reading there is
only the dirt they left behind them.'*

This is to be remembered – one of the most profound sentences:
'The men of old took all they really knew with them to the grave.'
When a buddha dies, whatsoever he knows disappears with him.
It has to be so, this is the way, this is how things are. We may not
wish it so, but our wishes are not the question. Whatsoever a
Mahavira knows disappears from this world when he dies. No, it
cannot be carried by scriptures, it cannot be carried by scholars.
Words will be repeated and memorized, written, worshipped, but
they are just dust, leftovers, dead things, graves. You can make
temples out of them, beautiful temples, and worship and go on
worshipping, but whatsoever a buddha knows disappears with him,
because that knowledge is not separate from a buddha – it is his
being. It is one with him, it is he himself. When he disappears, his
consciousness goes into the infinite, the river has fallen into the
ocean. You can go on worshipping that dry bed of the river, where
the river once was, but it is no longer there. You can make temples,
pilgrimages, but it is not of much use.

What is this wheelwright saying? He is saying that one should
always seek a living master; always seek the alive because only the
alive is here, only life penetrates the world of matter. And when a
buddha disappears, he simply disappears with all that he knew.
That is why buddhas are always in a hurry to teach, always in a
hurry to give, to find one who can learn, because the moment they
disappear, all they know will disappear.

And it has to be discovered again and again; it is not like
science. Science is a tradition; religion is individual. If something
is discovered by Newton, it will be there, written in the books in
the libraries; Einstein can be benefited by it. Really without
Newton there cannot be any Einstein, he has to stand on Newton's
shoulders. He may contradict Newton, but he stands on him, he

is the base. Whatsoever Einstein discovers will remain a part of humanity, always. That is why science goes on growing, progressively accumulating more and more speed.

But religion always disappears with the person who discovers it. You cannot stand on Buddha's shoulders. No, there is no possibility! You will have to stand on your own feet again and again and again. Religion has to be discovered again and again and again.

Religion is an individual discovery, it cannot become a tradition. Difficult, but beautiful also, because it cannot be borrowed. It is always fresh and young and new. It is just like love. Majnun and Laila loved, Shirin and Farihad loved, Romeo and Juliet loved, but you cannot stand on their shoulders and love more. Love cannot be an accumulative thing. When you fall in love the whole thing has to be rediscovered. When you fall in love, it is almost as if no one loved before you. Whether anyone loved or not, it makes no difference – you love anew, the discovery is again new. Every lover enters into the temple of love fresh. No footprints of past lovers are left, their love disappears with them. And it is good; otherwise even love will be just a tradition, a well-trodden path with maps. And when you walk on the path of love, where millions have walked, it is not worth walking. It becomes a superhighway, a market thing, a commodity – then it is no more a temple.

But when you love, you love for the first time. It is not a repetition of anybody's love, it is you. God loves through you again for the first time. This is the paradox – I say again for the first time, the mystery is revealed. This is how religion is, prayer is, meditation is. No, you cannot follow the dead, you can only be in the presence of the living ones. And you have to imbibe.

When *you* enter, this will be again for the first time. And it is good that when Buddha disappears everything disappears with him. You have to find the path again; it is an eternal hide-and-seek game. God again goes into hiding, you have to discover him again; otherwise Buddha has discovered him and we can put a sign there:

'Here lives God' – finished! Anybody who wants to can come. No! He again goes into hiding, and remember, he is a very skillful player. You will never find him in the old hiding place again. He is hiding somewhere else.

That is why old techniques become useless; new devices have to be discovered again and again, because God hides in new places. He finds new caves, he always vacates the old. He says: Now it is finished, this cave is finished. Now let worshippers worship here, but I will not be here.

CHAPTER 10

MAN IS BORN IN TAO

Fishes are born in water, man is born in Tao. If fishes, born in water, seek the deep shadow of pond and pool, all their needs are satisfied.

If man, born in Tao, sinks into the deep shadow of nonaction to forget aggression and concern, he lacks nothing,
and his life is secure.

Needs can be fulfilled, but desires cannot be. Desire is a need gone mad. Needs are simple; they come from nature. Desires are very complex; they don't come from nature, they are created by the mind. Needs are moment-to-moment, they are created out of life itself. Desires are not moment-to-moment, they are always for the future. They are not created by life itself, they are projected by the mind. Desires are projections, they are not really needs. This is the first thing to be understood, and the deeper you understand it the better.

What is desire? It is movement of the mind into the future. Need belongs to this moment – if you are hungry it is a need, and has to be fulfilled. And it can be fulfilled; there's no problem about it. If you are thirsty, you are thirsty here and now, you have to seek water. It should be fulfilled – it is a life need. But desires are not like that. You desire to be the president of a country. It is not a need, it is an ambition, it is an ego projection into the future. Or you desire heaven – that too is in the future; or you desire God – that too is in the future. Remember, needs are always here and now – they are existential. And desires are never here and now – they are nonexistential. They are just mental, in the mind. And they cannot be fulfilled because their very nature is to move into the future.

They are just like the horizon. It seems that just nearby somewhere the earth meets the sky: it is so apparent, you can walk there. But you could go on walking for ever and ever, and the distance will remain the same; always somewhere ahead the earth will be meeting the sky. But you will never reach that place, that point where the earth meets the sky. They never meet. This is just an appearance, what Hindus call *maya:* it appears, but it is not so. It appears if you are standing at a distance. The nearer you come the more you realize that it is not so. The horizon moves further ahead, and the distance between you and it always remains the same.

The distance between you and your desire always remains the same. How can you fulfill it? If you desire ten thousand rupees, you may get them some day, but by the time you get them, the desire will have gone ten thousand times ahead again. You have one thousand rupees; the desire will ask for ten thousand. Now you have ten thousand; the desire will ask for one hundred thousand. The distance remains the same. You may have one hundred thousand – it makes no difference. Ten times again, the desire will remain the same.

Needs are simple, they can be fulfilled. You feel hungry and you eat; you feel thirsty and you drink; you feel sleepy, you go to bed.

Desires are very cunning and complex. You are frustrated, but not because of needs. You are frustrated because of desires. And if desires take too much of your energy you will be unable to fulfill your needs also, because who is there to fulfill them? You are moving into the future, you are thinking of the future; your mind is dreaming. Who is there to fulfill ordinary needs of the day? – you are not there. And you would like to remain hungry but reach the horizon: you would like to postpone needs so that the whole energy moves towards the desire. But in the end, you find that the desire is not fulfilled, and because needs have been neglected, in the end you are just a ruin. And the time that is lost cannot be regained; you cannot go back.

There is a story told of one old wise man whose name was Mencius. He was a follower of Confucius and he died when he was very, very old. Somebody asked him, 'If you were given life again, how would you start it?'

Said Mencius, 'I would pay more attention to my needs and less attention to my desires.'

And this realization will come to you also. But it always comes very late and then life is no more in your hands. If you were given life again …

Needs are beautiful; desires are ugly. Needs are bodily; desires are psychological. But look at your so-called saints and sages: they always condemn your needs and always help your desires to be projected. They say, 'What are you doing? Just eating, sleeping, wasting your life? Try to reach heaven! Heaven is the ultimate desire. Paradise is waiting for you, and you are wasting your life on ordinary things – just vegetating. Stand up and run, because there is not much time left. Reach! Knock at the door of heaven! Reach God! But don't just stand there.'

They always condemn your needs and they always help your desires. That's why the world has become so ugly – everybody is full of desires and nobody's needs are fulfilled. That which can be fulfilled is neglected and that which cannot be fulfilled is being fed. This is the misery of man.

Chuang Tzu is for needs. Fulfill them and don't ask for desires. Simply drop the very idea, because there is no future; only the present exists. And how beautiful it is! When you feel hungry you eat – there is no future – and when you are so much into eating it becomes a paradise in itself. That's what Jesus says: Don't think of the morrow. Look at the lilies of the field: they don't accumulate, they don't think, they are not worried about the future. They flower here and now. Look at the blooming lilies – the tomorrow will take care of itself. You just be here and now. This moment is enough, don't ask for more.

This is the real sage – the one who lives in the moment, for whom this moment is enough. He is fulfilled. There is no heaven for him, he is heaven himself. There is no God for him, he has become divine himself. This will be very difficult, because whatsoever I am saying is against many centuries of teaching and poisoning. Eat when you feel hungry, and in that moment make eating a celebration. Celebrate! Because who knows, next time you may not be there. The hunger may not be there, nor this beautiful bread. Thirst may not be there – nor may this river be there. Drink it! Let yourself be so concentrated here that time stops. Because time is not moving – your mind moves. If you are in this moment, totally concentrated, enjoying it with your total being, time stops. There is no movement of time, there is no horizon and no running after it. But everybody is in a hurry to reach the horizon.

It happened that Mulla Nasruddin entered a hospital. The surgeon who was going to operate said to him, 'Here we believe in speed, and we don't waste any time. After the operation, on the very first day you have to walk for five minutes in the room; the next day, for half an hour, outside the hospital; the third day, a long walk of one hour. Here we don't waste time. Life is short and time is money. It has to be saved.'

Mulla Nasruddin said, 'Just one question – do you mind if I lie down for the operation?'

Everybody is in a hurry. Where are you going in such a hurry? Have you ever seen somebody reaching anywhere? Have you heard of anybody who has ever reached anywhere through hurry, through impatience, through speed? We have heard about a few people who reached by stopping, but we have never heard of anybody who reached by running. Buddha stopped and reached; Jesus stopped and reached; Chuang Tzu stopped and reached. You carry the goal within you, there is nowhere else to go. But desire leads you to distant lands, to distant times, to distant points in space. And the more you are desirous, the more you are in a hurry, the more you go on missing yourself – frustrated, tattered, you are just a ruin before you die.

But in that ruin the desire is still there. You have gathered a whole life of experiences of desire, and your mind says, 'You failed because you didn't make enough effort. Look, others have succeeded. Look at the neighbors, they have succeeded; but you have failed because you didn't run fast enough. Next time be ready.'

You gather all this attitude in a seed, then you are born again and the whole vicious circle starts again. Where are you going? Is there anywhere to go? And even if you reach somewhere you will still be yourself. Even if you are made a president this very moment, of this country or some other country, do you think anything will change? You will remain the same – the same frustrated being, the same ambitious being, with the same tension, the same anguish, the same nightmares.

Mulla Nasruddin once knocked at his psychiatrist's door. Said the psychiatrist, 'What is the matter now?'

Mulla Nasruddin said, 'I'm having a nightmare, it recurs every night. Help me! I cannot sleep, it has become a heavy burden on my head. Something has to be done now!'

He was really in trouble, his eyes were sore and his whole body looked as if he had not slept for many, many months.

The psychiatrist became concerned. He said, 'Tell me, tell me about the nightmare. What is it?'

Said Nasruddin, 'Every night I have a dream, a horrible dream. The dream is that I am on an island with twelve beautiful women.'

The psychiatrist said, 'I don't see the problem. What is horrible about it? Twelve beautiful women, and you are on your own with them! What is horrible about that?'

Nasruddin said, 'Have you ever tried loving twelve women, alone, on an island?'

But you are loving twelve thousand women. Every desire is a woman. And your whole life has become a nightmare – so many desires, so many horizons, so many things to be reached before life is lost. That's why you are in such a hurry – you cannot be anywhere. You go on running and running and running until you simply fall into the arms of death; that is the end of your whole effort.

Remember, the first thing is that needs are beautiful.

And this is the difference between other sages, so-called sages, and Chuang Tzu – needs are beautiful, desires are ugly. The distinction is: need comes from the body and desire is created by the mind. Happier are animals, the birds, the trees, because they have got no mind to desire; they are happy wherever they are. They live and they die, but they are never in anguish; the tension is not there.

This is the first thing to be remembered – the distinction, the clear-cut distinction between desire and needs. And accept needs, nothing is wrong with them, but drop desires – everything is wrong with them, because they don't allow you to be here and now. And that is the only existence possible. There is no other existence. Bloom like lilies in the field, sing like birds in the trees, be wild like wild animals.

And don't listen to the poisoners. Enjoy simple bodily needs. How many needs have you got? One needs food, one needs water, one needs shade, one needs a loving heart – that's all. And if there were not so many desires, the whole world would become a Garden of Eden this very moment. Because of desires we cannot pay attention to simple needs. And look … even animals can fulfill their needs, but man cannot fulfill his needs. Why is man poor? Not because the earth is poor but because man is mad; he puts more energy into desires. Reaching the moon seems to be more important than feeding the poor. What is the use of reaching the moon? What will you do?

But this is the whole trend of the mind. With the money America has wasted in reaching the moon, the whole of Asia could have been fed, all the backward countries could have been developed. And what have you gained by reaching the moon? The American flag is now on the moon – this is the gain. And there is nobody to even see it! And now other planets are the target. The moon has been conquered – now other planets have to be conquered. Why this moon madness? Why this lunatic craziness?

This word lunatic is very good. It comes from *luna*, the moon. A madman is always moon mad, struck by the moon; the moon has always been the goal of all the mad people. For the first time they have achieved the goal, they have reached the moon.

But what have you gained from it? When you have reached the moon, the goal shifts ahead, the horizon goes ahead. Now you have to reach another planet – and then another planet. Why so much wastage of energy and life?

And the so-called religions go on condemning your needs. This has become their slogan – not to enjoy is to be religious. 'Eat, drink and be merry' is their condemnation. Whenever they want to condemn anybody, they will say, 'He believes in "eat, drink and be merry."'

But Chuang Tzu says: Eat, drink and be merry. If you can be totally in it you have achieved the Tao, nothing more is needed. Be simple, allow nature, and don't force nature in any direction. Don't become a soldier, a fighter, a warrior with life. Surrender to life and let life happen through you. That is the first thing.

The second thing: everybody is in search of security. But then you are in search of an impossibility. And whenever you seek an impossibility, you meet frustration. It is not possible, it is not the nature of things to be secure. Insecurity is the very soul of life. Insecurity is the very taste: as the sea tastes salty, so anywhere you taste life it tastes insecure. Only death is secure. Life has to be insecure because of its very nature. Why?

Whenever a thing is alive it is changing; only a dead thing never changes. Whenever there is change there is insecurity. What does change mean? A change means moving from the known into the unknown. And the base of all insecurity is that you want to cling to the known.

Look at it in this way: a child is in the womb of the mother. If it wants to be secure it is better to cling to the womb and not come out. Can you get a more secure situation, a more secure position, than being in the womb for ever and ever? There is no responsibility for the child – no worry, no job, no office, no problem to solve. Everything is solved automatically. The child has not even to breathe on his own, the mother breathes for him. The child's heart beats through the heartbeat of the mother, the mother's blood goes on feeding the child. He is perfectly in heaven. Can you think of a better heaven than the womb? – comfortable, asleep, not even a dream flickers in a silent sleep. And then comes the birth! And psychologists say that birth is very traumatic because the child is thrown out, uprooted from his security. A convenient home, the most comfortable … we have not been able to create anything like it. No noise enters; it is as if the world does not exist at all. The child has not to make any choice and be divided; there is no training, no conditioning. He simply enjoys himself as if he is the very center of the world.

And then suddenly comes the birth. It is traumatic! Insecurity comes into existence for the child for the first time. Now he has to breathe; now he has to cry when he feels hungry, when he feels thirsty, when he feels uncomfortable. He has to make his own arrangements and he has to start being worried. If the mother is not there he is worried. He is wet, he cries and cries and nobody listens.

Now comes tension, insecurity; he is always afraid the mother may leave him. And the mother always goes on threatening, 'Listen to me, otherwise I will leave you.' Mothers even threaten the child, 'Listen, follow, otherwise I will die.' This is a threat. The child trembles to his very roots. He has to follow, he has to make arrangements, he has to become false and to wear masks. He has to play roles – even if he does not feel like smiling, if the mother comes, he has to smile. He has to become a politician and to take care how others feel about him, otherwise he will feel insecure.

Now he will never be as secure as in the womb. What should he do? Should he cling to the womb? And it seems that the child does cling, he does not want to come out. Many times the help of a doctor is needed to bring the child out – his whole being clings. He resists; he wants to be there as he is, the known. And can you think of anything more unknown, more strange for the child than the world? He opens his eyes and everything is strange, there are sounds all around. He becomes scared. And he will grow, and as he grows, more insecurity grows. Sooner or later he will be sent to school – now even the home is no more his base. And every child resists. You cannot find a child who is happy to go to school – unless the home is a hell. No child wants to go to school; he resists, he clings to the mother, to the house, because now he is being pushed into another birth – he is being thrown out of the home. And then he will start clinging to the school.

If you go to the university and look, and feel the pulse of the students, nobody wants to leave the university. There are many cases of people unconsciously making arrangements to fail again and again, because the university is again security. The father cares, he sends money, and you simply live like a prince. Still the world has not entered. But the whole world is pulling you into insecurity and sooner or later you will have to be thrown out of the university. It is not accidental that all over the world people call the university the mother. It is meaningful. It is the mother – you are still a child, and the society is taking care of you. But still, every day you are moving more and more into insecurity.

Mother's love has a security. The mother will love you whether you love her or not. It is a one-way traffic: she will love you naturally. But now you will have to seek a woman who will not love you naturally. You will have to love her. If you need love you will have to give love. With a mother it was different, everything was taken for granted. But with another woman it is not going to be so; you will have to earn your love with this woman; that's why there is a constant fight. A man wants his wife to be just like his mother. But why should she be a mother to him? She is not a mother, she is a wife. And she is in the same situation – she wants the man, the husband, to be her father.

What is the meaning of it? A mother's love is unconditional; it is given to you, she shares. A father's love is unconditional – just because you are his child, he loves you, there is no need to earn it. But when you move into the world you have to earn a husband's love, a wife's love. And any moment it can be withdrawn. Fear, insecurity ... Hence marriage has come into existence, because lovers are so insecure they want legal sanction. So the government protects them, the society protects them. Otherwise what would be the need for marriage? If love is really there, you need not get married. Why? There is a fear that the love may be here today but who knows about tomorrow? And if love goes, then what will you do? Who will you fall back on? The law, the court, the government – they become the securities. Then you can go to the court and you can demand love.

Every society makes divorce as difficult as possible, marriage as easy as possible. This seems absurd, it should be just the opposite. Marriage should be made as difficult as possible, because two persons are moving in an unknown world; let them wait, watch, think, brood, meditate. Give them time. To my mind it seems that at least three years should be allowed before the court allows anybody to marry. And I think that then nobody would get married! Three years! Impossible! After the honeymoon everything is over. Then people cling because of the law and the security and the problems that will come if they get separated. Children have come ... now marriage becomes a responsibility, not a bliss, not ecstasy.

And society is always happy if you are worried and not in ecstasy, because an ecstatic man cannot be exploited. Only a worried man can be exploited; only a worried man can be made into a slave. An ecstatic man can never be a slave, he is too dangerous for society. He is rebellious, he does not need society –

that is what an ecstatic being means. He alone is enough. And if he doesn't need society, then society cannot force things on him. Society wants you to be worried, ill at ease, then you will depend on it. Then you will go to the court and you will look towards the magistrate as if he were some god. Then the government, the state, the policemen, all become important, because you are worried. But if you are ecstatic … Lovers can forget them, but not married people. Lovers can forget the policeman, he is not needed at all. Their love is enough. But when love goes, then the policeman is needed to keep them united. A policeman is needed – now he will create trouble if you separate. And just to avoid that trouble, people go on living together.

Life is dangerous, but that is the beauty of it – it is insecure, because insecurity is the very nature of movement, aliveness, vitality. The more dead you are, the more secure. When you are in your grave there will be no danger. What can happen to you anymore? Nothing! Nobody can harm you when you are dead. But when you are alive, you are vulnerable, you can be harmed. But I tell you, that is the beauty of life. A flower in the morning cannot believe that by the evening it will be gone. But that is the beauty of it – in the morning it is so glorious, so magnificent, an emperor, and by the evening it is gone. Just think of a flower made of stone or plastic – it remains. It remains; it will never fade. But whenever something never fades it means it never bloomed. Marriage is a plastic flower, love is the real flower – in the morning it blooms, by the evening it has gone. A marriage continues, it has a permanency about it. But in this impermanent world how can anything real be permanent?

Everything real will have to exist moment to moment. And there is insecurity: any moment it can disappear. The flower that blooms will fade; the sun that has arisen will set. Everything will change. If you are too afraid of insecurity then you will make arrangements, and with those arrangements you will kill everything. A wife is a dead beloved, a husband is a murdered lover. Then things are settled – there is no problem. But then the whole life drags.

I'm not saying that love cannot be eternal – it can be. But insecurity is its nature; you cannot make it permanent. Remember: you have to move moment to moment. If it fades, you have to accept it; if it goes on blooming, you enjoy it. It depends. But you cannot be secure about it. How can you be secure about the future? Who knows whether you will be there or not? If even about yourself you cannot be secure, what about your love?

But you go on promising and you don't know what you are doing. When you love a person, you feel that you will love him for ever and ever. This is a feeling of this moment; don't make it a promise. Just say, 'This moment I feel that I will love you for ever and ever, but I don't know how I will feel about the next moment.' Nobody can say anything about the next moment, nobody can promise. If you promise, you live in a plastic world. A promise cannot be given.

And this is the truth, the honesty of love: it will not promise, although everybody wants the promise just to be secure. And the more afraid you are, the more promise you require. That's why women want promises more than men; they are more afraid, they feel naturally more insecure. They would like to make everything permanent, only then will they move a step. And then you go on giving false promises which cannot be fulfilled. Every promise is broken, and with every promise your heart is broken and the other's heart is broken. And with every promise disappearing, life becomes futile and meaningless; the poetry is lost, it becomes flat prose, a legal phenomenon. You come and make love to your wife, and it becomes a legal thing – you have to do it, it is not spontaneous. You have to kiss your child; it is not spontaneous, you have to do it, it is a duty. And duty is the ugliest thing, I tell you. Love is the most beautiful; duty is the ugliest.

Love is an unknown phenomenon, you cannot manipulate it.

Duty is a social by-product. Now the wife can say, 'You have to love me; this is your duty, and you promised!' And you know that you promised. Then what can you do? If the love has disappeared, or at this moment you don't feel like loving, or this night you don't feel like making love, what to do? Just to keep the promise of the past you have to be false and act. So you say, 'Okay, yes, I promised.' What will you do? Can you produce love on demand? Is it possible? Has it ever happened? Can you produce love?

You cannot, but you can pretend. That pretending will become more and more settled, because spontaneity is not allowed. And then everybody feels cheated, because a pretended love cannot fulfill. Everybody knows it is pretended, you can see through it. You make all the movements of love, but love is not there. It is just like a yoga exercise: the movements are there, the gestures are there, but the heart is not there. You are somewhere else, on duty or on demand, but you also feel, 'Yes, I promised.'

And I tell you that the promise may have been absolutely right, but every promise is for the moment. You cannot promise that you will be there tomorrow, how can you promise that your love will be there? You can say only that this is the feeling for this moment: 'Forever and forever I will love you, but this is a momentary feeling – if things disappear the next moment, what can I do?' But security creates the problem. In everything you need security; that's why everything has become false.

Life is insecure. Let this truth penetrate deeper and deeper in you, let it become a seed deep in your heart. Life is insecure; it is its nature and nothing can be done about it – all that you do will be poisonous. You can only kill … and the more secure you feel, the more dead you will be. Look at people who are really secure with wealth, prestige, castles around them – you can see they are dead. Just see their faces: the eyes look as if they are made of stone. Their faces look like masks, personas. Their gestures are automatic, they are not in them; they are encaged and not flowing – frozen and unmoving. They are not like rivers dancing, running towards the sea. They are dead, dull ponds, not moving anywhere, not flowing anywhere.

Every moment you have to face the unknown – this is the insecurity. The past is no more and the future has still to come into being. The future is unpredictable; every moment you are at the door of the unpredictable. This has to be welcomed. Every moment the unknown is the guest.

In India we have a very beautiful word for guest, no other language has that word. It is *atithi*. It means one who comes without giving any previous information, one who comes without giving any date that he is coming. *Atithi* means 'without date'; he has no date with you, he simply comes and knocks at the door. But we who are so mad and obsessed about security, we have even killed guests. If a guest comes he has first to inform you and ask for permission to come – because you have to make room for him and you have to make arrangements. Nobody can just suddenly knock at your door.

In the West, the guest has completely disappeared; even if he comes he stays in a hotel. The guest is no more because the West is more obsessed with security than the East. Of course, because of that obsession they have accumulated more wealth, more securities, more bank balances. Everything is insured, but the man is dead. Now no *atithi*, now no stranger knocks at your door – the unknown has stopped coming to you. Everything has become known, so you move in a vicious circle of the known. From one known you go to another known, from that known to another, and then you say, 'Why has life got no meaning?'

Meaning comes from the unknown, from the stranger, from the unpredictable that suddenly knocks at your door – a flower that suddenly blooms and you never expected it; a friend that suddenly happens to be on the street you were not waiting for; a love that blooms suddenly and you were not even aware that this was going to happen, you had not even imagined, not even dreamed. Then life has meaning. Then life has a dance. Then every step is happy because it is not a step filled with duty, it is a step moving into the unknown. The river is going towards the sea.

Insecurity is the nature of Tao. Don't make securities; otherwise you are cutting yourself off from nature, from Tao. And the more secure you are, the further away you will be. Move into the unknown and let the unknown have its own way. Don't force it, don't push the river, allow it to flow, and never promise a rose garden to anybody.

And when you love, be authentic and true. When you love, be authentic and true, and say only, 'At this moment I feel this – when the next moment comes I will tell you' … as if this moment is the whole of life. And I tell you, if you are so loving at this moment then the next moment you will be more loving, because the next moment is born out of this moment. But that is not a promise, not an insurance. If you have loved so totally in this moment you will love even more totally in the next. It looks absurd – how can totality be more? But it happens.

Life is absurd. If you have loved totally and authentically and truly and bloomed in this moment, why fear the next moment? You will bloom. Even if this flower fades, another flower will come. Don't be bothered with this flower. Life goes on blooming into this flower, into that one, sometimes on this tree, sometimes on another. But life continues, flowers fade. It means that form fades but the formless goes on moving. So why bother? But you are bothered because you are missing this moment, that is why you are afraid of the next moment. This moment you have not loved; that is why you are making securities for another moment. This moment you have not lived; that is why you are so scared of the unknown. You are making securities for how to live in the next moment. And this is a vicious circle, because you will be there with all your habits, patterns, with all dead routines you will be there. You kill this moment and you kill the next also.

Forget the future. Live in the present and be so totally in it that whatever comes out of this totality will be a blessing. Even if the flower fades it will be beautiful. Have you really observed a flower fading? It is beautiful. It has a sadness about it. But who told you that sadness is not beautiful? Who says that only laughter is beautiful? I tell you that laughter is shallow if there is no sadness in it. And sadness is dead if there is not a smile in it. They are not opposites, they enrich each other.

When you laugh with a deep sadness, the laughter has a depth. And when your sadness smiles, your sadness has an ecstasy to it. And life is not divided into compartments; life is averse to all compartments. It is your mind that creates airtight compartments. Life is overflowing – it does not know the difference between birth and death; it does not know the difference between blooming and fading; it does not know the difference between sunset and sunrise. It moves within these two polarities. These are the two banks, and the river goes on flowing just in between them.

Don't be worried about the future. Live this moment so totally that the next moment comes out of it golden. It will take care of itself. That is what Jesus says: Don't think of the morrow; tomorrow will take care of itself, you need not be worried about it.

Life is insecure, and if you can live in insecurity, that is the only security possible. The man who can live in insecurity is happy because he is the only one who is secure, secure in the arms of life itself. His security is not man-made; his security is that of Tao, of the ultimate nature itself.

Life takes care of you – why are you so worried about taking care of yourself? Why cut yourself off from life? Why uproot yourself from life? Life feeds you, life breathes in you, life lives in you. Why be so much concerned about yourself? A person who is too concerned about himself is a householder; a person who is not concerned about himself is a *sannyasin,* one who says, 'Life takes care of me.' This is what I mean by *sannyas*. It is not a renunciation of life, it is a renunciation of the ego concern. It is not renouncing life, it is renouncing the worry, the concern, the too great an identification, the too much pushing of the river – that is what it is renouncing. The river moves by itself, you need not push. The river has brought you up to this moment, to this shore, and the river will bring you up to many other shores. Why be worried?

Birds are not worried, trees are not worried. And man is the most conscious being, why should he worry? If the Tao takes care of a rock, if the Tao takes care of a river, if the Tao takes care of a tree, why do you doubt that life will take care of you? You are the most supreme flowering of life at this moment. Life is bound to take care of you more than anything else. Life is more concerned with you because more is at stake with you – you are a challenge. Life is becoming conscious through you; life is becoming more and more aware through you. You are reaching a peak – life is trying to reach a peak through you. So life will take care. To allow life and not to be concerned with your ego and yourself is renunciation – to me it is *sannyas*.

My *sannyas* is totally different; it is not the old concept at all. The old concept was to leave life, renounce life. The old concept was just the opposite of mine – it was to be very concerned with oneself. You had to take care of yourself, you had to care about meditation, your yoga, you had to care about your *sadhana*, and you had to take care that you reached God before anybody else did.

My *sannyas* is just the opposite. I say that you need not worry – you will reach, but you will not reach through worrying. You need not even make an effort. Be effortless. Let your whole life be a let-go and you will reach. Life takes care. In your own hands you are in dangerous hands; in Tao's hands, you are in the hands of a mother – the ultimate mother.

Now listen to these words:

Fishes are born in water, man is born in Tao.

Chuang Tzu says that as fishes are born in water, so man is born in Tao. The water takes care of fishes, the Tao takes care of you. You are fishes in Tao, nature – you can call it God. Chuang Tzu never uses that word deliberately, knowingly, because it has been overloaded with so much nonsense. He simply uses Tao – a more neutral word. The Vedas use the word *Rit* – 'Rit' means Tao, nature. Man is born in Tao, that is why we cannot feel it. Fishes cannot feel water, they know it too deeply because they have been born in it. They have lived with it so much; there has never been a separation. The fishes never know what water is. They move in it, they live in it, they die in it, they come into it and disappear in it, but they don't know what water is.

It is said that once a young fish became very worried because she had heard so much about the ocean and she wanted to know what the ocean was. She went from one wise fish to another wise fish. She searched for a master, a guru. There were many – fishes have their own masters and gurus. They said many things, because when you go to a guru even if he does not know, he has to say something just to save his gurudom. They said many things about the ocean, but the fish was not satisfied because she wanted a taste of it.

One guru said, 'It is very far away and it is difficult to reach; only rarely does somebody reach the ocean. Don't be foolish. One has to prepare for it for millions of lives. It is not an ordinary thing, it is a great task. First purify yourself and do these asanas' … one part of the eightfold path of Patanjali.

Another was a Buddhist, and he said, 'This won't help. Move on the path of Buddha. The eight disciplines of Buddha will help – first become purified absolutely, no impurity left, and then only will you be allowed to see the ocean.'

Then somebody else said, 'In the *Kaliyuga*, this present age, only the chanting of the name of Rama will help. Chant "Rama, Rama, Rama" – only by his grace one reaches.'

And the fish was always in the ocean. She searched and searched, consulted many scriptures, consulted many doctrines, doctors, visited many ashrams, but reaching nowhere she got more and more frustrated. Where is the ocean? It became an obsession.

Then one day she met a fish, a very ordinary fish – he must have been like Chuang Tzu, just ordinary. Nobody ever thought that this fish could be a guru, just living an ordinary fish life. This fish said, 'Don't be mad, don't be foolish. You are already in the ocean. What you see all around is the ocean. It is not very distant, it is so near – that is why we cannot see it.' Because to see a thing a distance is needed; to have a perspective, space is needed. 'It is so near you cannot see it; it is outside you, it is within you. You are nothing but a wave in the ocean – a part of it, a concentration of its energy.'

But the seeker didn't believe. The seeker said, 'You seem to be going mad. I have visited many masters and they all say it is very distant. First one has to purify, do yoga asanas, cultivate discipline, character, morality, be religious, go through many rituals – and then after millions of lives it happens. And if one does reach the ocean, that too is through the grace of God.'

But Chuang Tzu is true: the ocean is all around you. You are in it, you cannot be otherwise. How can you live if God is not breathing in you? Who is breathing in you? Who moves in your blood? Who digests your food? Who dreams distant dreams in you? Who gives birth to poetry and love? Who beats in your heart with the beat of the unknown? Who is the music in your life? How can it be possible that God is distant? If God is distant and far away, how can you be here? How can you exist? It is not possible, because God is life and you are a crystallization of life itself.

You are God – maybe miniatures, but you are gods. And I don't say that someday in the future you will be like gods – I say here, this very moment. Whether you know it or not makes no difference, you *are* gods – otherwise is not possible. It may take millions of lives to realize this; but that is not because the distance is vast but because you behaved foolishly; it is not because you were impure, but because you were ignorant. No discipline is needed except awareness: just becoming aware of the near and the close, just becoming aware of that which is already touching your skin, of that which is throbbing in the heart, of that which is flowing in your bloodstream – just becoming aware of the close and the near. And to come to the close you have to live in the moment, because if you move into the future you have gone into the distance. Then you are on a far-off journey. and God is here; you have already left him behind.

Says Chuang Tzu:

> *Fishes are born in water, man is born in Tao. If fishes, born in water, seek the deep shadow of pond and pool, all their needs are satisfied.*

Needs – yes; desires – no. If a fish becomes a politician, no. But they are not so foolish as to become politicians. Fishes are not as foolish as man. They simply live, they enjoy; they eat, drink and are merry. They dance. They are so grateful for the littlest pond that has been given to them; they delight in it. Look at the fishes in a pond, jumping, delighting, running hither and thither. It seems there is no goal for them, no ambition; their needs are fulfilled. When they are tired they move into the shadow in pond and pool; they rest. When energy comes they move and dance and float and swim; when they are tired again, they move into the shadow and rest. Their life is a rhythm between rest and action. You have lost the rhythm. You act but there is no rest. You go to the shop but you never come back home – even if you come, the shop comes in your head. You never seek a shadow in the pond, in the pool. That is all that meditation is – to seek the pond, the shadow. That is all that prayer is – to move from activity into inactivity. That is all that religion is about.

Action … You have moved too much, you have lost the balance; now be inactive so the balance is regained. Be active, but don't forget that inactivity is needed as much as action. Because action is to move into the world, inactivity is to move inwards. It is just like the rhythm of anything else. In the day you are awake, in the night you sleep. It is a rhythm. In the day you are conscious, in the night you become unconscious. You eat and then you have to fast for a few hours. Again, hunger comes and you eat, then again you have to fast for a few hours. If you simply go on eating you will go mad, and if you simply go on fasting you will be dead. A rhythm is needed. A rhythm of the opposites is the most secret key of life. Always remember the opposite.

But the mind says, 'Why the opposite? What is the need? Why be contradictory? If you can be awake then be awake. Why go to sleep?' There are a few scientists who go on thinking that if they can save man from sleep then more life will be saved. They say, 'If you are going to live for ninety years, thirty years will be lost in sleep; this is too much of a waste.' Scientists are more wise than Tao – too much of a waste! And your mind will also say, 'Yes, if thirty years can be saved, life will be much enriched.' But I tell you: you will just become mad. If your thirty years of sleep are lost, you may be awake for ninety years, but you will be maniacs. The world will be a nightmare. Just think of a man who has not slept for ninety years! It will be impossible to live with such a man because he will never relax; he will be continually tense. The whole world will become a madhouse – it is already!

A rhythm is needed: you have to be awake and you have to move into sleep. And sleep is not an opposite in life, it is opposite only in logic. Because when you sleep deeply you become capable of more activity and more awareness in the morning. If last night you slept beautifully, deeply, you enjoyed it, you relaxed completely into it, you forgot yourself totally, then in the morning you will arise completely reborn, fresh, full of energy to move into action again. And if you have been acting the whole day with tremendous energy, not lukewarm, really active, then you will have a better sleep again. Action done totally brings relaxation; relaxation done totally brings more action.

Life is enriched through the opposites, but logic believes that opposites never meet. And because of logical thinking, the whole West has become 'imbalanced'. It always goes on cutting sleep out because it says you enjoy only when you are awake; in sleep there is no enjoyment, so go on pushing your wakefulness deep into the night. So in the West, when they go to sleep, half the night has already been passed in dancing, eating, meeting friends, discussing, arguing, gossiping, clubs, hotels, theaters. As much as you can be awake, be awake, and push wakefulness deep into the night. And they push it so much that when they go to bed, they go always half-heartedly, because it seems that if it had been possible to be awake the whole night they would have enjoyed more – they could have visited one more theater, had a few dances more, met a few more friends; or they might have accumulated more money, gambled a little more. Always they go to bed half-heartedly and then they complain of having insomnia – they cannot sleep. Deep down you don't want to sleep!

I have never seen an insomniac who really wants to sleep. If he wants it, sleep will be there. He does not want it. Deep down he wants an active life, completely active, no rest. Because through rest you cannot earn money, that is the problem; through rest you cannot win elections, through rest the shop will not become bigger, through rest what can you achieve? Rest cannot fulfill ambition – ambition needs action. Desires need action; politics, money, everything needs action. Sleep is sheer wastage. If your mind is obsessed with desires you go half-heartedly to bed, as if it is a compulsion – and then you feel you cannot sleep. Half-hearted, you create resistance. And because you have moved too much into desire, into action, they continue in the mind. The body wants to go to sleep, but the mind continues being active.

Just the other day a man came and he said, 'When I meditate, thoughts continue. How to stop them?'

So I told him how to. Then he said, 'But I love thinking.' Then why try to stop it? And he said, 'Because of those thoughts I cannot go to sleep, and I cannot relax. But still I love thinking.'

This is the problem. You love thinking because thinking can become instrumental in achieving something: you can become a great thinker, or, through thinking, you can become a great leader. Through sleeping have you ever heard of anybody becoming a great leader? They all condemn sleep, they all condemn laziness. They all condemn people who simply enjoy life and are not too active – they call them hobos or bums, vagabonds, and condemn them. But have you ever observed the fact that the world has never suffered from any lazy man – because no lazy man can become a Hitler, no lazy man can become a Nixon, no lazy man can become a Mao, a Ghengis Khan, a Napoleon? No lazy man can become active. Action has brought all the wars. Action is the most mischievous thing in the world.

And still we go on saying that action is needed – because everybody is ambitious. If you drop ambition you will become lazy and active in proportion. Then your life will be a rhythm. You will move to this and then you will move to the other, and inside you will balance yourself – in the day active, in the night asleep. Action and meditation should be together. That is why I never suggest to anybody to move to the Himalayas and renounce the world, because then you will be simply lazy and sleeping – again imbalance. Be in the world, but when you come to your home, really come to your home; leave the office, leave it behind, and don't carry the files in your head. When you are inactive, enjoy inactivity, and when you are active, enjoy activity – and let the body feel and move according to Tao, not according to your mind.

If fishes, born in water, seek the deep shadow of pond and pool, all their needs are satisfied.

If man, born in Tao, sinks into the deep shadow of nonaction to forget aggression and concern, he lacks nothing, and his life is secure.

Deep down within you are the roots. You are like a tree: half of the tree is open above the earth, half of the tree is hidden deep in the earth, in the darkness of the earth. There are the roots. Flowers flower; you can see them, but they flower because of the roots which you cannot see. Invisible are the roots, visible are the flowers.

Let your actions be your flowers, visible, but let your inaction be your roots, the invisible. And keep a balance: the higher the tree goes in the sky, the deeper the roots have to reach. Small trees have small roots; big trees will have big roots. And it is always proportionate: if the tree goes fifty feet high, the roots go fifty feet down. The same should be for you: move into action, but then move into inaction every day. Make it a rhythm, a harmony.

If man, born in Tao, sinks into the deep shadow of nonaction to forget aggression and concern, he lacks nothing, and his life is secure.

In inactivity you dissolve into the ocean, the fish becomes the ocean. In sleep who are you? The ego is there no more, the fish has dissolved. In deep sleep, where are you? You don't occupy any space, you have become one with existence. The same happens in deep meditation.

Hindus have said that deep meditation is just like deep sleep with only one difference: you are alert in meditation and not alert in sleep. In deep meditation, when you seek the cool shadow, you are alert, inactive, but conscious. You know where you are moving. You know that the whole being is settling. You know that it is as if a dead leaf falls from the tree, moves toward the earth, floats a little in the wind, then by and by settles on the earth and falls into deep sleep.

When you move towards meditation from the world of activity, you are falling like a dead leaf or a feather of a bird. There will be a few shakings, waverings on the breeze, here and there you will move, and by and by you go deeper until you settle on the earth. You have reached the root and everything settles. Then there is no worry, no thought, no world, no you – only that which is remains. That is Tao. Then enriched, rejuvenated, you come back to the world, and by and by it becomes as easy as coming out of your house and going in. It becomes that easy.

When you want to, be active, but remember that this activity should follow your bodily need, not your mental desire. Become active when energy is flowing and you feel the energy has to be used – because energy needs action, energy delights in action. If you cannot do anything, at least dance. And remember, energy needs action. If you suppress energy then you will become aggressive – don't suppress energy. This is one of the deepest problems for modern man.

Primitive man needed much energy for his day-to-day life. Going for a hunt needed much energy – eight hours running in the forest, fighting with the animals, and by the end of the evening you might be able to get your food, but that too was uncertain. Much energy was needed for ordinary day-to-day affairs.

Now everything is done by machines; technology has relieved you of much work. What to do? You become aggressive, you fight, you get angry. Without any rhyme or reason, you become angry – suddenly you flare up. Everybody knows that this is foolish, even *you* in your cooler moments know that it is foolish, but why did you flare up unnecessarily? The excuse was not enough. The real reason is not that there was some situation; the real reason is that you have so much energy, so much petrol overflowing, inflammable, that any moment it can be active. That is why after anger you feel relaxed, after anger you feel a little well-being coming to you.

For the modern man this is going to be so – that is why I insist on active meditations, not silent meditations. Because your energy needs acting out, it needs catharsis. You have too much energy with no action for the energy. And rich food is available and food creates more energy. It is a fuel. This age is the most well fed age in the whole of history. And there is no work. Even if you go to the office or the shop or somewhere else, the work is mental, not physical. Mental work is not enough. Man is physically a hunter. He needs much activity to be relaxed.

So choose, but according to your bodily needs. Don't force the body, don't compel it; just feel the body and what it needs. If it needs action then go for a run, go swimming, go for a long walk, or, if you cannot do anything else, dance. Meditate and be active – let the energy flow. You melt into existence through action. And when the energy is gone and you relax, then be silent. Find a cool spot in the pond and relax there.

Action can lead you to Tao; inaction can also lead you to Tao – because there is nothing else than Tao. If you become aware through action you will also meet it. Action is pouring your energy into the Tao, and in inaction Tao pours energy back into you. Look … it is like this. This river flows into the ocean, pours itself into the ocean. This is action. Then the ocean becomes clouds, moves toward the Himalayas, pours down in rains, fills the river again. This is inaction. Now the river is not doing anything – now the ocean is doing something.

In action you give, in inaction you receive – and a balance is needed. And the more you give, the more you will receive, because the emptier you are, the more you will be able to receive. A small river will receive little, a big river will receive much. When the

Ganges pours herself into the ocean, the ocean has to return the same Ganges – again and again it happens. In action you share, you give, you overflow; be delighted, be happy, be dancing while you give. And then there is inaction: the Tao pours into you.

And if you go dancing, the Tao also comes dancing. God always comes to you the same way you go to him. If when you sit silently you feel sad, it means that in action you were not happy. You gave, but you gave grudgingly. If you gave really happily, then when you feel silent, and sit silently, you will feel so much bliss. But it depends on you. And remember this: People come to me and say, 'If we sit silently everything becomes sad and we feel very depressed.' That shows that when you are giving, you give grudgingly, you don't give whole-heartedly. God comes to you the same way you go to him. And it cannot be otherwise, because God is just the returning – if you reach him dancing, he reaches you dancing. If you are acting as if you are a martyr, if you go to the office saying, 'It is because of duty. The wife and children are there, and I have to, and I am just waiting until I retire ...' then God will come the same way to you. It will be a duty for him to knock at your door. He will say, 'I have to' – then he will come crucified. But if you go dancing in your life, he will come with a flute.

Remember this: God is a response. It is a resounding of your being. If you go to the hills and you say something, the hills resound with it. The whole existence resounds with you. Whatsoever you do will be returned to you; this is the law of karma. It is not a question of details: you have insulted somebody so the same man is going to insult you in some life. Don't be foolish! Don't be silly!

But the law is exactly right. It says: Whatsoever you give, you will receive; whatsoever you sow, you will reap. God comes to you the way you reach him.

OSHO MEDITATION RESORT ™

The Osho Meditation Resort is a place where people can have a direct personal experience of a new way of living with more alertness, relaxation, and fun. Located about 100 miles southeast of Mumbai in Pune, India, the resort offers a variety of programs to thousands of people who visit each year from more than 100 countries around the world. Originally developed as a summer retreat for Maharajas and wealthy British colonialists, Pune is now a thriving modern city that is home to a number of universities and high-tech industries. The Meditation Resort spreads over 40 acres in a tree-lined suburb known as Koregaon Park. The resort campus provides accommodation for a limited number of guests, in a new 'Guesthouse' and there is a plentiful variety of nearby hotels and private apartments available for stays of a few days up to several months.

Resort programs are all based in the Osho vision of a qualitatively new kind of human being who is able both to participate creatively in everyday life and to relax into silence and meditation. Most programs take place in modern, air-conditioned facilities and include a variety of individual sessions, courses and workshops covering everything from the creative arts to holistic health treatments, personal transformation and therapy, esoteric sciences, the 'Zen' approach to sports and recreation, relationship issues, and significant life transitions for men and women. Individual sessions and group workshops are offered throughout the year, alongside a full daily schedule of meditations. Outdoor cafés and restaurants within the resort grounds serve both traditional Indian fare and a choice of international dishes, all made with organically grown vegetables from the resort's own farm. The campus has its own supply of safe, filtered water.

www.osho.com/resort

For more information: www.osho.com
a comprehensive web site in several languages that includes an on-line tour of the Meditation Resort and a calendar of its course offerings, a catalog of books and tapes, a list of Osho information centers worldwide and selections from Osho's talks.

Osho International
New York
Email: oshointernational@oshointernational.com
www.osho.com/oshointernational